ROUTLEDGE LIBRARY EDITIONS:
WELFARE AND THE STATE

Volume 23

I0028153

THE UNSERVILE STATE

THE UNSERVILE STATE
Essays in Liberty and Welfare

Edited by
GEORGE WATSON

Routledge
Taylor & Francis Group

LONDON AND NEW YORK

First published in 1957 by George Allen & Unwin Ltd

This edition first published in 2019
by Routledge
2 Park Square, Milton Park, Abingdon, Oxon OX14 4RN

and by Routledge
711 Third Avenue, New York, NY 10017

Routledge is an imprint of the Taylor & Francis Group, an informa business

British Library Cataloguing in Publication Data
A catalogue record for this book is available from the British Library

ISBN: 978-1-138-61373-7 (Set)
ISBN: 978-0-429-45813-2 (Set) (ebk)
ISBN: 978-1-138-61036-1 (Volume 23) (hbk)
ISBN: 978-1-138-61046-0 (Volume 23) (pbk)
ISBN: 978-0-429-46577-2 (Volume 23) (ebk)

Publisher's Note
The publisher has gone to great lengths to ensure the quality of this reprint but points out that some imperfections in the original copies may be apparent.

Disclaimer
The publisher has made every effort to trace copyright holders and would welcome correspondence from those they have been unable to trace.

THE
UNSERVILE
STATE

ESSAYS IN
LIBERTY AND WELFARE

EDITED BY
GEORGE WATSON

RUSKIN HOUSE

GEORGE ALLEN & UNWIN LTD

MUSEUM STREET LONDON

FIRST PUBLISHED IN 1957

© GEORGE ALLEN & UNWIN LTD 1957

PRINTED IN GREAT BRITAIN
in 12 pt Fournier type
BY ROBERT MACLEHOSE AND CO. LTD
THE UNIVERSITY PRESS, GLASGOW

PREFACE

THIS is the first full-scale book on the attitudes and policies of British Liberalism since *Britain's Industrial Future* (1928), the decisive Yellow Book fathered by David Lloyd George and numbering Hubert Henderson, John Maynard Keynes, Lord Layton, Ramsay Muir and Lord Samuel among its contributors. It is in the light of their achievement that this book has been written. But there is little that is similar in our undertakings. The Liberals of the late twenties wrote for a world in which Liberal attitudes were familiar and widely understood, if widely rejected: but in the Britain of the 1950's the Liberal Party, though united, active and rising in strength and in support, is still the most mysterious element in our political life. It appeals to generations that have never known a Liberal Government. Its philosophy, lucid and consistent as it is, is not likely to be widely understood outside its own ranks. The *techniques* of Liberal administration and economics, on the other hand, are better understood than ever and are being extended to one Commonwealth country after another, while many hundreds of economic and statistical studies have appeared in the last thirty years to occupy the territory into which the Yellow Book boldly ventured as a pioneer.

We have not tried to write another technical study. Instead our object has been to re-define Liberal attitudes in the round, especially at their most problematical, and our central theme has inevitably been the prospects of liberty in the Welfare State. No other Party would have allowed to a group of its members such freedom in publicly expressing their views; in no other, perhaps, in an age of political apathy, does the certain conviction survive that such a book is worth writing at all. We have no doubts on either score. But we are bound to emphasize that this book, explicitly Liberal as it is, does not at every point define the official policy of the Liberal Party, a task for which we have no authority. Responsibility lies with the Editorial Committee alone, which stands as the corporate author of the book as a whole, though it cannot be expected that each member of the Committee should feel himself bound by every recommendation. Initials of contributors are appended to the chapters for which they primarily are responsible.

CONTENTS

BOOK ONE

THE
LIBERAL
OUTLOOK

I
Liberty and Welfare

II
The Reform of Parliament

III
Civil Liberties

IV
Property and Equality

CHAPTER I

LIBERTY AND WELFARE

IT is no coincidence that 'Liberty' and 'Liberalism' have the same root. Historically the two have been so closely associated that it is almost impossible to think of one without the other. The word 'Liberal' was first adopted as a political label in Spain, in the Cortes at Cadiz in 1810, to denote the opposite of 'servile'[1]. A Liberal is 'unservile', insubordinate. On account of its association with the *idées libérales* of the French Revolution it was taken up by reactionaries in this country as a 'boo-word' to disparage the champions of reform as unpatriotic and pro-French, but as it was already familiar in a laudatory sense the reformers were glad to accept it, and in course of time it provided a common banner under which the Whigs, with 'their sedate loyalty to their traditional creed of civil and political liberty',[2] and the more fiery Radicals could work together. Eventually the Whig Party, having shed its more conservative elements to the Tories, dropped its title altogether and became generally known as the Liberal Party.

Everywhere the Liberal movements were identified with the cause of political and civil liberty — and with the cause of national liberty also, British Liberals showing consistent sympathy with

[1] Wilhelm Röpke, *International Economic Disintegration* (1942), p. 91, and the article by Juan Marichal, 'España y las raíces semanticôs del liberalismo,' *Cuadernos* (Paris), March-April 1955.

[2] Ramsay Muir, article on 'The Liberal Party' in the *Encyclopaedia Britannica*. The first British writer to use the term as a political label seems to have been Robert Southey (*Quarterly Review*, October 1816), who in an unsigned article against Parliamentary reform reviewed the crimes of Napoleon and dubbed him scornfully 'This perfect Emperor of the British *Liberales*' (p. 240).

'peoples rightly struggling to be free'. Everywhere, too, Liberalism was identified with economic liberty, in its simple sense of freedom from State interference;[1] but in Britain the Whig or Liberal Party never wholly associated itself with the views of the Classical Liberal economists, nor were the latter ever completely *laissez-faire* or so lacking in compassion as has been represented in popular legend.[2]

As time has passed, moreover, British Liberalism has become increasingly identified with Welfare — or, as one might put it, with 'economic liberty' in its modern sense. The first steps in establishing what has come to be known as the Welfare State were taken by Whig or Liberal Governments — e.g. the Factory Acts of 1833 and 1847, the legalization of trade unions (Trade Union Act, 1871), the 'liberalization' of taxation through graduation according to ability to pay, death duties, supertax, etc., the funds thereby raised being used to finance social improvement; the initiation of Old Age Pensions (1908) and of Health and Unemployment Insurance (1911). While the Liberal Party, during its sojourn in the wilderness, has been opening up new ground in the study of economic and social problems (for example, the famous Yellow Book of 1928 and the more recent reports on Trade Unionism, Co-ownership in Industry, Education and the Problem of the Aged), it may fairly be claimed that everything which other Parties have subsequently done in the way of Welfare has been merely a development of its achievements when it was last in office.

Thus in Liberal thought and action Liberty and Welfare have gone together, but during the period in which Liberalism has been in eclipse there has been an increasing tendency to set them over against each other. The 'new' freedoms (economic) are contrasted

---

[1] This phrase has undergone a striking change of meaning, being commonly used nowadays to signify social security — freedom from want, unemployment, etc. — which involves a great deal of State interference with 'natural' economic processes.

[2] See Lionel Robbins, *The Theory of Economic Policy* (1952), *Capitalism and the Historians*, ed. F. A. Hayek (1954), and pp. 113–116, below.

with the 'old' (civil and political), and in some quarters which make much of the former there is a disposition to devalue the latter. This tendency, which vitiates much of Socialist thought, is seen at its logical extreme in Communism. 'Libertarians', on the other hand, are apt to deny that the new freedoms are freedoms at all, to dwell on the restrictions their establishment has involved, and to use 'Welfare State' as a term of disparagement.[1]

Liberalism — true Liberalism — repudiates this antithesis. It regards Liberty and Welfare as complementary, and both as means to the same end — the creation of opportunity for men and women to become self-directing, responsible persons.[2] Concern for the human person is Liberalism's prime inspiration. 'It is here', says Walter Lippmann, 'on the nature of man, between those who would respect him as an autonomous person and those who would degrade him to a living instrument, that the issue is joined.'[3] Liberals are in no doubt on which side they stand.[4] The unique significance of the person is an ethical concept. Christians would say that it is based on the theological ground that men are children of God and immortal souls. Humanists accept the conclusions

[1] The divergence in emphasis is well illustrated by the papers produced to assist UNESCO in drafting the Universal Declaration of Human Rights (*Human Rights,* 1949) where the contrast between the Western and the Eastern contributions is most marked.

[2] In a famous dictum Acton declared, 'Liberty is not a means to a higher political end: in itself it is the highest political end'; but the qualifying adjective 'political' should be noted. At its highest politics can never be more than an instrument, and a political end must always have an end beyond itself. We may agree that Liberty is the highest *political* end and yet continue to insist that it is a means to something further — the full and harmonious development of the human person.

[3] Walter Lippmann, *The Good Society* (Allen & Unwin, 1937), p. 387.

[4] It is significant that when (in his book of that title) Mr Victor Gollancz wrote of 'Our Threatened Values', and stressed respect for personality as the greatest, he designedly spoke of them as 'liberal' rather than 'socialist' values — though it is only fair to add that he went on to say, 'Because in the world of today liberalism can only preserve itself by flowering into socialism, the reader will understand that by liberalism I mean a liberal and humanistic socialism, wherever the context permits' (*Our Threatened Values* (1946), pp. 18–19).

without accepting the premise. But both found their convictions about the way in which men should be treated in society on an assumption which is unprovable: they make a leap of faith. This faith is the motive-force of Liberalism.

Liberals are sometimes described — indeed, they sometimes describe themselves — as individualists. Inasmuch as they are primarily concerned with individual human beings, the description is correct; but if by individualism is meant the atomistic conception which regards men and women as isolated units, each pursuing its own selfish interest regardless of the rest, then we must emphatically reject the name. The individual human being cannot live to himself alone. Willy-nilly he is involved in a complex of social relationships, and it is only in the interplay of mutual claims and obligations that he can develop as a person. Of all people Liberals are most conscious of this fact, and accordingly they are better described as 'personalists', aiming to make men responsible as well as self-directing, stressing their interdependence as much as their independence.

Liberty means being free, in the sense of not being prevented by external prohibitions or coercions to do something one chooses. The factor of choice is crucial. 'Personality', as has been said, 'is decision.' Men may choose good or evil, wisely or foolishly, but so long as the choice is their own they have liberty. Whether, in the interests of maximizing opportunity for the development of personality, it is good that they should be at liberty in this, that or the other particular way is another question, to be judged by the effects which their exercise of this particular liberty may have on the liberty of others. As for the equivocation of politicians asserting that they stand for 'liberty, not licence', the cliché camouflages a confusion of thought. Licence *is* liberty, but liberty (according to the views of the speaker) abused. Where the line should be drawn is a question that will be answered differently in different societies; but that it must be drawn somewhere is evident. If every man were (theoretically) free to do just as he liked, the result would be an anarchy in which no man, save the strongest and most ruthless, would be able to do anything he liked. One man's rights may mean another's wrongs. Restraint is the other side of freedom, and restrictions have to be placed on liberty in the interests of liberty itself. The conflict between claims ('Who shall be at liberty to do what?') is a perennial problem. The situation is constantly changing and the disfranchized of one generation may be the tyrants of the next. For Liberals the criterion must always be whether by conceding or denying a particular claim the sum total of liberty (or, rather, of opportunity for the development of personality) will be increased. We shall be constantly occupied with this problem in this book. It is *the* problem of a free society.

What then of the relations between Liberty and Welfare? We argue that Welfare is actually a form of Liberty inasmuch as it liberates men from social conditions which narrow their choices and thwart their self-development as truly as any governmental or personal coercions. At any rate both, in the Liberal view, have this in common that they should be regarded as means to the full and harmonious development of persons. But the 'new' freedoms differ from the old in that they call for positive measures, whereas the 'old' freedoms require simply the abolition of restraints. Their establishment, though in many ways extending the field for free action, involves restrictions which did not exist before. A great machine is needed to administer them and more machinery still to prevent their abuse — an extensive system of rules and regulations, a vast amount of red tape and an army of officials who cost a great deal to maintain and whose bureaucratic methods are often strongly and rightly resented.

Nor is this all. A not unimportant liberty is the liberty to get and spend one's income as one likes. This is seriously curtailed by the heavy taxation required to finance the social services and the contributions required from 'insured persons', who benefit from the ways in which their money is used but have no choice in its spending.

Once again the conflict of claims arises — 'Who shall be free to do what?' The question is whether, taking the members of society as a whole, the net effect of the means adopted to spread

Welfare more widely is to increase or diminish their scope for self-direction and responsibility. Under totalitarian systems, where civil and political liberties are reduced to zero and the benefits (such as they are) are liable to be withdrawn if their recipients show any sign of independence, there is plainly an overwhelming surplus on the debit side. In free societies, though so far in Britain there can be little doubt that the pursuit of Welfare has resulted in a net increase in effective liberty, a constant watch is needed lest the balance should tip against it. It has been inevitable that as the range of the State's concern for the Welfare of its citizens has increased, so has its control over their lives. But has not this gone unnecessarily far? Is not the control both too pervasive and too detailed? That many abuses exist is unquestioned. How are they to be remedied without weakening the structure itself? How are the subjects of the Welfare State to be secured in the personal rights they have enjoyed so long? How are its agents to be made amenable to the Rule of Law? How can the Executive be brought under more effective Parliamentary control? How can the anonymous arbitrariness of official persons be checked? These questions — discussed in Chapter III — go to the very foundations of a free society.

Again, it is sometimes alleged that 'all this spoon-feeding' is sapping the British character — that when the State does so much for the citizen he loses the impulse to do things for himself. Is this true — and if so how true is it? The gloomy conclusion that security is fatal to initiative and enterprise is certainly unjustified. History attests that. But it is undeniable that some of the present symptoms warrant anxiety, and these, coupled with the inescapable fact that more State provision means more State control, prompt yet a further question.

Are the social services to be regarded as crutches, necessary while so many are unable to walk freely as they would like, but to be discarded as soon as they are able to use their own legs? Or are they to be considered as permanent features of a Liberal Society? With the value they attach to self-direction, Liberals must naturally desire that people should be able to make more adequate provision for themselves than many can do now, instead of relying on the State to make it for them. They certainly do not regard the present structure of the social services as sacrosanct, and favour substantial changes in organization and administration. On the other hand they are keenly concerned for the less fortunate and passionately believe in the principle of mutual responsibility. With these considerations in mind, is it possible or desirable to cut down the provision which the State now makes? If not, when? and to what extent? How far would it be practicable to introduce more choice in the State-run systems — in health insurance, for instance, or in education? These questions, bristling with difficulty, are also examined in subsequent chapters. If the results may be anticipated and summarized, we may say that while whole-heartedly approving of Welfare (i.e. of some social arrangement that will ensure subsistence and protect the citizen against economic misfortune) our aim is a 'Welfare Society' rather than a 'Welfare State'.[1] We recognize that the State must remain responsible for those for whom other sources of Welfare are not available; but in a Liberal society we should look increasingly to the release and stimulation of private endeavour and voluntary agencies of service and mutual aid to diminish the rôle of the State. Eventually society, i.e. individuals and groups of individuals, would be able and ready to provide most of its welfare for itself.

In the introduction to his *Full Employment in a Free Society: a Report* (1944)[2] Lord Beveridge has stated that his purpose was 'to propose for the State only those things which the State alone can do or which it can do better than any local authority or than private citizens either singly or in association, and to leave to those other agencies that which, if they will, they can do as well as or better than the State' (p. 36). Wilhelm Röpke has extended this principle, which he calls 'the principle of subsidiarity', to apply to the whole hierarchy of society, from the individual through family, parish, district or county up to the central Government.[3] This is

[1] For this distinction we are indebted to Lord Beveridge, and for his permission to use it (apparently for the first time) in print.

[2] London: Allen & Unwin.   [3] Wilhelm Röpke, *Civitas Humana* (1948), p. 90.

the principle by which we propose that the existing Welfare State should be transformed by stages into a Welfare Society.

In the past many social organizations have undertaken the task of providing Welfare. In the Middle Ages there was a Welfare Church. The Reformation, by sequestering Church property, made it imperative for some other body to step in: this was the (lay) Welfare Parish. But social changes put an increasing strain on the parish, and the Industrial Revolution rendered it completely incapable of these functions, limited though they were. This fact was recognized by the Poor Law of 1834, which set up the 'Union' in place of the parish. But the Union became a name of odium and Bumble the personification of its central feature, the workhouse. There followed a period in which attempts were made to humanize the administration of the Unions, and in which a variety of private Welfare organizations — friendly societies and insurance companies, with trade unions and co-operative societies fulfilling some similar functions — sought to mitigate the hardships caused by uncontrolled social and economic developments; but these proved quite insufficient and, while the Royal Commission in 1909 recommended drastic reforms in the Poor Law system which were not carried out until after the first World War, the Liberal Parliament in 1911 borrowed a leaf from Bismarck and his Prussian Welfare State by initiating National Health and Unemployment Insurance. Thus the foundation of our own Welfare State was laid.

This was a notable advance: but as the years have passed and the system thus initiated has assumed such comprehensive proportions it has become evident that a State monopoly in Welfare has certain illiberal consequences, and our conviction is that the time has come to provide, not Welfare merely, but a varied and competitive Welfare. Much can be done by devolution (back to the parish, as it were): and more, we claim, in a dynamic and expanding economy, by encouraging personal effort and by some reversion to the spontaneous Welfare organizations in which the nineteenth century put too early and too complete a trust.

Set, here as everywhere, on creating conditions favourable to

the development of personality, Liberals are necessarily distributists. Concentration, which has grown so portentously in so many
fields, is the great robber of personal dignity and significance.
Liberals therefore seek to spread wealth, ownership, power and
responsibility as widely as possible. Thanks largely to their initiative, much has already been done to spread income. It is arguable that this process has gone too far: that in the laudable effort
to level up, levelling down has reached danger-point. Certainly
the inordinate tax burden weighs with particular unfairness on
some of the most talented elements in the nation. Little or
nothing, however, has been done to spread property; yet this, as
is emphasized in Chapter IV, is vital to the spreading of choice
and the creation of greater equality of opportunity.

'Greater equality of opportunity' — not equality of possession.
The distinction is crucial. Equality of possession, whether in
property or income, is not practicable, or at least only practicable
in a totalitarian society. On the other hand, equality of opportunity is, in a rough sense, feasible, and is essential if all citizens
are to have a fair chance of developing themselves to the full. But
we should face the evident fact that greater equality of opportunity
is likely to tend to less, not more, equality of possession, since
talents previously condemned to 'fust unused' will be set free and
will earn greater rewards; and watch will have to be kept lest a
new inequality of opportunity should result at next remove owing
to the effects of inheritance.

Other aspects of the distributism which is such a distinguishing
mark of Liberal thought and policy — all considered in this book
— are devolution from Westminster; the energizing of local
government; the re-distribution of population; the breaking down
of monopoly; the regionalizing (where possible) of the nationalized
industries and services and the institution of competition between
the various units; and the spreading of co-ownership in industry.

Welfare has to be paid for. The extent to which it can be financed depends on the national wealth, and this emphasizes the need
for greater dynamism in our society, discussed in Chapter VIII.

It is true that a free economy, though it may maximize national
wealth, does not necessarily promote the spreading of the product and thus the creation of greater equality of opportunity. A
nation, indeed, may grow very rich as an entity, yet its wealth
may be so maldistributed as to frustrate the self-development of
many — and also, by way of nemesis, to create frictions which
impede the wealth-producing process. But the antithesis of a free
versus a planned economy is false, thus crudely stated. A totally
planned economy is, of course, irreconcilable with freedom; but
planning at certain central points is necessary in order to maintain
the institutional framework favourable to liberty and even to preserve the freedom of the economy itself. A free economy needs to
be upheld by law (which means denying freedom to those, e.g.
some monopolists, who would pervert it), and steps must be
taken to 'redress the balance of private actions by compensating
public actions'.[1]

At this point, perhaps, a caveat should be entered. Man does not
live by bread alone, and, important though economic progress
may be, Liberals do not make the mistake of regarding economic
ends as necessarily supreme. Sometimes an economic sacrifice has
to be made to attain more human purposes. Moreover, material
progress may hinder moral and spiritual. A nation may grow rich,
its wealth may be widely spread, yet the consequence may be a
vulgarization of values that cripples its members' development as
persons. It is here that education has such a crucial part to play (see
Chapter VII).

Welfare must always be considered in an international setting.
Other nations do not owe Britain a living — certainly not such
Welfare as it enjoys. The needs of defence and the policies of other
nations may restrict the capacity for expenditure on Welfare (see
Chapter XII). On the other hand (see Chapter XIII) the need for
Welfare in a free society is as true beyond Europe as within it, and
it is our plain duty to spread Liberty and Welfare throughout the
Empire and Commonwealth.

[1] Walter Lippmann, *The Method of Freedom* (1934), p. 46.

But do men want Liberty? In Liberal circles fifty years ago it would have been regarded as almost blasphemous to raise this question, it being taken for granted that men everywhere were longing to be free. Today, however, we are only too keenly aware that this is a delusion — in so far, at least, as freedom involves responsibility. In many countries the burdens of freedom have been felt too heavy to bear and dictatorships have been welcomed. They have worked, they have been wildly popular. Even in Britain there are many people who are afraid of having too much liberty — they prefer to have things ordered and provided for them: 'a quiet life and not much trouble.' This is one of the facts that libertarians have to face. But the fact is not a hopeless one. People everywhere do tend to react against *particular* denials of liberty — for instance against foreign domination or exploitation by other classes. Everyone (or nearly everyone) wants freedom to eat enough, to choose their occupation and to be decently housed; above that level liberties may be ranked in an ascending scale of value according to the encouragement they give for personal decision.

It is essential to maintain the 'higher' liberties — of thought, worship, research, etc. — even though they may be desired by a minority only, since their use by this minority makes for intellectual, moral and even material progress and creates an atmosphere encouraging to the pursuit of liberty generally. The Liberal aim is to provoke an appetite for liberty, even where it hardly exists. Certainly it is impossible to *make* men self-directing, responsible citizens. They must do this for themselves. But society can create opportunities for them to become so, and encourage them to take them. Here again education has a vital rôle to play. A full circle has been turned in British politics in the last half-century and circumstances today seem combining to give many a livelier interest in liberty. There is a high state of awareness more widely spread than ever; the full effects of free compulsory education are only now becoming apparent. There is a new and critical attitude towards authority, especially in our youngest school of writers. At the same time it has become increasingly plain to everyone that authority — not merely Government, but also the great industrial combines, the T.U.C., etc. — has over-extended itself and is failing to grasp its duties.

Evidence of this greater awareness may be seen in the unexpected resilience of the Liberal vote since the War — not sufficiently noticed because unreflected in terms of seats; in the high morale in Liberal Party circles during the last few years, and in an influx of youth into the Party which has transformed it from the oldest to the youngest political Party in Britain. The change may be measured by the fact that whereas between 1945 and 1950 few people would have been surprised if the Liberal Party had thrown up the sponge, the political extinction of Liberalism today is inconceivable, and the upsurge in Liberal ideas has been noteworthy far beyond the Party. Before the war most intellectuals and uncommitted persons talked Marxism-diluted; now they talk a form of Liberalism (e.g. Mr Arthur Koestler and Mr J. B. Priestley). Significant too is the shift in political issues between the major Parties (in so far as there are any) from Marxist-imposed issues (nationalization or no) to Liberal-imposed issues (monopoly or no). It is true that the cynicism and sense of impotence bred during the post-war years, when Tories and Socialists — regarded by so many as the only available choices — have competed with each other in lack of vision and political incompetence, are still widespread. These have encouraged the feeling that, lamentable though the erosion of liberty has been, nothing much can be done about it. But a spirit of conviction and resolution has begun to assert itself, and its contagion is spreading.

Much of the Liberal advance since the war, in Britain and abroad, has been obscured and impeded by the persisting, but mistaken, use of linear classifications — 'Left', 'Right', 'Centre'. Originally 'Left' and 'Right' meant libertarian and anti-libertarian, as in post-Napoleonic France. They have now come to mean (if anything) something like the reverse. Though still carrying the 'hurrah' suggestions of something more advanced, Leftism has come to be measured by the extent to which a Party stands for State ownership or regulation. Thus Communists are still represented as 'progressive', and Tories (posing as champions of 'free enterprise') as 'reactionary', with Liberals teetering somewhere in the middle. In consequence those who think of themselves as Radicals are apt to be much tenderer towards tyrannies of the so-called Left than to those of the Right.

All this is nonsense. The true criterion — if linear classifications are to be accepted at all — must remain concern for opportunity for the individual person. And by this criterion many of the so-called Leftist Parties are the most reactionary. Communism gives no scope for personal self-determination whatever — it is an intensely *aristocratic* system of society — and the more 'Left' the Socialist groups are the more they approximate to this position. The Tories are the true 'Centre' of British politics, a dead centre dedicated neither to enlarging nor to restricting opportunity for the ordinary person, but to the *status quo* and 'don't rock the boat' — with a bias in favour of *beati possidentes*. By any strict use of language Liberals are the true Left, the real progressives. The widespread failure to recognize this fact is a measure of the defeat the Left has sustained since the beginning of our century.

Progress is only meaningful in terms of purpose. The Liberal purpose — let it be said again — is 'the creation of opportunity for men and women to become self-directing, responsible persons'. This means the simultaneous pursuit of Liberty and Welfare — or, if that way of putting it is preferred, of Welfare as an element in Liberty. It is because Welfare has come to be dissociated from Liberty, or set in antithesis to it, that Liberty has lost so much of its appeal; that Liberalism, falsely identified with Liberty as against Welfare, has suffered decline; and that the Statist parties (Communist and Socialist) have gained such unwarranted prestige with progressives. The business of Liberals today is to show by a practical and relevant programme how Liberty and Welfare can be consistently pursued with the aim of giving 'more abundant life' to the individual person — Liberty conceived as not merely freedom from restrictions, but as the enlargement of scope for the exercise of responsible citizenship: Welfare conceived, not merely as cash and comfort, but as providing opportunity for moral, intellectual and cultural development such as is frustrated when men are obsessed by anxiety about the bare business of living; and both encouraging adventure, experiment, colour, variety and eccentricity. Thus may Liberals re-establish themselves in their natural position as the acknowledged leaders of the Left — a consummation towards which we hope in this volume to make a contribution.

E. D.

CHAPTER II

THE REFORM OF
PARLIAMENT

PARLIAMENT is the traditional guardian of our liberties. How well does it guard them? And, since liberty depends on effective government, how efficiently does it govern?

I. THE NEW RÔLE OF PARLIAMENT

The rôle of Parliament is very different from what it once was. Formerly its main function was to stop the Executive from interfering too much with the life of its subjects. Now the boot is on the other foot. Individual Members of Parliament habitually urge the Executive to intervene more, to do more and to spend more. In fact resistance to more State action and more spending now tends to come from the Executive, not from Parliament. And in this change alone there is a threat to individual liberty. The Executive is not by its nature a reliable guardian of personal liberty. As its power spreads the need for more adequate checks upon its innumerable activities grows.

But so far people probably feel that though there are instances where the Government has overstepped the boundaries of what is tolerable, the advantages outweigh the disadvantages. We support the redistribution of income that has taken place. We want the Welfare Society and are prepared to pay for it. We approve of sumptuary taxation and are ready to give special assistance to industries, districts or classes of the population in special difficulties. But we should not blind ourselves to the erosion of the defences once erected against the Executive.

2. THE MEMBER OF PARLIAMENT

Let us look, first of all, at the membership of the House of Commons. It has always been fashionable to decry politicians, but, though no one would claim that M.P.s today are the *élite* of the nation the general standard is probably as high as it ever was. Yet unless first-rate men can feel that they will be given a chance to do useful work in Parliament they will not come forward — and there is a danger that they will soon feel the burden not worth the result unless Parliament can be made more efficient. Fortunately, there were indications at the 1955 election that personalities counted more than in other elections since the war, and there may be a natural reaction against blindly voting the Party ticket. After the 1945 election the House of Commons contained three completely independent Members and a few others such as Mr Lipson who were not official candidates of their Party. All the Independents together with the Labour dissentients such as Pritt, Platt-Mills and Zilliacus were defeated in 1950. Since 1945 no Independent has been elected.

But there are in the first place other factors which militate against independence. About 100 Members are directly connected with trade unions. Unions pay up to 80% of the election expenses of some Members. They contribute to constituency expenses of those elected in some cases and provide secretarial assistance, etc., in addition to paying pensions to many ex-trade-union officials. It is surprising that there has been so little comment on this practice. We should be shocked if anyone proposed a return to the old pocket-borough system, but we seem indifferent to the pocket-boroughs under our noses. Trade unions nominate candidates to the local Labour Party selection committees for certain seats. These nominees are usually selected. Once selected they are often as certain of election as any nominee for a pocket-borough. This system has its advantages and, as was the case with pocket-boroughs, many good members reach Parliament as a result. But they are hardly free agents. Nor are trade unionists the only Members who must look over their shoulders, so to speak. Members who rely on some business for part of their livelihood, or for a pension, may be as much in its power as trade unionists. Though in fact the dependence of Members on outside interests is free from most of the worst abuses that might arise, the direct support of Members by outside bodies is surely in principle bad and should be unnecessary. It is a far more serious danger to independence than holding an office of profit under the Crown.

This is particularly serious today from the point of view of democracy when some trade-union practices could affect efficiency and freedom and the unions seem sometimes bent on the establishment of an *imperium in imperio* regardless of the general interest. Members should be put in a position where they can unquestionably live in the style required of them without such payment. This is a strong argument for increasing their pay. The criterion should be that any Member can live on his salary and discharge the normal expenses which are inevitable in his position, and £1,000 a year plus a modest allowance is not enough. It need not be increased so that it offers rewards comparable to business or the top ranks of the professions, but £1,750 a year would not be excessive and should free anyone from any possible need for dependence on outside sources.

There are of course people who have a horror of paying M.P.s too much in case they become professional politicians. But politics in the end is concerned with the exercise of power: men and women become Members of Parliament to do things or stop them being done. Parliament is the seat of power. It needs considerable concentration and study. It is not enough for Members to use it as a platform from which to conduct outside interests nor as a debating society in which views can be aired. Today more than ever a proper exercise of power — however indirect it may be — by the ordinary Member needs time and thought. Certainly those who want the back-bench Member of the Commons to exert more influence must saddle him with more, not less, political work. We may be told that the House of Lords is regaled with wisdom wonderfully distilled by men of experience who are not politicians. Would not the House of Commons too (so the argument runs) be much poorer if shorn of its ex-public servants, business and trade-union leaders, farmers and lawyers? Should we not actively encourage politicians to take up other activities or men with other activities to take up politics? These arguments are only partially true. The criterion is not that every politician should have another job but that some politicians can have other jobs, or some people with other jobs can be politicians. There are certain fallacies in the demands for fewer professional politicians. The House of Lords is not as good as it is painted; and many of its best members, such as Lord Salisbury, Lord Samuel and Lord Swinton are first and fore-most politicians. Nor is the contribution made to the Commons by men in other trades or professions outstanding. How can it be? How can a first-rate business man or lawyer find time to give of his best in the Commons?

Another chain on a Member is his electorate. This, on the whole, is the one limitation on his freedom that Liberals can be expected to approve, but constituency associations have been apt to make excessive demands on a Member's pocket and time. Nor are they usually favourable to eccentric views. Their power, therefore, has not always encouraged the man or woman with wide interests, little money and an independent mind. The aspirants recommended by the Whips, though of course strictly on the Party line, have often been more distinguished than local nominees.

The candidate has usually given some hostages to local inter-ests before the election. If he is elected for a seat with ties to a particular industry he is soon made to feel the reins. Few great sayings are more honoured in the breach than Burke's that a Member of Parliament is a representative but not a delegate.[1] In point of fact the power of constituency and other interests is un-duly magnified by many Members. It is surprising how successful well-organized lobbies can be — such as the Sunday Observance

[1] 'Parliament is a deliberative assembly of one nation, with one interest, that of the whole. . . . You choose a Member indeed; but when you have chosen him, he is not Member of Bristol, but he is a Member of Parliament' (*Speech to the Electors of Bristol*, 1774).

THE REFORM OF PARLIAMENT

lobby — though they represent only a small number of voters. It is asking a great deal of a Member from an agricultural constituency to oppose subsidies to farmers even if he were converted to the view that in the general interest they were wrong. Each constituency has its own interests; intimate connection with a constituency must influence a Member's judgement and tend to limit his freedom.

Indeed the time may now have come to question the sacred cow of regional representation. What do we want to see represented? Originally, towns and countries had a community of feeling and interest. Regional Members represented this common feeling or common interest. Today Welsh Nationalists, trade unionists, farmers, doctors and Liberals may feel far more in common with their colleagues elsewhere than with their fellow-citizens in Merioneth, Manchester or Barons Court. The slicing-up of large cities into arbitrary blocks corresponds to no community boundaries. But do we want *interests* to be represented? Is this Fascism? Or why not divide up the electors alphabetically, giving 70,000 of those whose names begin with A one Member? At all events regional representation is often an anachronism in the modern world. Proportional Representation would give us a House of Commons more reflective of various trends of thought, though it would not of course abolish sectional interests entirely.

Luckily some pressures cancel each other out. Those who deplore the loss of independence among Members must bear in mind that if the power of the Party Whips is diminished, the power of selfish interests may be increased. One example may bring this home: so long as we have purchase tax it is only by the enforcing of discipline by the Government that any justice or order can be maintained in its application. Many Members are engaged in pressing for a reduction on commodities their own constituents make or use and if they were free to follow their voices with their votes chaos and unfairness would result. No doubt this particular difficulty arises from certain bad characteristics of the tax. But it is only an extreme example of what is fairly general: if

you release the pressure of the Whip you do not necessarily increase the freedom of Members.

3. LIBERTY IN PARLIAMENT

What are the results of these limitations on Members' freedom?
How far do they militate against Parliamentary efficiency and
weaken Parliament as a safeguard of liberty?

As far as liberty is concerned, it will always find champions
when votes and popularity are to be won upholding it. Parliament
has plenty of spokesmen against *unpopular* infringements of
liberty. But it is more difficult to assess how far it can be trusted as
the guardian of liberty in cases where the person threatened is himself unpopular or when there are strong arguments for curtailing
liberty. The test cases should be those under 18B. It is a little soon
still to judge how fairly that order was administered or to say how
much of the credit for its success was due to the particular Home
Secretaries and their advisers who administered it. But administration of the restrictions on liberty in the war does seem to have
been a success after some panic internments. Nevertheless, Parliament does not react as vigorously or wholeheartedly against
tyranny — petty or great — as a Liberal would wish. It took a
long time to get action on Crichel Down and there again the
prestige which accrued to Parliament in the end was partly due to
the self-sacrificing attitude of the Minister for Agriculture; and the
case of Seretse Khama, the comparative acquiescence in some of
the anti-Mau Mau measures and the lack of reaction against Russian tyranny are disquieting.

There are some subjects which may be badly handled by
Parliament because of their electoral implications: to give two
examples, very little protest is made against attacks on individual
liberty by organized labour and the Zionist lobby has sometimes
been able to drown the case for the Arabs, whatever its merits may
be.

The willingness of a Member to react against excessive infringements of liberty is clearly bound up with the Party system.

The Party not only does its best to ensure conformity but in general is anxious not to stir up trouble. It does not encourage original thought. It frowns upon any protests against stupidity or tyranny which are more likely to lose than win votes. Worse perhaps, the Party numbs the originality and frustrates the good intentions of many of its Members. The Party is the Lord Melbourne of modern politics too often declaring, 'It is not much matter what we say, but mind, we must all say the same.'

The Party Whips esteem silence and good health, with administrative competence. But these should be the virtues of a civil servant, not a politician. The result is to accentuate the centralizing tendencies of modern government. The position of the Prime Minister and the Cabinet is enhanced. A mass of colourless and unnecessary legislation is constantly before the House. Too little thought is given to wider or longer ranges of politics — the ranges which are becoming more and more important to our survival.

And the sanctions against a Member asserting himself are very strong: constant attendance at the discussion of trivial matters; ultimately, the withdrawal of the Whip. Once a Member has been disowned by his Party Organization, as several Labour Members were between 1945 and 1950, his career is seriously jeopardized if not ended. Admittedly he can go a fair way before this happens. To begin with, back-benchers can speak with freedom and with considerable influence in the Party committees, which meet in private (sometimes not as privately as they would wish). When the issue comes before the House of Commons the real battle may be over. Labour back-benchers have forced concessions from their leaders on the case of Seretse Khama and the '14-day ban'. Conservative back-benchers prevented a Teachers' Pensions Bill which they disliked ever reaching the House of Commons for a Second Reading.

In the House itself back-benchers can speak against the official line of their Party without risking more than a rebuke and a black mark against their chances of office. Nor are such speeches without effect. The House of Commons is sometimes accused of staging sham fights. It is true that the result of the debate is a foregone conclusion and that few votes — except on the rare occasions of a

B

free vote — can be influenced. There are no Independents in the House now and the Liberal Party cannot by itself change the result of the vote. But it is there to be won over on many issues by the speeches made. It must be remembered too that the work of Parliament is a continuing process. Speeches remain on the record in Hansard to be read and pondered upon. If the weight of argument is clearly against the official line it may well in the long run change it, especially if the rebels gain wide public support. A speech which may seem quite ineffective in the debate in which it is delivered may nevertheless have later repercussions. And, of course, there are the conversations in the lobby and the smoking room. The official views of Parties are not so rigid as they are sometimes thought to be.

Nevertheless, the power of the Whip has grown very much and ought to be curtailed. Free expression in the Party meetings and the delayed effect of speeches and conversations are not enough. In the totalitarian countries there are no doubt acrimonious discussions among the members of the ruling junta; but these are concluded before the decision is brought before any public or democratic assemblies. Discussion by Party meetings is the Communist method. We are rightly scornful of Reichstags and should beware of sowing the seeds within our own system.

4. THE CONGESTION OF PARLIAMENT

Furthermore, the complexity of modern government means that any Member must take a good deal on trust. He cannot study every problem and every Bill and must often take his Party's word for it that their general line as expounded by the Party's experts is reasonable. Nor in fact could the business be carried by 'dull M.P.s in close proximity all thinking for themselves'. The Government must have some pattern and coherence in its policy. Ministers would be in an impossible position if many of their Bills — or clauses within Bills — were continually defeated. Implications much more far-reaching than might appear to the ordinary Member would be felt throughout their programme.

But more serious than the pressure of constituency, Party or livelihood on the private Member is the weight of governmental business, relentless, impersonal and perpetual. More and more troubles are brought to the House of Commons or the Government with requests to do something about them. The mill of debates, questions, correspondence, legislation grinds ever more relentlessly. It must here be said that the present Government has unnecessarily cluttered up Parliament with a spate of minor Bills.

The British Parliamentary system depends upon obvious responsibility. We can see at various levels those who have the power. That the power may be circumscribed and the responsibility an illusion is sometimes true; nevertheless the illusion has enough reality for the Parliamentary system to retain prestige. In each constituency there is one Member, one representative. He is not a name on a list. He is a thing of flesh and blood who on the platform or at his committee rooms can be questioned. He is unique. Through him ultimately the choice of the electorate runs up to the leader of the Party — the actual or potential Prime Minister. We do not elect our foremost political leaders direct as in the United States, we elect an M.P. — even though he may prove a Party hack.

At the next stage responsibility is again pin-pointed. Every day in Parliament Ministers come to be seen and questioned in public. It is this which makes the House of Commons a place of incomparable drama. It is this which rivets on it the attention of the Press. These are the people who have the power to do something. There they are being told in public what to do. They cannot send experts to represent them; they must stand on their own feet and speak with their own voices. Personal responsibility is the justification for many features of our system — and the strongest argument for single Member straight-ballot constituencies.

But we pay a heavy price for this clear and individual responsibility. Ministers are broken on the wheel of routine long before they can turn to fundamentals. The Reform of Parliament itself, the Reform of Local Government and legislation on the reports of several Royal Commissions have been shelved. Our taxation system is badly in need of a calm review. It is difficult to believe that on Foreign Affairs, Commonwealth Affairs or Defence Ministers can sit back and make a long-term assessment. Indeed the strain on Ministers, increased by their habit of flitting about the globe, can only be borne by those with great constitutional strength and phlegmatic temperaments. Mr Francis Boyd, a most experienced lobby correspondent, considers that Mr Butler when Chancellor of the Exchequer arranged his work most carefully to keep strain to a minimum, yet he gives the following terrible description of his life: 'He arrived (at the Treasury) about 9.45 a.m. and left about 7 p.m. with a bag of official papers made up for him. Attendances at official dinners or at the House of Commons took up many evenings, but he liked to get to bed at about 11 p.m. He aimed at finishing his papers before going to sleep. They were collected, with Mr Butler's comments upon them, at 8.30 a.m. and the staff at the Treasury got to work on the comments before Mr Butler arrived. At the week ends, Mr Butler liked to get away to his country house in Essex. A bag of papers was made up for him on Fridays, and another was sent down on Saturdays. He kept this routine without much trouble because he had developed a flair for seizing the essentials in the papers submitted to him and could thus dispose of them rapidly.'

The individual Member is becoming more and more of a general father-confessor and welfare officer. His help is sought on every manner of personal and local problem, many of which are not political at all. As it is still the admirable tradition that all Member's letters and questions are thoroughly investigated by Ministries, the amount of work created is very considerable. Nor is it the weight of work alone which is so serious, so much as its variety. A mass of information, demands, correspondence, entertainment, pressure to speak and lecture, beats on every Member. He is provided with few defences. He has not a desk, let alone a room of his own. He must provide his own secretary, use a corner of the library, be ready to see constituents or answer the division bell, serve on committees discussing subjects in which he may have no interest and on top of everything there is the time-honoured, time-wasting and most inefficient method of organizing House of Commons business. We do not intend in this chapter to go into the various suggestions for detailed changes in the methods of the House. It is enough to point out that it is not at present set up adequately to do its work. As a result, there is not enough concentration on important matters. People who have a serious contribution to make on major political subjects either do not become M.P.s or, if they do, they either sink back into easy and superficial acquiescence in the prevailing opinions of their Party or at best strive to make their views felt behind the scenes.

Debates on Commonwealth or Foreign Affairs are particularly spasmodic. In the last six years there have been no debates about many of our colonies and dependencies, e.g. in the Pacific.

5. THE EFFICIENCY OF THE MACHINE

Some of the same forces which beat upon each Member and circumscribe his sphere of independent action also gravely affect the efficiency of the Government machine as a whole. The public scarcely realizes the extent to which it depends upon unpublicized public servants. The pressure on the higher ranks of the Civil Service must be very heavy and we must be sure that we do not tear the Service to pieces. We expect our senior Civil Servants to be a mixture of rare and contradictory qualities: they must be prepared to take responsibility; they must be exceedingly good at their job, yet they must have no itch to express their personalities; they must build up with equal enthusiasm good and bad Ministers. Nowadays too they must be ready to undertake jobs which are not 'Civil Service jobs' in the Victorian sense at all, since some departments are in business and have many contacts with business. They must watch their public relations. They must deal continually with individual cases and with powerful industrial firms requiring licences or advice. No longer can they live as an almost monkish order shrouded in anonymity dealing on clearly defined lines with a limited number of general problems. The top Civil Servants need judgment of the highest order, and should we fail to get replacements of sufficient calibre the whole Parliamentary system of government would suffer severely.

We believe that we are right not to budge yet from the doctrine of ministerial responsibility. But of course it is more than ever true that the Ministers cannot know all that goes on even at the top of their departments. It may be that with the size of the Civil Service and the multiplicity of the jobs which it undertakes we have to think again, and there are signs that whether they like it or not Civil Servants are emerging more into daylight. Already we have experienced the effects of a Horace Wilson. Today one cannot help suspecting that the senior staff at the Home Office exercise an influence not always wholly in accord with Parliamentary opinion. The development of the Civil Service tradition in the modern world poses very difficult questions indeed.

The inevitable increase in the power of the Civil Service makes it all the more necessary that there should be close scrutiny of its work. Civil Servants must not be left to judge political opinion nor (this criticism applies equally to politicians) are they trained business men. Some minor Government Bills lately introduced to Parliament seem to be the work of Civil Servants more intent on 'tidying up' legislation than following the rules of common sense. Decisions, too, that a postal charge should be increased 80% at one leap or that a nationalized industry should be authorized to spend £1,200,000,000 in sweeping changes in its methods on little satisfactory evidence that the outlay would be justified in higher profits, or that the lamp standards in a High Commissioner's house were reasonably priced at £117 each, do not give great confidence in the practical outlook of all Civil Servants.

Besides the Civil Servants there is another vital group behind the scenes — the Parliamentary Clerks. They have a delicate task. The Civil Servants are lions under the Minister's throne: the Clerks not only keep the business of Parliament going but are to some extent watch-dogs upon the Ministers and their lions, acting for Parliament as a whole and particularly the back-benchers.

Upon both these groups the growth of Parliamentary business has imposed great strain. It is quite logical under our present system that if the State takes a hand in so many things from wigs to jet-aircraft production the public should pester their Members about them. But when the innumerable points, questions and demands for debates come to be passed on either to the Clerks and to the Civil Service they impose much extra work in addition to the organization or preparation for Government and Opposition official business. And much of this extra business is not 'political' in the old sense at all. Yet to increase the numbers of key officials will hardly relieve the pressure, first because it is doubtful how far the supply of suitable men can be extended and partly because you cannot go on extending the tip of the pyramid without altering its character and indeed creating more work. Some unscrambling is needed. Work unsuitable to direct democratic control must be abandoned if Parliament, the Government and the Civil Service are to do their real work efficiently.

6. THE CONDUCT OF THE HOUSE

The main business of Parliament can be divided under three headings: there is legislation — principally the Second Readings, Committee, Report and Third Readings of Government Bills. There is the voting of supply, principally used for the discussion in general debate of subjects chosen by the Opposition; there are 26 Supply Days in the year. And there is the time devoted to private Members' points, notably Question Time.

As far as legislation is concerned, the Government is nearly always pressed for time. One day, occasionally two, are given for the debate on the principles and main features of a Bill; at this stage the Government is ruthless in insisting on a solid vote in the lobby. No one can blame it for this. But there are signs that the evolution of Parliament is opening up two dangers even in the treatment of the principle of major Bills. It is difficult to believe that some of the Bills which have been brought forward have received adequate consideration even in outline before they reach the light of day in the House of Commons. Secondly, once the Government's flag is nailed to the principle of a Bill there are now

no checks in the Constitution sufficient to make it think again. It is
a little frightening that a Labour Government without a majority
for Socialism in the country could pass nationalization measures
which even Socialists now admit would have benefited from more
consideration.

But again a warning must be given against expecting too much
of Parliament. While we would agree that some greater control of
the nationalized industries, for instance, is desirable, let no one
think that more and more debates or another brood of committees
are necessarily going to improve their efficiency. Again, it must be
stressed that Parliament is a political body concerned with political
power. It is not set up to run the Coal Industry. Nor will M.P.s
give more than a limited amount of attention to matters which are
not bound up with the political battle — the state of the House
when private Members' motions are being discussed is some
measure of that. We have yet to discover any adequate substitute
for the market in economic affairs. Having withdrawn certain
industries from the market it is certainly vital to find the best substitute we can, but piling the Pelion of Select Committees on the
Ossa of public boards is not enough.

The same sort of considerations lead us to believe that the
problem of 'delegated legislation' has been rather mis-stated. It is
true that the system is open to abuse. Its abuses are well known
and we do not intend to reiterate them here. Its effects on civil
liberty are considered in the next chapter. The difficulty is a genuine one and arises again from imposing on Parliament tasks which
it cannot fully discharge. The details of schemes for agricultural
subsidies or alterations in purchase tax are not always suitable
matters for democratic control except in principle. However much
time you provided for the debate of many orders, you would get
little enlightenment and a lot of sectional pressure. If you want the
Government to cover such an enormous field, then the best for
which we can hope is a thorough discussion of the principal Acts
from the point of view of the country as a whole, a first-rate Civil
Service, and constant vigilance for omissions and injustices. The
ultimate sanction of the public is to get a new Minister or a new

Head of a nationalized board. This should be made easier. No committee of Parliamentarians can teach the public boards their business.

But must Parliament attempt so much? There seems to be no instrument more effective than an occasional 'Geddes Axe' in pruning the growth of Government Departments while the attempt to keep the nationalized industries outside day-to-day Parliamentary pressure — which is desirable from Parliament's point of view as well as from that of the industries — has led to their floating in a world of their own largely insulated from political or economic control. The answer seems to be that the Government should get out of a lot of the business in which it still dabbles. It should try to reduce its commitments, e.g. in the Ministry of Supply; to hive off more welfare undertakings and to exercise general control over industry and finance rather than creating nationalized monopolies. If some industries must remain largely nationalized some sections or firms might be left in private hands to give us a measure of their efficiency and their success in meeting consumer needs. The welfare services might be run locally or by specialized bodies.

There is a conflict of view between those who think that a Bill is best considered by a committee of 50 Members, most of whom may be assumed to have some knowledge of the subject, and those who believe that on a Bill which raises important issues or affects the great majority of the people every Member has a right to make his views known. On the whole we favour sending more Bills 'upstairs', simply because it clears the floor of the Commons for other purposes. Fighting a Bill line by line, delaying it by endless repetition during the Committee Stage and dragging out its passage is usually unprofitable. The saga of the all-night sitting may rouse the battle spirit of M.P.'s, but the public are unimpressed and the Bill none the better for it. Short and informed criticism is what is wanted. Secondly, the Government should be able to allow much more freedom of voting on the Committee stage. Even if it feels it must insist on its point of view eventually it can still do this on report. Cross-voting used to be much more common. The fault at present is not so much that too little time is given to Bills in Committee but that much of the available time is wasted by repetition, by speeches for constituency consumption, by 'playing politics' and by ignorance of the back-ground to the subject. A Bill which should be closely examined may slip through if it does not make good propaganda while a comparatively straightforward Bill may be delayed *ad nauseum* if the Opposition find it is fertile in Party points.

In general debates the salient problems are the lack of Parliamentary control over expenditure and the nationalized industries and the difficulty of dealing adequately with Commonwealth and foreign affairs. The Gas and Electricity Industries were not discussed at all in the session 1954–5. The work of the North of Scotland Hydro Board merited three written replies only. The administration of Airports, Cable and Wireless and the Bank of England were not debated. Railways got one day, and the National Coal Board a statement by the Minister. The work of the Ministries supposed to control the nationalized industries is rarely looked into. In the House of Commons itself the estimates as such are hardly ever examined. When they come up the Opposition initiates a debate on a special subject such as civil aviation or takes the opportunity to air a grievance. These discussions are valuable, but they are not a substitute for detailed examination of the estimates, nor are they sufficient for the exercise of Parliament's immense responsibilities. In fact there is no effective and continuous watch by Parliament over the departments of Government. A reformed Parliament would find more time for detailed examination of the estimates and an informed vigilance over such questions as our colonial policy.

7. THE SYSTEM OF CHECKS

But there are two important qualifications to our general assertion that Parliament is failing to exercise effective control over the Executive. First, there is still Question Time. Spasmodic, ridiculous and evanescent as questions must sometimes appear, too often drafted for personal publicity or constituency appeal as many of them are, this is still the most distinctive element of Parliamentary work and often the most effective. And secondly, there are the many committees outside Parliament itself with which Members are concerned and through which influence may be exercised, such as the special committees of the political Parties and private societies such as Chatham House and the Africa Bureau. There are the two committees set up by the House itself to watch expenditure, the Estimates Committee and the Public Accounts Committee. Finally, there is the Auditor-General.

The handicaps under which such bodies labour are obvious. Some have no official standing and all have a limited access to information. Those that can call Civil Servants before them, as the Public Accounts Committee can, have no power to question policy and even the Estimates Committee is usually examining water which has already flowed over the dam and exposing extravagances too late. They have insufficient authority. They have, on the whole, inadequate information. They cannot anticipate events or influence decisions to any great extent. But they must be borne in mind as means, and often influential means, for bringing informed criticism to bear on policy.

8. THE HOUSE OF LORDS

A subject having had its quota of attention in the Commons is also, unless it relates directly and solely to finance, open to examination in the Lords.

The Parliament Acts, in reducing the power of the Lords to the point at which they can at worst delay Bills other than money Bills, have not in practice diminished their actual powers as much as might have been expected. But changing times and traditions have done much in this direction, and it can be said that the Lords will neither reject nor mutilate a Bill unless it is either a very minor one or is felt to be contrary to the will of the people. They still feel entitled to make fairly copious minor amendments to Bills, though ultimately they will give way in nine cases out of ten if the Commons insist on their amendments. Few questions are asked. But they debate general subjects frequently and it might be thought that a great many of the shortcomings of the Commons could be remedied in the Lords. To some extent this may be so. But it remains true that the Lords in its present form will not stand up to examination as a useful Second Chamber. First, its membership is not so distinguished as it is sometimes painted. The distinguished members are usually verging on retirement if not actually retired. Secondly, as its members are unpaid they are naturally unable to devote very much time to its affairs. And again, as they have no democratic authority their powers are circumscribed in their very nature.

Nevertheless, the Lords have had several useful debates on economics in the past year and their work on some of the Nationalization Bills should be remembered. They sent 91 Amendments back to the Commons on the Coal Industry Nationalization Bill and 289 on the Town and Country Planning Bill. In addition, in the session 1948–9 over 600 amendments on other Bills were passed in the Lords, 15 successful Bills initiated by the Government, 18 Private Bills and 11 Consolidation Measures. The Guillotine may prevent all discussion of some clauses in the Commons; in such a case the only consideration given to important matters may be in the Lords.

The case for reforming the House of Lords is evident and compelling. Certainly the House should not be abolished. Checks and balances are still essential bulwarks to freedom. A minority view in a Party may foist its policy on the people though perhaps 80% of the nation is against it. The protection for minorities and individuals is more slender still. If you have no written constitution at a time when the jurisdiction of the Courts have been pushed aside in so many ways, the extra security of a Second Chamber is necessary. Further, a strong and effective Second Chamber would relieve the Commons of some work.

But there is little sign of agreement on reform of the House of Lords, and Parliament needs a wide measure of agreement on such an issue before it can act. At present the only modification of the

Lords which has even the vaguest chance of gaining general agreement is the addition of life peers, such peers to be created on the advice of the Prime Minister and to be paid. And even this proposal, though it would meet with the support of many Tories and Liberals, would be opposed by strong factions within these Parties and by a majority of the Labour Party. Indeed it is doubtful if it measures up to the needs of the case. If the House of Lords is to be reformed at all, then the hereditary principle must collapse. The best way to form or strengthen an hereditary Second Chamber can hardly be the creation of life peers at the behest of the Executive. Reform, if any, must be radical. There are ingenious schemes for filling the Lords with the holders of certain offices mixed up to taste with peeresses, bishops and anyone thought to be wise; but such a medley would have neither the sanction of tradition nor any argument of logic on its side. All schemes for life peers or a mixed House ignore the fact that politics is not a matter of argument by good men but of argument directed to action; and action will only be effective in a democracy if it springs from contact with the people.

Far better would be a Second Chamber of perhaps 250 Members elected for 9 to 12 years in three blocks by Proportional Representation in very large constituencies. This would seem to answer some of the present needs: a more adequate representation of minorities would be achieved; some Independents and some distinguished figures who shun the Commons would almost certainly be elected; and Members would be much freer from both constituency and Party pressures. A Member elected fifth on the list for Lancashire to serve a nine-year term would be freer from pressure both by cotton interests and the Whips (who would have no power to recommend dissolution) than a single Member for a cotton town. Such a body could also be expected to take a considerable amount of work off the Commons.

The powers of such a House or of any Second Chamber are as difficult a question as its composition. Delay in itself should not be the main function. As we have — and rightly — no system of referendum, the public cannot pronounce directly on the matter in dispute between the Houses, during the period of delay. Merely to prolong the process of legislation may lead to boredom and irritation. And, of course, it is a weapon which is at its sharpest in the last year of a Government's life when it may not be most needed. It is true that after four years of office a Government may no longer represent the majority view. But it will be conscious that it has to face the electors soon. And in its exhaustion it may be more in need of stimulation than restraint.

Nor can a Second Chamber take the place of a written constitution by having particularly strong powers over certain categories of 'fundamental' rights. Such a change would be so alien to our form of government that it could scarcely be grafted on. Anyone who studies the actual experience of trying to work Second Chambers within the British system of Parliamentary government must admit that it is discouraging. But the debates of a Second Chamber of the type suggested would exert a considerable influence on the Government, the Civil Service and on the public and the House of Commons. It could be entrusted with the initial discussion of many Bills before they ever came to the Commons, and it could undertake, after discussion in the Commons, considerable revision at a Committee stage. If conflicts with the Commons arose provision could be made for a conference between the two Houses. Some delay would be acceptable, but ultimately the view of the majority in the Commons would have to prevail. Since democratic government presupposes that discussion should precede and influence executive decision, one main function of the Second Chamber would be to discuss and watch the long-term problems which are at present neglected in the Commons. Their other functions would be to revise in committee and perhaps initiate moves on matters which the House of Commons finds thorny — such subjects as the Criminal Law and the Marriage and Betting Laws. They might also spend a considerable time on Commonwealth questions, and if representatives from the Commonwealth could be persuaded to attend this would be a valuable addition.

THE REFORM OF PARLIAMENT

9. PARLIAMENT AND THE PRESS

There is a tendency for Members of Parliament to get out of touch with what the people at large are thinking. They are inclined to overestimate 'House of Commons opinion' and their own importance. One sign of this was the clamour for privilege raised between 1945 and 1951, another was the 14-day ban on broadcasting.

The Press therefore has an important two-sided job: it interprets the country to Parliament, and Parliament to the country. It also plays the rôle of a 'Third Chamber' by its own discussion of events. One result of the interaction of Members and the Press is harmful to the Parliament: the trivial, the ridiculous, the stunt often makes the best news. No Member can be indifferent to publicity, but a few go too far out of their way to purvey what the popular Press wants. The public therefore gets a distorted view of politics and the real issues and personalities. It would be revealing to take a Gallup Poll among the public and ask them to name the 20 best known M.P.s of each Party and then to ask the Tory and Labour Parties who are considered ablest or most influential in their Parties. The work of the House and its committees is sometimes clogged up by speeches aimed at the local Press. Some debates might well be more effective if no publicity could be attached to them at all. In fairness, however, to the Press it must be said that the prime fault lies with Members too eager for publicity.

But the harm done to Parliament by the interaction of a few Members with the more sensational columns of the Press is far outweighed by the immense service that the Press in general performs. To begin with, the newspapers give good coverage of Parliament. Even when they seem to concentrate too much on inessentials which happen to make good news they are in fact bringing some knowledge of Parliament to people who naturally have little or no interest in politics. Further they put the best construction on the intentions of Members. They go out of their way to paint the House of Commons in a favourable light. Even the most sensational papers such as the *Daily Mirror* produce such admirable aids to political understanding as its 'Spotlight on the Trade Unions'. But more important still, newspapers' leading articles, particularly, of course, those in the more serious papers such as the *Manchester Guardian*, the *Daily Telegraph*, the *Times*, the *Yorkshire Post*, the *Scotsman* or the *Observer*, are a most valuable part of political discussion. In fact they go a long way towards rectifying some of Parliament's shortcomings. Leader-writers of influential papers are reasonably independent within the general orbit of their papers' policy. They react against infringements of liberty. Most important of all, they are free from sectional interests and on the whole treat problems from the standpoint of the nation as a whole. The light they shed on current affairs is all the brighter from the knowledge they have of their subject — greater than that of most M.P.s.

But although daily leading articles and weekly articles, such as those in the *Economist*, give admirably professional comment on current issues, it is felt that there is a gap in political journalism. The political correspondents of some papers are no more than gossip-writers. That is right and, indeed, in so far as it stimulates interest in politics is an important job, but there does seem to be a dearth of Lippmanns, Mowrers and Vernon Bartletts. It is not that men of their calibre do not exist, but they do not seem to be encouraged to treat the dominant issues and long-term trends in everyday politics. Nor do minorities such as Scottish or Welsh Nationalists, Marxists, Free Traders or Credit Reformers get much space in the press or time on the air. The Press or the B.B.C. or I.T.V. are not to be blamed for this — but such minorities excluded from Parliament are also excluded to a large extent from other platforms of discussion, with grave injuries to politics as a whole.

The B.B.C. has steered a remarkably successful course in its political reporting. If it and the I.T.A. have not been able to do as much as they could have done to blow some fresh air into political discussion this is largely the fault of Parliament, though the timidity of the broadcasting authorities must bear a little of the blame. On the whole, however, both by daily reports and by brains trusts the B.B.C. has greatly helped Parliamentary government.

10. THE CASE FOR REFORM

The case for Parliamentary reform is complicated by the need to recognize that atmosphere is more important than Standing Orders. And the present atmosphere of the House of Commons is a good one. It draws out the better side of its Members, though perhaps not the more adventurous side. The established conventions, especially those existing between the Parties, are satisfactory; they allow for an interchange of ideas, if only rarely for conversions. In rooting out weeds in the Parliamentary system we must be careful not to scatter the very soil in which Parliament grows. But an impression remains that we are as a people too self-satisfied with our system of government. Some reforms are needed, and that of the House of Lords has already been considered. As far as the individual Member is concerned he wants more room to work things out for himself. The pressure of organized pressure groups, constituency interests, the Party machine and welfare work should be relaxed. Parliament as a whole needs more freedom from domination by the Executive and some release from the grind of miscellaneous business so that it may really contribute of its best on important problems. Debates should not be merely conventional nor conducted solely with an eye to popularity and the daily Press. We must try to restore some of the checks and balances of the constitution and establish some Parliamentary control over finance and the running of the various business undertakings of Government, as well as of the departments themselves. Most important of all, the electorate must be given the feeling that the Government is their Government and not the prerogative of a politicians' caucus cynically designated as 'they'.

i. *The Committee System*

The House of Commons and the Second Chamber should adopt something similar to the continental system of committees.

This system is subject to two major criticisms: first, that the committee or its *rapporteur* may accumulate such power as to usurp some of the Minister's authority; and second, that the members of such a committee may come to form a trade union on a particular subject, to the disadvantage of themselves and the House. The nearest thing we have to such a committee is the Scottish Grand Committee composed of all Scottish Members and a few English representatives weighted so as to give the Government a majority. It considers matters of purely Scottish interest, both Bills and estimates. It is difficult to say if it has proved a success. Certainly, since the Scottish Ministers dominate it, they have not suffered from its creation. But it is inevitably too large, its field is enormous and its members are uncertain whether its creation is a triumph or a dismissal of Scottish interests.

But the advantages — if the system is rightly used — should greatly outweigh the disadvantages, which are in any case largely hypothetical. A small committee of Members interested in a particular subject, meeting regularly, could be kept supplied with information and could take up points with the Minister and discuss them in a more useful way than can be achieved in Question Time. No committee, of course, can achieve the drama and authority of a debate in the House of Commons. But if small working committees could establish a tradition of short speeches and attention to essentials, they would be a useful adjunct. Room must, however, be made for them by reducing the total amount of work to be done by Members. Government itself, as we have suggested, should abandon some of its functions; there should be fewer minor Bills; and more Bills should be considered by committees at the Committee stage, instead of by the whole House.

ii. *Electoral Reform*

If the Second Chamber is to be a mere modification of the present House of Lords by the creation of life peerages, then the case in the House of Commons for Proportional Representation except in some sparsely populated areas is very strong. The system by which Independents are squeezed out, minorities under-represented and in the end a wholly false result achieved, not as an exception but as a rule, cannot be defended as long as the majority in the House of Commons is free from all effective checks. Whatever the advantages of single-member constituencies (and some of the oft-cited advantages are to a considerable extent disadvantages), the damage to democracy must outweigh them. Nor will the arguments about 'strong and stable' government stand much examination. France does not suffer from a plethora of governments because she has proportional representation. She has never had it. Her troubles arise from the temper of her politics and the lack of any weapon such as dissolution in the hands of her Prime Minister. Many Parliaments elected by proportional representation, such as the Swedish, have few Parties and long periods with one Government in power. We export P.R. to our dependencies and should not be shy of experimenting with it ourselves.

iii. *Devolution and the Reform of Local Government*

The time has also come for a radical reform of Local Government. There is a strong case, apart from nationalist sentiment, for allowing Scotland, Wales and regions of England to run their own affairs on a federal basis. We shall consider it in closer detail in Chapter VI. It should relieve Parliament and the central government of some work. It would revivify democracy by allowing more people to play a part in it. It would also allow some differentiation in legislation in each region to suit local needs. The over-centralization of government is having dire results in places which do not fit into the general pattern. It is absurd, for instance, to pretend that the same agricultural policy can suit Shetland, Inverness-shire, Norfolk, Cardigan, Yorkshire and Kent. There are probably greater local differences in tradition, climate and occupation within Britain than in any other comparable area. But an overworked and over-centralized government has to design one policy to suit all districts. It ends by legislating for the big blocks of population, with the result that the peripheries are neglected. If we want the amount of government we have today and want to exercise better democratic control over it we must send more representatives to conduct it. You cannot expand the House of Commons. But you can fortify it with 'national' legislatures. The 'Imperial' Parliament would keep control of foreign affairs, defence and major taxation; the 'national' Parliaments would be confined to strictly defined subjects.

It is important, however, that the central Government should not be left with all the unpopular jobs. Further, it must retain its primacy. The arrangements for finance certainly present peculiar difficulties but the change would allow for the introduction of a new system of local taxation to take the place of the present rating system. The tendency for Local Authorities to become more and more dependent on central grants — some obtain 90% of their finances from London — while their contribution is raised by a chaotic rating system is neither efficient nor democratic.

If they are coupled with the reform of Local Government, these proposals can stand up to the strongest argument which may be directed against them: that they will lead to an intolerable number of elections and all the paraphernalia in expense and officialdom that goes with every legislature. At the present time we have in theory a three- or four-tier system of Government. In London there is already the L.C.C., the borough and the relics of a parish system. The trouble is not that the system inflicts too many elections on the electorate but that democratic control and ordinary efficient administration suffer from our attempt to carry on with a system of Local Government which is out of date. There is no reason why the election of a local body of County Council status — though perhaps with different powers and boundaries — a 'national' Parliament and a House of Commons should prove intolerable.

At the same time the strictest watch must be kept to see that such devolution genuinely spreads the work of government more widely and does not merely create new jobs, new functions and new committees making work for themselves. Special measures might be necessary to provide adequate services at all these levels, and the supply of able Civil Servants and Parliamentary Clerks may in the short run prove a limiting factor. But one effect of such 'national' Parliaments, which need not sit for more than half a day for half the year, combined with a reformed House of Lords with an enlarged capacity for work, would surely be a more effective House of Commons. It would be relieved of some of its burdens. It could reduce the length of its sessions and free some Members for outside activities. Together with reforms already suggested, increased salaries and the creation of some standing committees, Party bonds could be loosened, cross-voting could become more common and a more open political atmosphere created.

It must be emphasized, however, that Parliament works not in theory but in a real world, and reforms can only succeed if they are generally accepted. No reform is so good in itself that we should sacrifice the harmony of Parliamentary government for its sake. Much should be surrendered for the sake of continuity, and the reforms we have suggested ought only to be attempted with caution and in stages. But the present shortcomings of Parliament are real and grave. We are in the curious position that while more and more work is thrown on M.P.s and Governments, they are in some respects more divorced than ever from important currents in modern life and less able than ever to control events. There are signs that politics here may go the way of France. Here admittedly we make our intrigues and arrangements within the big Parties instead of between different Parties; but the tendency for political commentary to concentrate on the manipulation of groups around personalities is here for all to see, and to some extent it corresponds to reality. Our failure to deal with inflation or pursue a bold policy in our Commonwealth springs from the need to conciliate various groups. As a result people have turned away from politics and important decisions, if taken at all, lie in the hands of Civil Servants, industrial managers and the trade unions.

J. G.

CHAPTER III

CIVIL LIBERTIES

THE aim of Liberals is to secure for each individual the liberty to do what he wants without harming others, and to this end to restrict the ability of the State or of any other group to interfere with him. To attain both these objects, power (defined by Bertrand Russell as 'the production of intended effects')[1] must be diffused throughout society. We shall therefore discuss in this chapter not only actual restrictions on the liberty of the individual, but also concentrations of power within and outside the State which by their very existence pose a threat to liberty.

I. THE STATE

In the eighteenth century Montesquieu examined the British system of government and first formulated what is now a well-known doctrine — that the Executive, the Legislature and the Judiciary should be separated in order to limit the power of each and protect the individual from oppression by the State. Even if complete separation were possible in theory, it could only be realized in a small community like the Greek city-state; it did not exist in eighteenth-century England and it does not and could not exist today. Nevertheless it is always desirable to restrict as far as possible the incursion of any one of the three departments of State into the spheres of the other two, to maintain a reasonable equilibrium among them and in particular to divorce judicial from executive and legislation functions. In the last fifty years or so this principle has been ignored to an increasing extent as the Executive has grown in size and power.

[1] *Power: a New Social Analysis* (Allen & Unwin, 1938), p. 35.

Clearly a larger Executive is required by a Welfare State than by a *laissez-faire* State. Once the necessary economic and political decisions have been made the problem of restricting the growth of the Executive becomes primarily one of administrative techniques. Unfortunately every bureaucracy, whether public or private, has an inherent tendency to expand. The *Economist* (19 November 1955) has ironically suggested that there is a mathematical formula ('Parkinson's Law') by which the rate of growth can be measured. Outside bodies may enquire into departmental organization from time to time for particular purposes, but the only effective control is to limit the funds available to pay staff. Financial control is exercised in the first instance by the Chancellor of the Exchequer and the Treasury and ultimately by Parliament on Supply Days or acting through the Public Accounts Committee or the Select Committee on Estimates. These methods are quite inadequate, and there is an urgent need for stricter Parliamentary control of expenditure.

It is impossible to classify or enumerate completely the powers now vested in Government departments. Some are discretionary; others impose a mixture of judicial and administrative duties; many are coupled with power to legislate by issuing regulations. The provisions of post-war planning legislation cover the whole spectrum of Executive power — a metaphor that is particularly appropriate, since some of the powers granted are almost invisible except to the expert. The Agriculture Act 1947 vests in the Minister of Agriculture a duty to review annually the general economic conditions and prospects of agriculture and to consult with representatives of producers; he has power to extend the list of products enjoying guaranteed prices and assured markets and to make supervision orders against those who own agricultural land but do not fulfil their statutory obligation to farm it in accordance with the rules of good estate management. An equally wide range of authority is vested in the State by the legislation dealing with Town Planning, the National Health Service and National Insurance.

Parliamentary control is very tenuous. Questions can be put to

Ministers verbally or in writing and this is probably the most
effective check on the activities of their departments; but, as we
have shown, Parliamentary debates afford only a very limited
opportunity for pressing individual grievances, since there is so
little time available.

(a) Delegated Legislation

A matter for particular concern is the extensive use of delegated
legislation. Examples can be found as far back as the sixteenth
century, but it is in the years since 1867 that the practice has developed as the State has intervened more positively in the
direction and control of the nation's economy. The business of
Parliament has grown enormously and there has been progressively less time available for each subject which has come under
review. Members have been unwilling or unable (because of ignorance of the subject or Government use of such devices as the
closure) to deal adequately with more than the broad principles of
legislation which has come before them. As a result delegation has
become standard practice in all Acts of Parliament except those
which are short and simple.

A typical modern example is the National Insurance Act, 1946.
S. 69 provides that

> 'Without prejudice to any specific power conferred by any of the four
> last foregoing sections, regulations may be made for facilitating their
> operation or the introduction of the system of insurance established by
> this Act, including in particular regulations providing —
>> (a) for modifying, as respects the period before the appointed day, any
>> enactment repealed or amended by the foregoing provisions of this
>> Part of this Act. . . .'

This is only one example chosen at random from an Act which
is merely a framework into which numerous regulations are subsequently fitted by the Ministry of National Insurance. One M.P.
remarked in relation to this procedure:

> 'Indeed, if only Moses could have known this technique, he would
> never have committed himself to anything so precise, and occasionally so
> inconvenient, as the Ten Commandments. When he came down from
> Mount Sinai, he would have taken power to make regulations.'

In theory power to legislate may be delegated to any person or body; in practice delegation is usually to Ministers, the Privy Council or to Local Authorities, who may in certain cases subdelegate. The volume of delegated legislation considerably exceeds that of original legislation.

Control of delegated legislation is exercised by Parliament in various ways. During the passage of the Bill, which will enable regulations to be enacted subsequently by some other person or body, both Houses have the normal opportunities to consider, criticize and vote on the relevant provisions. They also have an opportunity of reviewing delegated legislation, if the enabling Act so provides: e.g. regulations may be laid before either or both Houses with a provision that they shall not operate until approved by resolution of the House or that, if within a specified time a resolution is passed by the House annulling or modifying the regulations, they shall be annulled or modified accordingly. There is no general Statute which requires regulations to be laid before either House and the procedure in each case depends on the enabling Act.

In 1932 the Donoughmore Committee on Ministers' Powers recommended that both Houses should have a Standing Committee to consider and report on Bills conferring law-making powers and on legislation made pursuant to such powers. The House of Lords has had a Committee since 1925 dealing with some aspects of delegated legislation, and in 1944 a Select Committee was appointed by the House of Commons to scrutinize all regulations which came before the House requiring affirmative or negative resolutions and to determine whether the attention of the House should be drawn to any such regulation on various grounds, e.g. that

(1) it is made in pursuance of an enactment containing provisions excluding it from challenge in the Courts;

(2) it appears to make unusual or unexpected use of the power delegated;

(3) it purports to have retrospective effect where the enabling Act does not expressly authorize this;

(4) there appears to have been unjustifiable delay in publication or in laying before Parliament.

By convention the Chairman of the Select Committee has always been a member of the Opposition and the members work in comparative harmony, so that it would be difficult for an outsider to know to which political Party individual members belonged. Since 1944 the Committee has examined about 8,500 regulations and drawn the attention of the House to just over 100. If the Committee has a query to raise it usually calls on the Department concerned for an explanation before it reports to the House; this can cause delay which may be serious in the case of regulations which can only be annulled by a negative resolution laid before the House within a specified time.

In February 1956 Sir Cecil Carr argued in the course of a public lecture that the dangers of delegated legislation had been exaggerated in at least two respects: there was no progressive annual increase in the number of regulations and it was not true to say that many regulations were the work of irresponsible Civil Servants and were promulgated without their Ministers' knowledge. He gave figures to support the former contention[1] and cited in support of the latter the conclusions reached by a Parliamentary Committee which examined the position in 1953. Nevertheless it is still true that a very considerable reserve of power to legislate is vested in the Executive, even though much of it may not be in current use. The Donoughmore Committee gave instances in their report of powers to legislate on matters of principle, to oust the jurisdiction of the Courts and to confer on Ministers such wide discretions that it was almost impossible in some cases to know what limit Parliament did intend to impose.

Powers to delegate should be scrutinized more closely *before* they become effective. There are obvious limits to what can be done by Parliament as at present constituted but it has been suggested that the first reading of a Bill should be less of a formality

[1] Annual totals of general statutory instruments: 1949, 1,379; 1951, 1,166; 1953, 829; 1955, 657.

and that some opportunity should be afforded to the House on that occasion to consider proposed powers to delegate. Further opportunities might be found by sending more Bills to committee and by having advisory committees drawn from both Houses and attached to each Department; these would consider proposed regulations with the officials concerned, before they were issued.

Delegated legislation impinges on many routine activities today and the sheer complexity of its form is a constant irritant to those who have to deal with it. Since 1954 Hire-Purchase and Credit Sale agreements have been subject to restrictive orders from time to time as a result of the Government's economic policy; one of these (S.I. 1956 No. 180) commences as follows:

'The Board of Trade in pursuance of the powers conferred upon them by Regulation 55 of the Defence (General) Regulations, 1939, as having effect by virtue of the Supplies and Services (Transitional Powers) Act, 1945, as extended by the Supplies and Services (Extended Purposes) Act, 1947, and the Supplies and Services (Defence Purposes) Act, 1951 and continued in force by the Supplies and Services (Continuance) Order, 1955, hereby order as follows:—'

Memoranda are frequently attached to these orders explaining their purport in fairly simple language. These should include an explanation of the chain of original and delegated legislation which has led to the order and this should be consolidated and reviewed by Parliament as often as possible, if only to reduce the necessity for laborious research and cross-reference.

(b) Special Tribunals

Another development which parallels the growth of delegated legislation is the establishment of special tribunals outside the organization of the Courts which are in many cases part of the Executive or strongly influenced by it. The development of railways in the last century involved the compulsory purchase of land and objections by individual land-owners were often considered by the House of Commons itself at the committee stage of the Bill. This procedure slowed up the work of Parliament and was expensive for those concerned. The Judges were not anxious to get involved in questions which had an administrative flavour and the procedure in their courts was slow and cumbersome. As a result tribunals were established to deal with such questions and the same procedure has been adopted subsequently in numerous Acts of Parliament. The following are three fairly modern examples:

Medical Practices Committee

This was established by the National Health Service Act, 1946 and hears applications by doctors to practise in the Committee's area. The Chairman and eight members are appointed by the Minister after consultation with medical organizations. A doctor whose application is refused may appeal to the Minister.

Enquiries under the New Towns Act, 1946

If the Minister of Town and Country Planning receives objections to proposals for developing a new town, he must cause a public local enquiry to be held. The enquiry is conducted by an Inspector who is appointed by and who reports to the Minister. The report must be considered by the Minister, but when he has done so he may proceed with the proposals subject to such modifications as he thinks fit and there is no appeal from his decision.

Lands Tribunal

This was established by the Lands Tribunal Act, 1949, and hears rating appeals and various other matters which relate to land or the value of land. The President and other members are appointed by the Lord Chancellor and there is a right of appeal on points of law to the Court of Appeal.

Special tribunals have been frequently criticized. In 1929 the Donoughmore Committee heard evidence from Civil Servants and from various associations and individuals concerned and eventually reported that there was 'nothing radically wrong about the existing practice of Parliament in permitting the exercise of judicial and quasi-judicial powers by Ministers and of judicial power by ministerial tribunals, but that the practice is capable of abuse, that dangers are incidental to it if not guarded against, and that certain safeguards are essential if the rule of law and the liberty of the subject are to be maintained'.

In defining its terms the Committee suggested that a true judicial decision presupposed an existing dispute and involved:

1. the presentation by the parties of their case;
2. the ascertainment of the facts by evidence adduced by the parties;
3. if the dispute is a question of law, the submission of legal arguments by the parties;
4. a decision which disposes of the whole matter by a finding upon the facts in dispute and an application of the law to the facts so found including, where required, a ruling upon any disputed question of law.

A quasi-judicial decision also presupposes an existing dispute between parties. It involves the first two requisites: it does not necessarily involve the third: and it never involves the fourth, which is replaced by administrative action, the character of which is determined by the Minister's free choice.

The Committee's main recommendations were as follows:

1. Parliament should always be reluctant to entrust purely judicial powers either to Ministers or to tribunals; but, if it does so, a tribunal is to be preferred to a Minister.
2. Quasi-judicial matters should be referred to tribunals.
3. Whenever judicial or quasi-judicial matters are delegated to Ministers or special tribunals:
    (a) the High Court should have the right to prevent either exceeding its statutory powers;
    (b) any party aggrieved by a decision should have the right to appeal to the High Court within a short specified period;
    (c) Ministers and tribunals should observe the principles of natural justice, i.e. a man should not be judge in his own cause, no party ought to be condemned unheard,

each party should know in good time the case which
he has to meet and both parties should be given reasons for the decision which is finally reached.

Both the recommendations and the definitions referred to
above have been criticized as inadequate and the former have
been largely ignored in practice. After the Committee reported,
numerous powers with a judicial element were vested in Ministers
alone and several new tribunals were established, such as Rent
Tribunals, in many cases with no right of appeal. Criticism
mounted again and in 1956 a committee was appointed under Sir
Oliver Franks as Chairman to consider the constitution and working of tribunals and related matters.

The principal grounds of attack on special tribunals can be summarized as follows:

1. Tribunals often sit privately and the public does not know
   and cannot find out how they work.
2. Many tribunals give only a bare decision without explaining
   the reasons which have led to it.
3. The rules of evidence and procedure adopted by tribunals
   are insufficiently precise so that issues are not clearly formulated and the investigation into questions of fact is of
   poor quality.
4. In many cases no legal representation is allowed.
5. Members of a tribunal may be appointed by or be members
   of Departments which are themselves parties in cases before
   the tribunal.
6. The right of appeal from a tribunal's decision is often restricted or non-existent.

In the case of certain tribunals there may be some force in these
criticisms, but general attacks on special tribunals as such are of
limited value in view of the number of such tribunals which now
exist and the wide variety of subjects with which they deal. Many
critics assume too readily that the existing organization and procedure of the Courts is satisfactory and represents an adequate
criterion by which to measure the inadequacies of the tribunals. In

fact some tribunals compare favourably with their nearest counter-parts within the judicial system: the comparison is perhaps more apparent to the parties than to counsel who represent them. For example, the Lands Tribunal and the Chancery Division of the High Court both deal with the type of covenant which is frequently imposed on land, restricting the use to which it can be put or the type of building which can be erected on it: the former considers applications for the cancellation of such covenants and the latter deals with cases in which a breach of covenant is alleged. In the Chancery Division counsel always have to be instructed to settle pleadings and to appear in open court: documents for the use of the Court have to be typed or printed in special ways; there are several formalities before trial which require the personal attend-ance of solicitors or their clerks at Court and it is not possible to deal with any of these by letter or telephone. Some of the pro-cedure may have a certain Dickensian charm but it is grossly un-economic. Before the Lands Tribunal formalities are reduced to a minimum and are as far as possible conducted by correspondence or over the telephone: counsel may but do not have to be em-ployed and there is much less room for the development of un-necessary and uneconomic expertize; the atmosphere of the tri-bunal is considerably less forbidding than in the High Court, where a litigant often feels that he is merely being allowed on sufferance to play a small part in a pageant staged *ad majorem legis gloriam* at his expense.

Many of the critics of tribunals have political axes to grind. Be-fore the War the attack on the tribunals was part of the general resistance to increasing State interference in the economic life of the community. This interference has increased since the War with the development of the Welfare State and criticism of the tribunals is frequently part of the general attack by anti-Socialist politicians on the Labour Party. In the debates in Parliament on the Restrictive Trade Practices Act, 1956, the Conservative Government advocated the establishment of a new division of the High Court to examine restrictive trading agreements, but the Labour Opposition argued that these functions would be more efficiently performed by a special tribunal. This is the first time for many years that a function of this kind has been assigned to the Courts rather than to a tribunal and it will be extremely interesting to see how the new Division operates.

In considering reforms in the system of special tribunals the aim should be to preserve their advantages while improving their organization. There is a general feeling, to some extent justified, that a number of tribunals which are nominally independent of the Executive are too closely influenced by it in practice. Is it therefore desirable to separate the judicial side of their work from administrative functions in so far as this is practicable. No general reforms can be made without a detailed examination of their probable effects on each tribunal concerned but, subject to this point, Parliament should pay more attention to the recommendations of the Donoughmore Committee and reforms should proceed on the following lines:

1. There should be a right of appeal to the High Court on questions of law. Most writers on the subject favour this, irrespective of their political views. It would strengthen the Courts in relation to the Executive and increase the independence of tribunals from the Executive by placing them under the aegis of the Courts in so far as they were dealing with questions of law.

2. A reasoned opinion should be given in all cases. There is very little justification for not adopting this practice. Apart from any legal issues involved, it is extremely frustrating to appear, for example, before a Rent Tribunal, argue that a standard rent should be fixed at a certain figure, wait while the tribunal considers the case in a room next door and then be told that the rent has been fixed at some other figure without any indication of why or how the decision has been reached.

3. Members of tribunals should not be appointed by Ministers who are interested parties in cases which come before them.

4. Hearings should be public and legal representation permitted, if individuals concerned so desire.

5. Wherever possible administrative and judicial functions should be separated. When enquiries are to be held under the New Towns Act or other planning legislation, inspectors should be appointed independently and should operate substantially in accordance with the rules which usually govern judicial proceedings; in particular they should hear evidence in the proper manner from all parties and publish a written report without at any stage in the proceedings consulting privately with any official in regard to policy.

(c) Judicial Control

No attempt is made here to do more than summarize the main principles which the Courts adopt in relation to the activities of the Executive and special tribunals. In nearly all cases the Courts have to consider the wording of particular statutes and regulations made under them and a decision on one set of words may only have a limited application in future cases, since there is considerable variation in the wording of legislation dealing with analogous situations. The Courts are often left with a certain discretion, which is exercised in different ways by different judges, and their conflicting decisions provide a rich field for academic lawyers searching for something to be academic about.

The main principles on which judicial control is exercised are set out below but Parliament can and does limit their application in particular cases:

1. There are a number of presumptions in law against officials of the State, e.g.

   (a) It is presumed that an act which would lead to civil or criminal proceedings if committed by a private individual will have the same effect if committed by an official, and it is for the latter to show that he is protected in some special way.

   (b) If an official is vested with discretionary power to perform an administrative act it is presumed that such discretion does not carry with it the right to interfere with private rights; in one case powers were granted

c

by Statute for the erection of a smallpox hospital, but the Court held that these powers did not allow the hospital to be built in such a way that it caused a nuisance.[1] This presumption can only be displaced by express statutory provisions but, if it is displaced, there is no presumption that an individual affected is entitled to compensation unless the relevant provisions cover this also.

(c) Where statutory powers can be exercised in alternative ways one of which is less harmful to an individual affected there is a presumption that it must be exercised in this way. In certain circumstances there is protection against the exercise of power in a negligent manner.

2. The Courts will restrain the exercise of powers beyond the limits prescribed by the enabling Act. Thus:

(a) Delegated legislation which is outside such limits can be declared *ultra vires* and invalid, but except in the case of by-laws made by subordinate bodies the Courts do not consider whether delegated legislation is reasonable.

In the U.S.A. the Courts have this power, and Mr Bernard Schwartz in comparing British and American procedure has suggested that the 'extension of the *ultra vires* doctrine to include the question of reasonableness is essential to the maintenance of effective judicial control in an age of expanding Executive power'.[2] It is difficult to formulate satisfactory criteria which the Court could adopt if any such reform were to be introduced here. But perhaps it could be applied in cases where individual rights are particularly vulnerable.

(b) An inferior Court or other body exercising judicial functions will be prevented from acting outside the limits of its jurisdiction.

[1] *Metropolitan Asylum District* v. *Hill*, 1881 6 A.C. 193
[2] *Law and Executive in Britain* (New York, 1949), p. 175.

3. In certain cases the Courts will interfere to prevent powers being abused, e.g. in the case of discretionary power exercised without proper consideration of all relevant circumstances.

The omission to exercise a power does not give rise to an action by any individual affected against the appropriate authority; but he may in some cases have a right of action, if the authority is under a duty to exercise the power.

4. The Courts will interfere with the exercise of judicial or quasi-judicial functions which does not conform to the rules of natural justice. Difficulties arise in applying this principle: in 1947 the House of Lords held that the procedure for a public local enquiry under the New Towns Act, 1946, referred to above is administrative in nature and that the rules of natural justice have no application to it,[1] although in similar cases under the Housing Acts orders were quashed because the Minister concerned did not act quasi-judicially.[2]

One of the principal features of planning and welfare legislation is the acquisition by the Executive of powers in which legislative, administrative and judicial elements are fused. The Lands Tribunal exercises functions in which the judicial elements predominate; it can be argued that an Inspector presiding over public local enquiries is performing judicial functions, but the Minister for whom he is acting is usually engaged in a complex mixture of legislative and administrative duties as he selects and develops areas for new towns. There are limits to the value of any approach based on attempts to discover and distinguish the metaphysical nature of particular powers and to base remedies on these distinctions. The important point to consider is the extent to which a particular power deprives an individual of liberty or property and to provide remedies accordingly.

Judicial control of the Executive should be strengthened by

[1] *Franklin* v. *Minister of Town and Country Planning*, 1948 A.C. 87.
[2] E.g. *Errington* v. *Ministry of Health*, 1935 I K.B. 249.

eliminating statutory provisions which oust the jurisdiction of the Courts and in cases where an individual suffers direct loss as a result of the exercise of a statutory power:

(*a*) There should be a presumption that he is entitled to compensation unless the relevant Act clearly provides to the contrary. The onus is then on the Government of the day to exclude this right and to justify the exclusion to Parliament.

(*b*) The exercise of the power should be subject to the rules of natural justice; the appropriate Department should put its own case clearly to the individual concerned, give him a proper opportunity to meet it and put his own case forward and then act reasonably and fairly.

(*c*) On appeal by the individual effected the Court should have power to enquire into the motives for the decision and to call for a statement of the facts upon which it was based and the reasons which led to it; it would then be able to check that the decision had been reached in accordance with the rules set out in (*b*) above.

These reforms will only work in practice if the procedure and organization of the Courts are adapted to meet their increased responsibilities. This should not present any difficulty. Patent and Trade Mark cases are dealt with by a Judge who has special experience in these matters; Judges often sit with lay assessors when dealing with Admiralty cases, and similar arrangements have been adopted under the Restrictive Trade Practices Act, 1956. There is growing support for the creation of an Administrative Division in which Judges would sit with ex-Civil Servants and experienced administrators and deal with all cases involving the Executive and special tribunals.

Judicial control of the Executive by the new Division will only be effective if it adopts modern rules of evidence and procedure and discharges its functions quickly and at the minimum cost. The laymen chosen to sit with Judges of this Division should take part in the preparation of the rules of evidence and procedure so that unnecessary and uneconomic technicalities are eliminated as far as possible. The rules which govern the issue of the prerogative writs will have to be improved; these are used in certain cases to initiate proceedings for compelling officials and tribunals to carry out their proper duties or to prevent them from exceeding their powers. There are a number of defects in this type of proceeding and in the remedies available to the Court.

If the individual litigant against the State is to have a fair chance of presenting his case, the latter should not have any special advantages. The Legal Aid system has done much to put litigants on an equal footing and post-war legislation has reduced Crown privileges in litigation. A few still remain and the most onerous of these is the privilege enjoyed by the Crown to withhold disclosure of documents to the Court, if the Minister concerned thinks that this would injure the public interest. A certificate or affidavit by a Minister on this point must be accepted as conclusive and the Court cannot enquire into the matter further; in Scotland the Court has an inherent power to override the Minister but this appears to have been exercised on only two occasions in the last hundred years. This privilege appears to have been abused by Ministers and has been the subject of caustic judicial comment on several occasions.[1] In June 1956, the Lord Chancellor announced that there would in future be more liberal disclosure of documents in certain respects, but essentially the position remains unchanged. Whatever views Ministers may have as to the public interest which makes disclosure undesirable, there is an equally strong public interest in preserving the liberty of the individual against arbitrary executive action and the final decision on a claim to privilege should be made by the Court and not by the Minister concerned.

The Legal Aid system should be extended to cover litigation in the new Division and advice to individuals before proceedings begin. Parliament will have to create and give the initial impetus to the new Division, but eventually it should be able to develop rights and remedies of its own volition. We should ultimately

---

[1] E.g. by Lord Radcliffe in *Glasgow Corporation* v. *Central Land Board* (*Times*, 13 October 1955).

have a new body of Common Law analogous in some respects to the French *Droit administratif.*

This chapter has so far been concerned primarily with powers vested in the Executive by planning and welfare legislation. Space does not permit a comprehensive treatment of all types of State power but there are certain restrictions on and rights to interfere with liberty of expression which are particularly objectionable in a country which is supposed to set an example to the rest of the world.

(d) The Official Secrets Acts

The principal Act (1911) was passed by the Liberal Government at the time of the Agadir crisis and strengthened by the Coalition Government in 1920. One of the Ministers responsible for the passage of the 1920 Act through Parliament was the Attorney-General, Sir Gordon Hewart, who later as Lord Chief Justice castigated official bureaucracy in *The New Despotism* (1929).

Several aspects of these Acts have been criticized; they are constantly being used to restrict legitimate discussion and criticism of State activities and in this connection S. 2 of the 1911 Act and S. 6 of the 1920 Act have caused the most trouble. The former makes it an offence for anyone to communicate to unauthorized persons various types of official information and documents including such as he may obtain 'owing to his position as a person who holds or has held office under His Majesty or as a person who holds or has held a contract made on behalf of His Majesty, or as a person who is or has been employed under a person who holds or has held such an office or contract'; S. 6 of the 1920 Act required any person on demand by a senior police officer or sentry to give any information in his power relating to an offence or suspected offence under the Acts and for this person to attend for interrogation. This section was modified in 1939 to exclude sentries and to require the prior permission of a Secretary of State before the powers under the section were exercised, except in a case of 'great emergency'.

In 1920 certain newspapers correctly forecast the arrest of Gandhi by the Government of India and their editors were interrogated under the Acts; in 1935 the Acts were used to stop a proposed sale at Sotheby's of letters written by the first Duke of Wellington to the British Ambassador in Paris.[1] Since the War threats of a prosecution under the Acts have been used to deter publication of information about the notorious Casement diaries and have prevented a number of ex-servicemen from recounting their war experiences as fully as they would have liked, although no harm would have resulted. A perusal of Sir Winston Churchill's war memoirs does not suggest that he has been troubled by the Acts in any way.

The wording of these Acts is unduly wide and since 1911 the number of situations and personnel to which they can apply has increased considerably as the business of the State has extended. They should be amended so that they apply only to genuine cases where public security or interest really would be affected by disclosure.

(e) Censorship

The Official Secrets Acts provide opportunities for indirect censorship, but direct methods are available. The theatre is subject to censorship by the Lord Chancellor, from whom there is no appeal. The effects of this are ludicrous: Music Halls in the suburbs of London and in the provinces are allowed to put on salacious 'variety shows'; performances of plays by such writers as Bernard Shaw and Laurence Housman have been banned but they can be published in book form; plays written before 1843 (e.g. Restoration comedies) can be performed quite freely. Censorship of films is operated through the British Board of Film Censors, whose certificates are accepted by Local Authorities. This has been used for political ends; before the last war licences were refused to pacifist films and, until opportunities for appeasement had been exhausted, to a number of anti-Nazi films.

The Common Law offence of Obscene Libel is invoked from

[1] *Times,* 4 July 1935.

time to time for censorship purposes by Home Secretaries and
senior officials with puritan inclinations. An inept nineteenth-
century judgement defined the test of obscenity to be 'whether the
tendency of the matter charged as obscenity is to deprave and corrupt those whose minds are open to such immoral influences and
into whose hands a publication of this sort may fall'.[1] This is a
vague objective test which would include innumerable works of
literature from Shakespeare to Wyndham Lewis, regardless of the
authors' and publishers' motives. A wave of prosecutions in 1954
was checked by a liberal judgment of Mr Justice Stable[2] and, if the
offence cannot be abolished altogether, the law should be reformed
to make the motives of the author and publisher the test of liability. In 1955 the Children and Young Persons (Harmful Publications) Act was passed in order to prohibit 'horror comics';
censorship of publications deliberately designed to corrupt children and young persons may be justified but it is significant
that the Government should have felt impelled to introduce this
Act quickly without at the same time feeling any urge to remove
the other and indefensible forms of censorship referred to
above.

(f) Interference with Postal and Telephone Services

The Government has power under the Post Office Act, 1908,
to intercept letters in the course of post and it claims a prerogative
power to listen into conversations on the telephone. Members of
Parliament have been unable to find out how often and under
what circumstances these powers are used.[3] They are supposed to
be confined to espionage and related cases but there can be no
assurance of this, unless the procedure is modified so that no
letters or telephone conversations can be intercepted without a
warrant from a Judge or Magistrate.

Employees of the State are not the only persons who may wire-
tap; any competent electrician can do so if he gains access to a

[1] Cockburn, C. J. in R. v. Hicklin 1868 LR3QB 360.
[2] R. v. Martin Secker Warburg Ltd, 1954 2 AER 683.
[3] Hansard, House of Commons, 31 July 1952 and Times, 5 July 1956.

telephone wire, but the process usually involves several civil and criminal offences and would doubtless be frowned on by the Electrical Trades Union. Conversations on the telephone can also be recorded on a tape-recorder by one speaker without the knowledge of the other and this pernicious practice is growing. It is already quite unsafe to talk to some people in the City by telephone except about the weather.

The use of electronic devices for spying and eavesdropping by police, reporters, private detectives and others may well become a serious problem in the future, as it has already become in the U.S.A. Miniature television cameras have been developed so that people can be observed secretly (e.g. by their employers at work) and there are devices whereby private conversations in a room can be overheard without hiding a microphone there beforehand.

Official use of all these devices should only be permitted within strict limits and their private use should be banned completely. The law relating to the invasion of personal privacy is not clear and should be strengthened to deal with these and related matters.

(g) Conclusions

The use of delegated legislation, special tribunals and discretionary powers is inevitable in a modern industrial society — particularly in a Welfare State. Generally they have worked reasonably well, but there have been injustices and it is urgent that a system of checks and balances should be built into the Welfare State so that the Executive power is contained by Parliamentary and judicial control, particularly where individual liberty is directly affected. For this there must be full information at all times on the activities of the State and secretive tendencies on the part of officials should always be resisted. Their powers to decide what adults may read in books and newspapers or see on the stage and screen must also be limited. 'Experience should teach us to be most on our guard to protect liberty when the Government's purposes are beneficent. Men born to freedom are naturally alert to repel invasion of their liberty by evil-minded rulers. The greatest dangers to liberty lurk in insidious encroachment by men of zeal, well-meaning but without understanding.'[1]

The British Constitution has developed in a characteristically empirical fashion by conventional practices and laws laid down by Parliament and the Courts which have a special sanctity and would only be overridden in a national crisis. But as legislation to control the Executive is introduced some of this existing law might well be codified and consolidated within the new Act to provide a comprehensive Statute for the protection of individual liberty which could be altered or suspended only in special circumstances. Liberal peers in the House of Lords have since the war repeatedly tried to win support for a Liberties of the Subject Bill which would enact some of the reforms we have advocated here. Their proposals were rejected by Lord Jowitt, the Labour Lord Chancellor, and later by his Conservative successor, Lord Simonds, who was a member of the Donoughmore Committee. Members of both major Parties are sympathetic but few would accept the changes required in Parliament and the Courts before they could effectively control the Executive.

Nearly all legislation enacted by Parliament today is initiated by the Government and concerned with economic and related matters; there is no authority which takes the liberty of the individual as its starting-point instead of the general good, and the kinds of reform we call for are usually effected only after years of agitation by individuals and groups of individuals. A new institution is needed to fill the gap with power to initiate legislation and with fixed days assigned to it for debates on civil liberties. Socialist lawyers have suggested a Ministry of Justice to deal with some of these matters, but this would be part of the Executive and too dependent on the Government of the day. We should prefer a body elected by back-benchers in both Houses with power to co-opt members from outside Parliament. It should have a permanent staff assigned to it and operate through a small executive committee. Its powers should include the right to initiate proceedings

[1] L. D. Brandeis, dissenting opinion in *Olmstead* v. *U.S.* 277 U.S. 438 (1928).

against the State and to act as *amicus curiae* in cases brought by other plaintiffs.

2. ORGANIZATIONS OUTSIDE THE STATE

'A well ordered society', Simone Weil wrote, 'would be one where the State only had a negative action, comparable to that of a rudder: a light pressure at the right moment to counteract the first suggestion of any loss of equilibrium.'[1] In fact the Welfare State takes positive action in numerous ways and therefore represents in itself a continual threat to equilibrium. Perhaps a wider distribution of property would enable its functions to be reduced, as suggested in the next chapter, but it will always be necessary to check undue concentrations of power in private hands and pressure on the rudder will often have to be exercised by the State.

The economic effect of monopolies and trade unions is considered in later chapters. But they have other effects which must be considered here.

i. *Private Monopolies and Trade Associations*

(a) *Effect on Freedom of Contract*. Maine discerned a movement in legal history from status to contract, from a situation where most of the rights and duties of the individual were fixed by an external authority to a free society where each was free to negotiate and establish his own rights and duties by agreement with his fellow-citizens. This freedom was largely illusory in many respects and we are now moving away from contract to a new kind of status. Since the war, for example, the State has intervened in the relationship of landlord and tenant to an increasing extent by according rights to the tenant which cannot be overridden by any agreement with the landlord. The Agricultural Holdings Act, 1948 protects tenant farmers from various onerous conditions and from eviction, and the Landlord and Tenant Act, 1954 has provided a code of protection for residential tenants on long leases and tenants of business premises.

[1] *Gravity and Grace* (1952), p. 151.

The Law of Contract provides a striking contrast. Every day of our lives we enter into numerous contracts with public and private bodies in the course of such routine activities as buying goods or travelling by bus, train or ship; but in relation to many of these the law does not recognize that there may be such gross inequality between the parties that a transaction which is legally a contract is often in practice a piece of private legislation by the stronger party which the weaker party is powerless to prevent. For example, it is difficult in many districts to arrange for laundry to be taken by a firm which is not a member of the Institution of British Launderers Ltd. The members of this organization adopt standard conditions of contract which are printed in their laundry books (as revised in 1946). These contain elaborate provisions limiting the laundry's responsibility for loss and damage and stipulate that in no case is its liability to exceed twenty times the amount charged for cleaning articles lost or damaged. Similarly, purchasers of articles such as watches and radios are frequently handed an impressive piece of paper with a coloured facsimile seal attached purporting to guarantee goods for a certain period. In fact such documents frequently deprive purchasers of the greater rights to which they would have been entitled under the general law and offer much less in return.

The Courts do not like such contracts and are always ready to interpret onerous conditions strictly against the party seeking to impose them or to find ingenious reasons for holding that they are totally inapplicable to a particular situation. But there are many cases where the party who suffers loss does not take his case to court and accepts an *ex gratia* payment by the company concerned, which thus sets itself up as legislator and judge in its own case.

The remedy here is to enact contractual conditions and warranties which are to apply in certain cases notwithstanding any agreement to the contrary.

(*b*) *Effect on the Arts and Freedom of Speech.* The tendency to larger economic units is a serious danger to the maintenance of a free Press. The situation was succinctly described by Mr Francis

Williams in an article on the position of independent provincial morning papers:[1]

'Eighteen of them have died since the first great scramble for popular circulation in the twenties, six since the end of the war, two in the last two years. And the concentration of newspaper interests in great London-based centralized groups has moved on apace to such an extent that of the close on 30,000,000 copies of morning and evening papers of all kinds that go into British homes each day some 60% are now produced by four major groups — the Mirror Pictorial group, Lord Rothermere's Associated Newspapers, Beaverbrook Newspapers and Kemsley Newspapers.'

Periodical publications of all kinds have been affected in a similar way. Many long-established magazines have disappeared or been absorbed into others, e.g. *The Leader*, *The Strand Magazine*, *Life and Letters* and *John O'London's Weekly*. Periodicals concerned with the arts and with political ideas have found it very difficult to survive: post-war ventures such as *Polemic* and *Sequence* did not last for very long, and *The London Magazine* has only survived with outside support.

The same tendencies have developed in the theatre and the cinema. Eighty-two theatres have had to close down since the end of the War and during the last fifteen years or so a group has emerged owning and controlling a large number of the West End and leading provincial theatres which are still operating. The group is headed by Mr Prince Littler and his associates and controls over 50% of the theatre seats in the West End and over 70% of the larger theatres in the provinces.[2] Cinemas are dominated by Associated British Cinemas Ltd and the Rank Organization, which together control about half the cinemas in London and the South-East and about 40% of the cinema-seats in the rest of the country excluding the North. The same groups own two of the four main studios for film-making. A number of cinemas are being closed as a result of competition from television, which is itself a rapidly expanding medium dominated by the State and by groups already powerful in other fields of entertainment.

[1] *New Statesman*, 10 March 1956.
[2] *Theatre Ownership in Britain* (1953), a report by Equity and others.

The publishing industry has been in great difficulties since the War and a number of smaller firms have either disappeared or been absorbed into larger groups. Many of the latter appear to retain their identity and the effects of their absorption are difficult to assess. Mr Aldous Huxley has suggested that rising costs are imposing an economic censorship which will force authors to form co-operative societies for duplicating books which ordinary publishers will not accept because of their limited appeal.[1]

The health and vitality of a free society depend on a diffusion of power in all the media of instruction, information and entertainment, but this is becoming increasingly difficult to achieve in practice. Sometimes the State sponsors or subsidizes ventures which give opportunities for creative work, such as the Third Programme of the B.B.C., but this is undesirable in principle. It is surely not the business of the State to intervene in cultural activities: it should rather create the economic conditions in which such activities can flourish by restricting the power of monopoly.

ii. *Trade Unions*

It is interesting to compare the extent to which company law and trade union law have kept pace with modern requirements. An elaborate code of statute law for companies has been in existence for many years, dealing with the rights and duties of shareholders and directors and containing numerous provisions to protect the public and minority shareholders from fraud and oppression. In 1945 the Cohen Committee recommended certain changes in the law; reforms were subsequently enacted in the Companies Act, 1947 and this was almost immediately afterwards consolidated with earlier Acts in the Companies Act, 1948. Unfortunately such alacrity is exceptional and many years usually elapse between recommendations for law reform and action by Parliament to give effect to them.

By comparison with company law, trade union law is in a primitive state. Laws have been enacted at various times to deal

[1] 'Censorship and Spoken Literature', *London Magazine*, October 1956, and in *Adonis and the Alphabet* (1956).

with particular problems, e.g. the political levy, but a number of essential points are still obscure. It is not even clear to what extent a trade union is a legal entity as distinct from its members. The unions enjoy considerable protection against litigation in respect of civil wrongs committed by them or on their behalf, and it has only recently been decided by the House of Lords that a registered trade union can be sued for damages for breach of contract.[1] There is a model set of rules which a trade union can adopt if it wishes, but there is virtually no protection of individual workmen from the iniquities of the closed shop and the system of sending to Coventry and, although membership of a trade union is a pre-requisite to certain types of employment, it is not certain that union committees must conform to the rules of natural justice when pro-ceeding to expel a member. The rules which should be followed have been summarized as follows:

1. Notice specifying the charge must be served upon the offending member.
2. The Committee must hold a proper hearing; the strict pro-cedure of a Court does not have to be followed but the Com-mittee must confine itself to the charge referred to in the notice and give the member an opportunity of defending himself.
3. The decision must be made *bona fide* and without malice and those adjudicating must not be the prosecutors in the case.

There is an urgent need for a Charter of Rights for union members which shall apply notwithstanding any union rules to the contrary; in particular, when a member has a dispute with his union, he should have an inalienable right of appeal from its decision to an independent body, which should consist of senior members of the T.U.C. sitting with a High Court Judge.

Until recently trade unions have been fairly successful in keep-ing their affairs clear of the law, but in recent actions by individual members the Courts have refused to give effect to inter-union

[1] *Bonsor* v. *Musicians' Union*, 1955 3 AER 518.

agreements in regard to the poaching of members.[1] These decisions, together with the affirmation of a member's right to sue a
registered trade union for damages, have raised a number of
awkward problems for the trade union hierarchy, who are
naturally anxious to avoid any general examination of trade union
law. It is most unfortunate that the law relating to trade unions
was not dealt with by Parliament at the same time as it considered employers' organizations, in debating the provisions of the
Restrictive Trade Practices Act, 1956. It will be much more difficult to deal with the subject separately.

In this section we have been concerned with unions of workmen, but legally the term 'trade union' includes unions of employers. Some of the criticisms made above apply to these and to
professional associations, but there are wide differences in their
rules and practices.

3. PERSONALITIES

In this chapter we have referred to a number of laws which vest
powers in the Executive and either limit or protect the liberty of
the individual in various ways. Their effect in practice depends to
a great extent on the individuals who exercise the powers or enforce the laws — on Town Clerks, Civil Servants, prosecuting
solicitors and police inspectors — and, where litigation ensures,
on the personalities of the lawyers and Judges engaged in it.

As far as the Civil Service is concerned, there has been a decline in financial status and possibly in intellectual and moral
standards. In the thirties many parents with vivid memories of the
slump thought that the service offered the best and safest career
for their children; but today, as a result of inflation and high taxation, the financial rewards of such a career are much smaller than
those offered by private industry, which is attracting men and
women of ability from Government service by offers of higher
salaries, generous expense allowances and opportunities for tax-

[1] E.g. *Spring* v. *National Amalgamated Stevedores and Dockers Society*,
1956 2 AER 221.

free capital profit. Examples of this tendency are frequently noted in the Press; in August 1956 it was reported that an official of the Ministry of Fuel earning £3,250 p.a. resigned from office and became a director of a furniture company, the directors of which earn an average salary of £5,600;[1] and at about the same time an official of the Ministry of Supply was reported to have left his job worth £4,500 and to have joined the board of a firm of produce merchants, each member of which earned an average salary of £5,500. A number of senior officials in the Treasury, the Foreign Office and the Board of Trade have left for similar reasons since 1947.

This development comes at a time when intelligent and efficient administrators are needed in greater numbers than ever and when the tasks facing them impose much more responsibility. The Crichel Down case is an example of what can happen when authority is vested in officials who are unequal to it.

It is difficult to press a case for an increase in Civil Servants' salaries at a time when the fight against inflation calls for a reduction in Government expenditure, but if we want administrators of high quality we must be prepared to pay an economic price for them, and if there is a wide difference between the financial rewards of business executives and Civil Servants the latter are inevitably more susceptible to corruption. This is a notoriously difficult offence to prove; business men complain of it at times, but often they are merely bitter at losing a Government contract; probably there is very little direct bribery in the form of payment for favours, but officials are open to more subtle temptations. Affairs of business are frequently conducted by men of powerful personality in an atmosphere of speed, tension and excitement accompanied by good food and drink; the world of the Civil Service is often humdrum, circumscribed by routine and the need for personal and departmental economy. A Government official may find it very pleasant to step out of his world for a time and feel not at the fringes but at the centre of power as he takes part in discussions with senior business executives and helps them to solve their

[1] *Evening Standard*, 28 August 1956.

problems (as it is his duty to do). A Managing Director may find
that a little flattery and a good cigar at the right moment are
sufficient to secure the desired result and the official concerned
may be quite unaware that he has been influenced in any way as
he recounts the day's events to his wife. Numerous examples of
this kind of approach to Civil Servants, M.P.s and Ministers were
cited in evidence before the Lynskey Tribunal.

Similar problems arise in regard to corruption of the police.
Their pay is modest and only about one-third of those who join
can rise above the rank of constable and raise their pay by more
than three pounds per week after twenty-five years service. It is
their duty half-heartedly to apply stupid and out-moded laws
relating to prostitution and street-betting so that the public can
indulge its weaknesses without facing up to their consequences,
and their work involves frequent contact with bookmakers, in-
formers, pimps and the like. The *camaraderie* which can develop
between hunter and hunted, sentry and prisoner, policeman and
criminal is a common theme in fiction and one has only to visit the
Magistrates' Court at Marlborough Street to see how difficult it is
to prevent this kind of relationship. Every morning prostitutes
trip smartly into the dock one after the other; they have been
there before and will be there again; most of them are well known
to the officer who gives evidence against them in court; he saw
them the previous night while on duty and will see them again on
his next round of night duty.

A kind of liaison can also arise between police and magistrates
since their work brings them into frequent contact with each other.
A bad example of this occurred in November 1955, when allegations of police corruption were made in the *Daily Mail*: the Chief
Metropolitan Magistrate at Bow Street attended there with two
other magistrates and made a special statement defending the
police from this attack.[1] Magistrates are supposed to approach
each case with an open mind and they should be particularly careful to keep at arm's length from the police, whose evidence they
frequently have to weigh against that of private citizens. The con-

[1] *Times*, 18 November 1955.

duct of the three magistrates on this occasion was precisely the reverse of that which their office requires; it was noted by many of those whose professional duties or private peccadilloes bring them into Magistrates' Courts and it added considerable force to the arguments of cynics that it is a waste of time and money to defend a police prosecution except in a serious case, since police evidence will always be accepted as correct by magistrates.

The police sometimes have a difficult task to perform at public meetings and demonstrations where they have to preserve order without taking sides. Inevitably their behaviour attracts a good deal of criticism from those taking part and much of this can be discounted. But there have been incidents which are disturbing in their implications and which have not been satisfactorily explained by the authorities. In March 1936 a meeting in Thurloe Square, South Kensington, was charged by mounted police without any warning and several persons were injured. Repeated requests were made for an official enquiry but these were refused, although an independent unofficial committee (consisting, among others, of Mr J. B. Priestley and Eleanor Rathbone) considered after hearing the evidence that the police had behaved improperly in several respects. In November 1956 crowds were demonstrating in Whitehall against the attack on Egypt by the Eden Government when they were charged by mounted police without any prior warning. Their behaviour was critized in some detail by a correspondent of *The Economist*, which described his report as 'frankly disturbing'.[1]

It is often alleged that there are undesirable links between those who occupy positions of authority at a higher level — particularly in the Civil Service, the B.B.C., the Church of England, the two major Parties and the more respectable newspapers. Those of limited education but sound instincts often refer to such people as 'they'; the more sophisticated now refer to 'them' as 'The Establishment'.[2] This phrase was used some years ago by Mr A. J. P. Taylor to describe the 'governing classes'. More recently

[1] *Economist*, 10 November 1956.
[2] *New Statesman*, 29 August 1953.

Mr Henry Fairlie has popularized the phrase but endeavoured to give it a more refined definition: 'By the "Establishment" I do not mean only the centres of official power — though they are certainly part of it — but rather the whole matrix of official and social relations within which power is exercised,'[1] and, 'it denotes not the oligarchs, but those who create and the pressures which sustain the climate of opinion within which they have to act.'[2]

It is naturally difficult to discover any accurate data in regard to such a nebulous concept, but as more information becomes available about the earlier history of this century evidence emerges of important links between persons of influence and authority which were hidden from the general view at the time when they were operating. The function of a governing group is to provide leadership and therefore to develop a point of view in advance of those whom they lead; the danger is that they may develop an outlook in opposition to the best interests of the people and in the process conceal vital information from them. 'Munich' and the Abdication both provide fertile ground for argument on these matters.

Governing cliques are inevitable in any society and our Establishment is preferable to most; it helps to maintain stability and to provide continuity between governments. Graham Wallas pointed out that the permanent Civil Service operates as a constitutional check or Second Chamber and the Establishment certainly contributes to this.[3] According to Wallas officials in the first decade of this century regrouped themselves after their day's work 'in the healthy London fashion, with labour leaders, and colonels, and schoolmasters, and court ladies, and members of parliament, as individualists or socialists, or protectors of African aborigines, or theosophists, or advocates of a free stage or a free ritual';[4] it is clear that the scope of their leisure activities has narrowed considerably since those days — particularly in the Home Office and the Foreign Office.

There are various ways in which the dangers referred to in this

[1] *Spectator*, 23 September 1955.   [2] *Ibid.*, 25 May 1956. 3
[3] *Human Nature in Politics* (1908), p. 249.   [4] *Ibid.*, p. 267.

section can be limited. The most important safeguard is a vigorous and free Press which constantly scrutinizes official activities and is not deterred from performing its proper functions by specious appeals to 'national interest' and 'good taste' or by legislation such as the Official Secrets Acts. In addition, the dangers of an Establishment can be reduced and its advantages increased if steps are regularly taken to prevent hereditary and nepotic influences playing any part in appointments to private and public posts of importance, and by ensuring that all classes in the community have an opportunity to compete. Considerable progress has been made since the War in reforming the conditions of entry to the Civil Service, but there is scope for improvement as far as private industry and the professions are concerned. For example, entry into both branches of the legal profession is still difficult for those with limited means, and for a barrister survival in private practice is almost impossible in the years immediately after call to the Bar without private means or opportunities to earn money from outside work such as coaching. Their position would be eased if they were allowed to work in solicitors' offices in their first years or if they were allowed to practise in partnership and earn a fair return for assisting successful barristers, who are always overloaded with work. Reforms in education would also improve the position and these are suggested in Chapter VII.

The general vigour and efficiency of our society would also be increased if there were greater mobility of labour among the senior positions in the Civil Service, private industry and the professions. An entrant to the Civil Service is expected to make it his permanent career and to work in it for the rest of his life; he rarely gets the opportunity at any stage in his career to leave the service for a year or two and gain experience in some other work related to that which he has been doing. Conversely, those who gravitate into the Civil Service from the professions are often men of moderate ability who fall back on the Service after failing to make headway elsewhere. There are a number of competent professional men who would like to work for the Government for a time and return to private practice later, but it is impossible for them to do so at present. Government, industry and the professions would all benefit from exchanges of this kind — for example between British Railways and companies operating road transport — and arrangements might also be made for the exchange of officials between this country, the Commonwealth and the U.S.A. We have referred above to various threats to the integrity of Government personnel, but in the last twenty-five years or so the most serious threat of all has come from the Communist Party. Those who deny or minimize the importance of this are either fools or knaves; either they do not understand the world in which they live or they deliberately aid the Communist Party by confusing the issue and playing down the effects of Communist infiltration. In dealing with the problem it is necessary to strike a balance between the measures necessary to protect the country and the limitations of personal freedom which these require. In this country Civil Servants threatened on security grounds with dismissal or transfer from secret duties can appeal to a tribunal of three advisers; they report to the Minister concerned who makes the final decision. This procedure was reviewed in 1956 by a conference of Privy Councillors, who found nothing organically wrong or unsound in it,[1] and a similar procedure has been adopted for security risks in private industry.

The *Times* described the conclusions of the Conference as 'refreshingly calm and sensible' and pointed out that 'in the final analysis the true safeguard of individual liberty is the climate of public opinion'.[2] But public opinion cannot operate as desired by the *Times* unless it has knowledge of the facts or confidence in those who discover and withhold them; at present it has neither. It appears that Communist infiltration into Government service is less extensive here than in the U.S.A., where there is no strong Social Democratic Party to provide an alternative attraction to the Communist Party for youthful idealists with a passion for social justice. But how competent has the investigation been? This task is in the hands of security services, who must work to a large extent in secret; but their public performances have not always been

1 Cmd. 9715.   2 *Times*, 9 March 1956.

very impressive, and they appear to draw a number of recruits from ex-servicemen who have only limited knowledge and experience of these matters and who derive most of their ideas on the subject from the works of 'Sapper' and George E. Rochester.

Much of the argument in these matters inevitably rests on supposition but on the facts at present available the present system is open to a number of criticisms. The status, powers and procedure of the three advisers are all rather vague; it would be much better for appeals to be conducted by a genuinely independent tribunal (drawn perhaps from the Privy Council and including at least one High Court Judge). It is not possible to allow security personnel and their witnesses to be cross-examined by the Civil Servant who is under suspicion, but he should at least have the opportunity to present his own case fully to an independent body and the satisfaction of knowing that those testifying against him have been carefully cross-examined by such a body. A certain amount of comfort may be drawn from the fact that Mr G. R. Strauss was a member of the conference of Privy Councillors who examined the position, since he himself was found guilty of Left-Wing deviationism by the Labour Party before the last war. One would like to be sure that those lower down the political and social scale who formerly advocated joint action with or owed allegiance to the Communist Party now have an equal chance of working their passage. Such people usually experience a 'Kronstadt', a moment of revelation when facts suddenly appear as they are and not as the Communist Party has interpreted them; there are plenty of published letters and articles to witness the 'Kronstadt' of, for example, Mr John Strachey; but former humble Party Members with no talent for writing may find it much more difficult to clear themselves. The Civil Service employs a number of these and they are entitled to the greatest possible protection and assistance. In particular they should be allowed legal representation when appearing before the three advisers. The denial of this elementary right is one of the most serious defects in the existing procedure.

P. M. S.

CHAPTER IV

PROPERTY AND EQUALITY

I. THE DECLINE OF PROPERTY

IT was not just a Marxian fantasy to divide society into classes, to interpret much of human affairs in terms of this division and to define class by its relation to ownership. Most Victorian thinkers of the Right and Left did the same: Disraeli, for instance, and Thomas Arnold. The erstwhile power of property lives on in our memory in many now inappropriate phrases and maxims such as 'Possession is nine points of the law' and 'May I not do what I like with my own?' When Hannah More began to found schools for the village poor a powerful farmer in one village objected: 'If a school were set up it would be all over with property, and if property is not to rule what is to become of us?'[1] William Paley, whose philosophical and theological writings would surely have made him a bishop, was often reckoned to have lost all chances of promotion by his comment on the institution of property: 'If you should see a flock of pigeons in a field of corn, and if (instead of each picking where and what it liked, taking just as much as it wanted and no more) you should see ninety-nine of them gathering all they got into a heap; reserving nothing for themselves but the chaff and the refuse; and keeping this heap for one, and that the weakest perhaps and worst pigeon of the flock; sitting round, and looking on all the winter, whilst this one was devouring, throwing about and wasting it, ... you would see nothing more than what is every day practised and established among men.'[2] He died

[1] M. G. Jones, *Hannah More* (Cambridge, 1952), p. 169.
[2] *Moral and Political Philosophy* (1785), I, iii. But he goes on to adduce ineluctable practical reasons for the institution of property.

an archdeacon, his dreadful *gaffe* forever refreshed in men's minds
by the sobriquet *Pigeon Paley*.

It is a different world today. There are no longer two classes,
the owning and the working. Private property confers hardly any
political power — certainly less than that conferred by a vote, and
much less than that which flows from membership of a trade
union. The classes have become social rather than political; they
differ by speech, education and occupation and avoid inter-
marriage. Differences used to be both subjective and objective;
now they are merely subjective. Income differences, especially
after tax, are small and are not related in any simple way to class
differences: bank-clerks earn less than steel workers. Political
power[1] determines class, not *vice versa*, instilling into M.P.s and
Civil Servants of the lower classes the habits and attitudes of the
upper middle class, though not necessarily changing their politics
thereby. Divorced from political power, property is also divorced
from class differences. With the exception of a few great noblemen
and the small business man nobody's property determines his
social class.[2] It hardly determines even his income, so heavy are
the taxes upon high and unearned incomes. He cannot dispose of
it at death as he would like, owing to death duties, and still less
while he lives can he 'do what he will with his own'.

Property, then, has been demoted in political importance almost as much as religion. There are two major reasons for this.
First is the growth of regulation and taxation. This has obviously
diminished the disposability of, and the power and income derived from, private property to an enormous extent. It needs no
discussion. Secondly there is the more interesting growth of
absentee ownership. Limited liability has vastly increased absentee
ownership as lenders diversify their portfolios and borrowers appeal to ever wider and ever poorer circles of investors. The ab-

[1] I.e. power in Westminster and Whitehall. In local government political
power has much less social effect.

[2] Except in the sense that a man may sell capital to buy his children a public
school education. Thus a father may *deprive* himself of property in order to
raise his child's class.

sentee shareholder in a modern limited company is the possessor
of a mere scrap of paper which entitles him to certain payments by
a remote and unknown agent. Nationalization does not worry
him much; it deprives him of no power he ever exercised and
merely substitutes one piece of paper for another. To be sure the
shareholder's power *can* be put to work against the directors, but
only by an individual or *ad hoc* committee holding the proxies of a
large percentage of the equity. This happens very rarely indeed,
and only after inordinate expenditure of initiative, effort and
money; when directorial control does pass by a shareholders' vote
from one group to another the event is a nine days' wonder
lengthily celebrated in the City columns. With every decade that
passes the large corporate body becomes more and more a legal
entity separate from its individual 'owners'. It can, of course, sue
and be sued. Its shareholders can sue it, e.g. for breach of the
articles of association; and it can even sue its shareholders, e.g. for
trespass on 'its' property. Its profits are subject to taxes that differ
more and more from income-tax; yet originally its profits were
merely its shareholders' income, and all the tax it paid was income-tax in their name. The regulations to which it is subject —
price-control, restrictions on the employment of women, safety
rules, etc. — are imposed upon it as a company and not upon its
shareholders. Muddled as modern theories on the subject are, no
one today would be childish enough to confuse the shareholders
with the company; difficult as it may be to define an economic,
legal or political entity that is not a human being.

Ownership, in fact, has little meaning any longer from the
point of view of power, and all advanced sectors of the economy
have fully passed through the Managerial Revolution. In such
sectors there are now no owners but only shareholders on the one
hand and managers on the other. Indeed in nationalized corporations there are no shareholders at all, and even 'the State' as owner
has only a control limited by statute. The very concept of ownership implies a pre-managerial economy.

Yet the question of private property cannot be so lightly dismissed, for the economy still has a large pre-managerial sector,

and even in its more advanced sector it still matters very much *who* its shareholders are, since upon this depends the distribution of national wealth. When nationalization hits the pre-managerial sector, as in the cases of road haulage and the Liverpool Cotton Exchange, the capitalists concerned react with all the sharpness a Marxist could wish. Even in the managerial sector an increase in dividends always stimulates a claim for higher wages. Above all, property is still most unequally distributed; the very high death duties of recent decades have scarcely begun to bite.[1]

This extreme inequality is an important fact indeed. It is true that property yields much less gross income than it used to do, and that incomes derived from it pay more in tax than earned incomes, not only because of earned income relief but because property incomes chiefly accrue to those whose incomes as a whole are large. But all this only mitigates the inequality of property incomes. The

[1] The following summary of the facts, based on Mrs Kathleen M. Langley's figures (*Bull. Oxford Univ. Institute of Statistics*, December 1950) is only a simplification but establishes that property distribution today is still essentially unchanged since 1911:

Property-owners	Percentage of total private capital			
	1911/13	1924/30	1936/38	1946/47
Richest 5% own	87	83	78	72
Richest 20% own	95	95	93	90
Richest 50% own	98	99	97	97

These figures merely show how little change there has been yet. But their accuracy is highly contestable: it seems that they much underestimate the capital in the hands of the poor. Mr H. F. Lydall (*Bull. Oxford Univ. Institute of Statistics*, March 1952) has shown that the poorest 52% of the population possess nearly £200 in small savings alone per 'spending unit' (which is more or less a family, and has an average of 1·6 adults in it). If we add to this the value of consumers' durables less personal indebtedness (which must surely be a positive figure of some kind), it appears that adults in the poorest 52% of the population average well over £100 of capital. These data come from a very thorough sample based on a careful and direct questionnaire. Yet Mrs Langley, by the indirect and inaccurate method of analysing death duties, makes the poorest 65% of the population appear to possess less than £100 per person. And this accumulation of consumers' durables in the hands of the poor has mainly taken place in recent years, so there is probably some trend towards equality, not shown by the death-duty figures.

capital value of property also has great significance, and the inequality of its distribution has not been changed in the present century. The wise sayings of the past are as true as ever on this theme:

> 'It is easier for a camel to go through the eye of a needle than for a rich man to enter the kingdom of God' (Mark, 19.25).
> 'Wealth is like muck: it is not good but if it be spread' (Francis Bacon).
> 'The man who dies rich dies disgraced' (Andrew Carnegie).
> 'The distribution of private property depends on inheritance, constantly modified by "thrift, ability, industry, luck and fraud" ' (Irving Fisher).

It is hardly too much to say that most of the social tensions surviving in Britain today are due to the unequal distribution of private property. Why else have rent-control (which in itself is almost wholly bad) if the few did not own and the many need houses? Why else speak of Labour and Capital as 'two sides' of industry? Yet this concept is the most poisonous of all economic fallacies — if only it really *were* a fallacy.[1]

2. REDISTRIBUTION OF PROPERTY

What we must abandon from the outset is the Marxist obsession with the 'Division of the Product of Industry'; yet it is difficult and dishonest to liberate ourselves from it entirely while it still retains some tatters of reality. Marx — and Ricardo before him — distinguished the classes by the *kind* of income they received, to wit wages, interest/profit and rent, which were derived from the provision of distinct factors of production, labour, capital/enterprise and land. For them each individual in a modern industrial society belonged to one class only, the peasants and artisans (who supply more than one kind of production-factor) being ground out of existence by superior large-scale techniques. They believed their classification to be exhaustive, and Marx and his followers

---

[1] The other great source of social tension is the national antipathy between managed and manager. Workers in co-operative societies, for instance, get on no better with their employers than in capitalist shops. The relations of managed and manager, as opposed to labour and capital, are discussed in Ch. IX.

held that of the three kinds of income only wages could be morally justified.

It is now clear that this analysis is false at many points. Peasants and artisans have by no means completely disappeared. By means of life insurance and the small savings movement some wage-earners have accumulated considerable capital from which they receive interest — and much of this capital is invested by the insurance company in industry itself. Above all the Welfare State has been created and now provides a very large fourth kind of income in which all classes, however we define them, can share. And the profit-taker is no longer, as we have seen, the man in power. All these things blur the sharp outlines of the Marx-Ricardo picture.

Blur, but not erase. A wage-earner can still feel, and not wrongly, that he is 'working for another man's profit'. People who work with their hands for wages are very unlikely in fact to get a significant income from privately-held capital. Social service payments are individually small except in cases of illness and un-employment, i.e. cases of incapacity to earn wages. Moral tensions will continue to arise from private property so long as it is dis-tributed in gross inequality. For it is, in the last resort and when current confusions have been cleared away, only the unjust, arbitrary and wildly unequal distribution of property that leads to scandal. That incomes derived from property are 'unearned' is, or should be, no objection at all, for they are payment for genuine factors of production: land and capital and enterprise. These fac-tors should, as we shall see, be paid for by those who use them, and it is natural and just that these payments be made to those who supply them. An income may very easily be deserved when it is not 'earned'; are not the social services unearned? But income is not deserved (and this is what concerns us) when it is based upon a system of property-distribution which is in itself unjust.

Many reasons can be urged in favour of gross inequality in the ownership of private property and in the income derived from it. Thus, non-governmental associations and activities should be strong and flourishing in a free society and they are most likely to flourish if there exist large private fortunes to endow them. Rich men, again, patronize the arts, especially innovations in the arts which contemporary popular taste mistrusts. They patronize progressive schools and, indeed, all eccentrics and eccentricities. They take sometimes absurd risks in investing their capital in new kinds of industry. They are often themselves eccentric. They save more than the poor, thereby making more investment possible (since more is voluntarily saved out of an unequally distributed national income than out of one equally distributed); and more investment, as we shall see, is one of the main sources of economic progress. Above all, it requires political, we may even say police, interference, to establish and to maintain equality of fortunes. True, equality itself is not opposed to freedom, but attempts to establish it very usually are, and Britain must be reckoned in this respect a singularly lucky exception. Men who hold equality to be the highest value usually underestimate individual differences between men and therefore underestimate the degree of freedom that men require. Moreover inequality as a matter of history has facilitated political freedom since it raises greater individual agglomerations of power over against the State. These individuals may, of course, dominate the State themselves, but if the constitution is democratic or merely subject to the rule of law this seldom happens. Usually the effect of powerful individuals with large private fortunes is to ensure political freedom, not only for themselves but also, by reflection, for others.

This case for inequality of private property does not outweigh the fact that most British citizens have an unalterable passion for equality generally, and particularly for equality in unearned income. This passion must not, of course, be exaggerated. If only they are vulgar enough, the very rich rouse admiration, not resentment, among the uneducated. Wide classes of the population will tolerate a millionaire, still more a millionairess, with the common touch and a zest for high life. But this is not so of the politically-conscious leaders of these same uneducated masses. Such leaders — and therefore in effect their followers too — will not accept the free-price mechanism, or indeed the very existence

of private property and many other good things including even
the rule of law itself, so long as there are gross inequalities of
ownership. And they are right to object. Professor Irving Fisher
has shown that it is inheritance — a matter of pure chance — and
not merit of any kind that distributes private property. There is,
in fact, no justice in its present distribution, however much ex-
pediency there may be. We may add that private property is not
distributed by any *economic* law either, and that the manner of its
passing from individual to individual contributes in no way to
economic efficiency. It passes simply by virtue of the decisions of
individual testators made under the existing legal system. It follows, then, that we must choose the lesser evil in establishing so
far as possible a greater degree of equality of private property and
of the income derived from it.[1]

3. REDISTRIBUTION OF INCOME

i. *Earned incomes*

First, however, we must consider the question of income distribution. The community can always achieve as much inequality
as it wishes simply by not controlling the distribution of earned
income. Such income approximately corresponds under the free-
price mechanism to the usefulness of each worker to the community. Experience shows the economic utility of individuals to
differ greatly by this standard. However, inequality of this sort is
accepted by most people as being fair; and it certainly encourages
efficiency and self-improvement. It is accepted even by the poorest
provided that private property is distributed in a reasonably equal
way and unearned income from the State ensures subsistence for
all. And so we argue for a revolutionary distributive principle:
that the abandonment of Marxist thinking, the equalization of
property and the assurance of a social minimum make desirable

[1] There is the minor matter of property accumulated — out of earnings or
clever speculation — in a single lifetime. The general sense of justice is much
less outraged by this and would surely be content not to hinder the accumulation being made but to disperse it at death.

laissez-faire in earned income. Now, curiously enough, however revolutionary the principle may sound our present practice is not so very different. Compared with other Western countries we have astonishingly little State interference with the distribution of incomes before tax. There is not even a legal minimum wage — and rightly not, for why should not the almost unemployable supplement their social minimum by whatever earned income they are in fact worth? Most of the regulation of hours of work — of which we have more — is also quite unnecessary, for when there are social services and full employment the worker really can drive a hard, rational bargain about hours, just as the Victorians supposed. It was only hunger and unemployment that ever made a labourer drive a foolish bargain, detrimental on balance to himself, in the matter of hours. He who today chooses night-work certainly gets himself paid extra for the inconvenience; and if the hours threaten his health or take him from his family he can always get himself a day job for less pay.

It is not, then, against the State so much as the unions that the principle of *laissez-faire* operates; not against public interference but against private monopolies of labour. Collective bargaining merely raises the earned incomes of particular monopolistic groups above what their value would be to the community under fair competition, while on a nation-wide scale it generates inflation and harms those whose money incomes are not, or not easily, increasable. There can be no valid notion of just wages or just profits: it is the *total* income that should be just, while wages and profits should correspond to the productivity of the individual and the cost of capital under fair competition. Indeed, granted subsistence for all and no gross inequality of property, *laissez-faire is the just way to distribute earned incomes.*

We have castigated above the Marxist idea, shared by most other kinds of Socialist and originated by the Classical economists, that the 'Division of the Product of Industry' is the essential question in economics. Where does the gross revenue of a particular factory go? How can the 'workers' increase their share of it? Are they being exploited? Are profits moral? These people are obsessed with the direct distribution of income by the market process, and behave too as if there were no other kind of income: they seem to have forgotten both that income from private property is distributed by no market process at all (except for the small part that comes from property acquired through current savings) but by inheritance; and that income is also distributed by the Welfare State on purely political or charitable grounds. If income directly derived from production does not ensure subsistence to all or leads to gross inequalities, this is no argument for suspending the price mechanism in this respect, still less for altering the whole social system. It is an argument for supplementing earned income through the Welfare State. The function of a distribution of earned incomes determined by the price mechanism is to attract labour into the trades socially most important at any moment, to encourage greater efficiency and to render promotion attractive. If the State does wish to interfere in this matter it should actually increase the inequalities brought about by the price mechanism — as in the U.S.S.R.

ii. *Unearned incomes*

Grant then private property more justly distributed and *laissez-faire* in the distribution of earned incomes: the main question is then whether unearned income from the Welfare State can be relied upon to ensure subsistence for everyone and to make the overall distribution reasonably 'fair' (meaning acceptable to the moral intuitions of most people). The answer is surely Yes. The distribution of unearned income ('Welfare') by the State is the greatest social development of the twentieth century. The State can now achieve virtually any income distribution that political opinion desires; the only serious difficulty is the tax burden. For the social services are largely financed by taxes and these, whether direct or indirect, must *ex hypothesi* be progressive. They thus cut into the marginal earned income of producers from work, which discourages over-time work and the effort to win promotion. Tax evasion, by the way, is not a serious issue in Britain though were we Frenchmen or Italians we should be giving it very much more

D

space. There are three great advantages in the distribution of unearned income by the State:

(a) It is the least totalitarian way to 'social justice', i.e. greater
equality of incomes. All attempts to establish social justice are in a
sense totalitarian and threaten liberty in so far as any serious alteration of the existing social system — unless that system be itself
totalitarian — may do so. But the threat is least when the State
merely hands out old-age pensions, family allowances, etc., while
taking in compulsory insurance premiums, various taxes and
death duties. For in this system there is no direct confiscation of
actual objects owned by particular individuals, no action is arbitrary, and the transfer of wealth from the rich is gradual, never
exceeding the amount currently required for the support of
the poor. The Inland Revenue is superior to the People's Court
or to Robin Hood.

(b) This system of redistribution is also the most delicate and
finely adjustable. It takes — or can take — from exactly the class
of person in the best position to contribute and gives — or can
give — to exactly the most deserving group. Thus the losers
should not be *any* rich people but those who are young or child-
less or, perhaps, live on unearned income. And the gainers should
be not unskilled workers in general but the old — whether they
have been 'workers' or not — and those with large families. This
point is extremely important: redistribution should not be between
rich and poor in the crude sense of profit-takers and wage-
receivers, or between the upper and the lower social classes. At
this point the fallacious obsession with the 'Division of the Product of Industry' raises its head again. Clearly if the Welfare
State is to live up to its name it must take from the rich who have
few or no responsibilities — and this includes bachelors among
the skilled working class — and give to the old and the infant.
Poverty is very much more a function of age and family status
than of gross income or social class.

(c) The system gives the community immense freedom of
action in other matters and makes the beneficent results of technical progress and the free-price mechanism perfectly acceptable.

Having assured a subsistence to all, we need not be constantly looking over our shoulders at the incidental redistributive effects of the measures taken for (say) economic efficiency, or reasons of foreign policy or defence; for whatever happens, none can starve and few can be much hurt. For instance, the case for free trade is that it ensures that each country contributes to the world economy that product which it makes most cheaply: in other words, it ensures the best possible division of labour between nations, and a free-trade world produces more, *ceteris paribus*, than a protectionist world. But to abolish a tariff which is not necessary on strategic grounds or for economic development is still to impoverish those employed in or profiting from the trade hitherto protected, and this has always been a chief obstacle to the removal of tariffs once they have been put on. This obstacle is slight indeed if we have full employment and a high unemployment benefit. Again monopoly — at any rate in its cartel form — leads to high prices on restricted outputs. Competition — or State control of the monopoly — raises the output of the product hitherto monopolized, thus diverting economic resources to better use than previously, but it reduces the price of this article and therefore the wages, profits, etc. of its producers. Consequently there may often be good social arguments for monopoly on grounds of income distribution; but never if the social services are sufficient and there is full employment generally. Above all, the State can promote and enforce technical progress without *arrière-pensée*: new machinery can be introduced, releasing labour for other employment: inefficient enterprise can be rationalized or even wholly suppressed and whole trades relocated. All these considerable disturbances to the labour force are possible and tolerable only because beneath them lies the cushion of the social services.

It is clear then that the obsession with the 'Division of the Product of Industry' not only leads to class war but also to economic stagnation. It is wrong that before proceeding to improvement in the pattern and location of economic activity we should have to ask how such changes will affect the incomes that are derived from the activity. For competition, re-organization and progress always

hurt *somebody's* earned income, and if we are too cautious improvement will come never or too late. And yet if basic or subsistence income is wholly earned, i.e. derived directly from production, such caution is inevitable. We must take advantage of the
Welfare-State mechanism unavailable to our ancestors to ensure
that basic incomes continue if earnings cease. In this way we can
break down or at least diminish that vested interest of all citizens
in the past or current pattern of economic activity which is the
great bar to progress.[1]

4. THE NEW IMPORTANCE OF PROPERTY

So far we have spoken in terms of high praise of the Welfare
State. Yet looking closer at the matter we see that we have been
praising, not the social services or progressive taxation in particular, but *any* just distribution of unearned income: any distributive
method, that is, that ensures to all citizens a basic minimum when
earnings are inadequate or cease. We turn now to the possibility of
bringing this about by the despised and improbable means of
private property in the means of production; and it will be seen
that this means is so superior that the whole Welfare State apparatus must itself be regarded as a passing phenomenon. Always in
the past desirable, the Welfare State at length became possible
through the raising of the level of the Civil Service and technical
improvements in communication, accountancy and filing systems.
But that very advance in the arts that made it possible will make it
undesirable before long. With good luck and good management,
we should see about one century elapse between its birth (*ca.*
1910) and its demise.

It needs, of course, few words to show that social justice should

---

[1] It may be objected that welfare arrangements will also break down the
vested interest in progress, i.e. the innovator's hopes for increased earnings.
But in practice all innovators are at present assured of a subsistence. They
never did stand to gain by more than an increase in their earnings, and that
prospect remains undimmed.

be obtained if possible without central administration, but instead
by the private means of individuals. For this diminishes the impersonal and bureaucratic side of life, secures individual freedom
from the State and makes for self-reliance and independence of
character. The point is so obvious that however crucial its importance we may assume its truth at once and pass to the practical
question: *how* do we distribute private property in a just and
equal way and keep it so distributed?

First and most obvious, by severe and progressive death duties.
True, all taxes are bad, but of all taxes death duties discourage
work the least. It is true that as a rich man approaches his natural
term he ceases to accumulate wealth in view of all the taxes that
must shortly be paid upon it; but his need for income is not
diminished and the whole effect is very slight compared with that
of surtax, which lessens very sharply the will to work of a rich or
highly-paid man all his life.

The object, however, is not to confiscate but to redistribute
property. We are Liberals, not Socialists, and must never lose
sight of this elementary principle, so ill reflected in current legislation. It is commonly suggested that there should be substantial
reductions in tax if the fortune is split up and devised to several
heirs, but this does not quite meet the bill. For in this way the
property of each individual rich man can easily be divided tax-
free among his rich relations, who all in turn make wills dividing
the property up amongst each other, so avoiding the tax again:
'You endow your nephew (= my son) and I'll endow mine (=
your son).' Thus a whole family could easily remain hereditarily
rich. What is wanted is tax rebates on legacies to charity or the
poor.[1]

Secondly, new property must be built up. In an expanding
economy there are ever more things to own per head of population: the only thing is to ensure that most people can own them.
The most effective means has hitherto been 'small savings':
National Savings Certificates, Post Office and Trustee Savings

[1] Who could be defined, roughly but well enough, by the size of their
income-tax payments in the last two years.

Bank deposits, Building Society deposits, Co-operative Society shares and deposits, etc. The simple and straightforward accumulation of funds by the poor will of course continue to be very important; but it will only remain so if these savings, like the equities bought by the rich, can make some show of keeping pace with inflation. A sliding scale must surely be applied to these accumulations based, doubtless with a suitable lag, or even a permanent discount, upon the cost of living index. Tax exemption, too, might well be extended beyond National Savings Certificates; it has a very great psychological effect on the poor, who would, apparently, much prefer tax exemption to a rise in the rate of interest, which would have the same effect.[1]

A more promising line of approach than small savings has recently gained upon it: personal insurance. The superiority of insurance over sheer accumulation is very simply explained: it offers a moderate rate of interest on one's savings, and insurance against one's misfortunes as well. Only the very rich, the size of whose fortunes is ample cover against accident and disease, will prefer the higher interest yield of sheer accumulation. Of the various forms that insurance takes this is not the place to speak. Enough for us that there is scarcely any kind of private property more suited to a poor man. Insurance will grow and should be encouraged to grow.[2] But it too must of course adjust itself to inflation.[3]

A third small savings channel is the purchase of one's own house. This is traditional, but strongly on the increase now. It

[1] Such is the opinion of Trustee Savings Bank officers.

[2] The so-called National Insurance has few of the essential features. Premiums and conditions cannot be varied at choice, policies cannot be taken out, let alone sold back to the issuer at the will of the insured. National Insurance is just a social service dressed up; which is not to deny, of course, that it has many advantages over a pure social service, but that is not here to the point. There is of course, nothing to stop the State competing with private companies to offer orthodox policies; indeed it would enjoy great administrative economies in such competition. Nor do we necessarily object to that.

[3] Cf. Garibian and Wiles, *Oxford Economic Papers,* July 1952.

should surely be encouraged, for instance by making it easier for municipalities to sell their houses to their tenants. Owner-occupancy has the particular advantage that it makes it easier to abolish rent-control; indeed unrealistically low rents dissuade very many from buying the houses they live in. On the other hand there is the objection that labour becomes less mobile; but the arguments in favour of *geographical* mobility, as opposed to mobility be-tween jobs, have been rather outdated by modern suburban trans-port. Except in country areas, where there really is a strong econ-omic argument for tied cottages and houses, it hardly matters where a worker lives or how strongly he is attached to his house.

Nowadays one can also buy *consumer's durables,* and this is a fourth way of promoting small savings. It has not hitherto been properly recognized as such, but it suffices to point out the fact for it to be admitted at once. A man is just as much a capitalist if he has his own washing-machine as if he possesses shares in a laundry.

For all these three sources of accumulation full employment is very important. When a man is out of work he spends his savings, and this is the main thing that in practice keeps the proletariat from making permanent accumulations. Economic growth and full employment, then, between them quite transform the pros-pects for small savings.

Fifthly there is co-ownership: the free or subsidized acquisition of the equity of the business by its own workers. It is chastening to set it out among the other channels of small savings: clearly unless the existing equity is confiscated and redistributed, co-ownership will never make much of a quantitative contribution to the problem. Merely to give the workers some claim on the growth of the equity is statistically very small beer. Again, unlike the other items, there are whole classes to whom it does not apply: Civil Servants and professional men particularly. Even the employees of very small businesses, farms in particular, could hardly be affected: the equity of such businesses is too personal to split or share, and the relation of employers and employed is already so personal that most of the psychological advantages claimed for co-ownership fall to the ground.

Co-ownership, then, is not mainly a device for redistributing private property, though it will do that in some degree; it is a psychological device for closing the gap between labour and capital in large firms. This is precisely where the gap is greatest, and the proportion of workers employed by such firms tends to increase with every generation. The object is, of course, to make the worker work for his own profit as well as someone else's: not merely to give him piece-rates or a bonus to wages, but a *right*, identical with that of any other shareholders, to the final dividend, and the correlative right to vote on directorial appointments, etc. It is thus the most radical of all solutions to the quarrel between labour and capital.

The problem of co-ownership is first among the problems treated in Chapter IX. It is enough to say here that practice has proved it to have excellent effects in labour-management relations and in the attitude of workers to their work. But we may rely as well upon natural processes for such effects: rises in real wages, more effective education, the autonomous decay of the Socialist tradition and the accumulation of other kinds of capital by wage-earners. Co-ownership has never been offered as a panacea and it has always been clear that it is too delicate, various and complicated to be imposed by law according to a single pattern. But it is an effective way of redistributing capital and, still more, it is the most effective measure of all for improving relations between capital and labour in modern large-scale industry.

5. THE IRRELEVANCE OF NATIONALIZATION

We must now consider, if only to dismiss, the classical solution to 'inequality' in any or all of its aspects of the first half of our century: nationalization. There are few phases in recent history so difficult to explain as the phase of Socialist dominance of British political thought (*ca.* 1918–50) and the fascination and repulsion of the concept of State ownership during those years. For it is now clear, as it should always have been clear, that *nationalization with compensation* (and the Labour Party was never pledged to any other kind) is a negligible change. So much so that while the ancient statist traditions of which it is a remnant are profoundly illiberal, it is in itself too feeble to be dignified with any such condemnation.

The rationalization of an industry by subjecting it to State ownership is not really our subject here, though it is an 'illiberal fact', not to be shrugged off but squarely accepted, that the State can sometimes take hold of an industry traditionally split up haphazardly among small and inefficient firms, and by rationalizing, specializing and above all reducing the number of these tiny units make the industry a better servant of the consumer and a better employer of labour. Liberals who put their heads in the sand rather than admit this do their cause much harm. Their proper answer is to insist that in order to rationalize such industries the State need not own them. It should rather proceed on the model of a liberally inspired land reform: the value of what individuals own should be preserved and even enhanced by the new efficiency of the industry. It is not private ownership but inefficient management that so often calls for reform. Certainly, in such cases, the structure of management should be altered and many owners deprived of their managerial powers. But the State should step in to improve, not to grab. If a child's leg is growing crooked we should straighten it, not amputate it; the fact of rickets does not establish the principle that artificial legs are best. All this was recognized and has ample precedent in the Railways Act of 1921.

Freedom and private enterprise, in other words, are subject to diseases. There is nothing alarming in that. All good things can go wrong. And sometimes only the State can be the doctor. Call in the doctor, then, rather than deny the obvious fact of illness when it occurs. But reject the fatuous suggestion that the doctor should be ceded in perpetuity all the rights of *paterfamilias*.

In most cases, however, nationalization does *not* improve efficiency. In these cases it is an unnecessary tampering with private ownership, and since in Britain it has always been accompanied by compensation it makes little difference even to that. However, it excludes the hopeful possibility of co-ownership and limits the beneficent increase of the value of property in private hands, the compensation stock being on a fixed-interest basis. Control may be quite unaltered — as with the Bank of England or Cable and Wireless — or altered for the worse, as may be the case with British Railways. Whatever the changes, they are bad; but they are also small. No workman, no consumer, is impressed by the difference. And above all the changes are gratuitous; they represent State action that might have been avoided, a waste of Parliamentary time and Civil Service skill.

Most other accusations against single acts of nationalization are misconceived. It involves, in itself, no threat to freedom, except in so far as the new Corporation may be monopolistic and Parliament unable, as it is in practice unable, to keep its policy under effective review. Again, the policy of management may be altered by nationalization even where its efficiency is not; many Boards, for example, during the Labour Governments of 1945–51 adopted a soft attitude to Labour which included surrenders to absurd wage claims and a tolerance of restrictive practices. But this is a fault not of the essence of nationalization and we may doubt if it will last. Nor does nationalization necessarily over-centralize; this too is a legacy of 'Labour misrule', especially in the case of the Coal Board, which can and should be reformed. Competition is entirely possible within a nationalized industry and between nationalized industries, as between the Gas and Electricity Boards and among grammar schools. No doubt nationalization does sometimes create monopolies, as it did in the British coal industry, and this is a black mark against it — mining is naturally competitive and should be made to function in that way. But nationalization might have been used to enforce a keener, fairer and more vigorous competition. Evidently the mistakes of 1945–51 are not permanent, but their correction is overdue.

Ministerial control is a more serious matter. Our pre-war public corporations were treated as independent trustees and carefully shielded from the responsible Ministries — or rather from the

Ministries which might have been made responsible for them. The Labour Government conceived of a public corporation almost as a Department of State, more obedient to the Government than private enterprise and consequently favoured by it; and it gave the Minister most excessive powers. Or at least on paper. An amusing and unexpected result of 'Labour misrule' has been that the personalities in charge of public corporations, and the prestige of the corporations as such (do they not 'belong to the people' and 'stand for the workers'?) have overwhelmed the Ministers supposed to control them. Ask any Civil Servant: he will tell you the nationalized industries are like bulls in china-shops, vastly more difficult to control and plan than private enterprise, almost as refractory as Local Authorities. A particularly bad case is the Electricity Authority's refusal to charge higher prices at peak hours, and its consequent waste of capital in building generating stations to cover peak loads it might have shifted to the troughs. And if the Minister's control over his corporation has become a myth, the control of Parliament is and has always been the merest fairy-tale. A Parliament which, as we have shown in Chapter II, is too congested to fulfil even its traditional duties is in no shape to deal with new ones. Yet if we are bound to condemn the ineffectiveness of the Minister when he does not act, we see no more reason to commend him when he does. Such arbitrary Ministerial decisions as the imposition on the Board of a five-day week in the coal industry or the surrender over the Board's dead body to wage-claims on the railways are obviously illiberal, and so is the Minister's power to appoint subordinate regional Boards.

What then should be the Liberal attitude to nationalization? Primarily one of amused contempt, as of an ichthyologist towards a coelacanth; certainly not a heated one. It is an act which, in the vast majority of cases, no Liberal could approve, but not necessarily one he must filibuster to prevent or undo the moment he reaches power. It doesn't necessarily threaten freedom, it doesn't make for happier workers, it doesn't satisfy the consumer, it doesn't necessarily create monopolies, it doesn't — much or in a rational way — redistribute wealth. If it lowers efficiency it is for chance reasons; it it raises it, the proper course for Parliament was to rationalize the industry while leaving it in private hands. Ministers ought to have less power over the private affairs of the nationalized industries and more courage to keep them in the queue for scarce capital or scarce dollar goods. Since it excludes co-ownership, indeed any form of private property, nationaliza-tion must one day go, but there is no hurry. It is not important.

6. CONCLUSION

Rightly enough Liberals have never been interested in econ-omic equality as such, whether in property or in income. Our con-cern is with liberty, and our objection to *extreme* wealth and *ex-treme* poverty is based on the recognition that both are, in their separate ways, violations of liberty — extreme wealth because it confers privilege, extreme poverty because it stunts the person-ality. But this is no objection to moderate gradations of wealth; in fact our first commitment to liberty obliges us to accept such gradations. We are offended by economic inequality only when it is so gross that equality-before-the-law and equality-of-oppor-tunity, i.e. liberty itself, are threatened by it. Here is the real urgency in this debate: to recognize that in the Socialist use of the word *equality* at least three incompatible ideas are confused — equality of property, equality of income, equality of opportunity. It is imaginable that the first and the second might be achieved to-gether, though it would take a totalitarian society to do it; what is unimaginable is that the first should ever co-exist with the third Great opportunities inevitably lead to great accumulations. Hence in some measure there must also be inequality of property, even if it be only of houses and consumers' durables. Moreover, *equality of earned incomes means direction of labour.* If people are not to be induced to go where they are wanted, they must be forced.

We really must choose. For the bitter fact is that the more Socialist equality we achieve the less of Liberal equality we are likely to retain, while the more we seek equality of opportunity the less equality in terms of wealth we shall have. For Liberals, fortunately, this is an easy choice, and we made it a long time ago. Our purpose now is twofold: first, to insist upon a more rigid use of language in the current debate on equality and a recognition that Liberal and Socialist ideas on the subject are radically opposed; and second, to define the consequences of our own attitude. It is clear that present inequalities in income are too small to represent any threat to liberty at all, and the Welfare State, which is an elaborate mechanism for redistributing income, is of declining importance and will eventually wither away. Inequalities in property, on the other hand, are gross, unjust and practically unchanged since Edwardian times, and it is only the diminished *power* of property which has made public opinion so indifferent to this standing injustice. In respect of property, as opposed to income, Liberals are outright distributists. Our object, in fact, is a society in which differences in property and income are wide but not too wide: moderate enough to ensure that poverty is abolished and opportunity is not defeated by the magnate, extreme enough to make opportunity, for the individual, something worth believing in.

P. W.

BOOK TWO

LIBERTY IN THE WELFARE STATE

V
Welfare in the Liberal State

VI
The Geography of Liberty

VII
Education

CHAPTER V

WELFARE IN THE
LIBERAL STATE

OUR purpose now is to examine the logic of the Liberal position on social policy. There are three main questions:

(i) To what extent does the Liberal of today accept the views on social policy expounded by the great Liberal philosophers and political economists of the eighteenth and nineteenth centuries?

(ii) What principles determine the scope and the form of State intervention in order to achieve the aims of a Liberal social policy?

(iii) What reforms in our present-day social policy are suggested by these principles?

I. THE TRADITIONAL ATTITUDE

It is often claimed that the great failure of Liberal political philosophy in the nineteenth century was its failure to define the scope of economic rights in the democratic State. The evidence usually offered is the supposedly negative attitude of nineteenth-century Liberal economists to the problem of poverty and their emphasis on non-intervention in economic life. But this attack has been largely misconceived. There is abundant evidence that Liberal economists and political philosophers were deeply concerned with the condition of the working classes.[1] It is true they

[1] See the ample evidence provided by Lionel Robbins, *Theory of Economic Policy in English Classical Political Economy* (1952), Lecture iii. Adam Smith, for example, insisted that 'no society can be flourishing and happy of which

argued that poverty was often self-imposed, either because of laziness or fecklessness, but this did not prevent them supporting measures to remove great inequalities of wealth, particularly inheritance taxation or such measures to increase the earning opportunities of the poor as State education. They were more sceptical, perhaps, of a social policy which contained a strong element of income redistribution, such as social security schemes requiring relief in money or in kind.

Is there any reason why the Liberal of today should abandon the position taken up by the great representatives of the nineteenth-century Liberal tradition in regard to social policy? So far as sentiment is concerned, none at all. So far as economic logic is concerned, we have learnt in recent years to respect their emphasis on the conflict between economic progress and a social policy requiring a redistribution of incomes, even if we do not think their logic impeccable. It must be remembered that they did not reject State intervention to relieve poverty because they thought that State intervention was undesirable in principle: they rejected it because they thought that it would be ineffective. The heirs to the Liberal tradition have cause to abandon the position of their political ancestors only in so far as they have come to question the *technical* foundations of their arguments.

The technical foundations consisted of two main supports. The first was the Malthusian principle of population. The relief of poverty by State intervention brought with it the danger of encouraging early marriages and a higher birth-rate. It was for this reason that Malthus insisted that one of the main subjects to be taught in elementary education should be the principle of population. The remedy of the poor was thought to lie in their own hands — the voluntary restriction of their numbers. The second support was the theory of economic development: the rate of economic progress depended on the level of saving, and if this

the far greater part of the members are poor and miserable. It is but equity, besides, that they who feed, cloath and lodge the whole body of the people should have such a share of the produce of their own labour as to be themselves tolerably well fed, cloathed and lodged' (*Wealth of Nations* (1776), I, viii).

proposition were accepted any radical redistribution of income through the State would be incompatible with the eventual relief of poverty because redistribution would hit the savers — the rich.

But these foundations of the nineteenth-century Liberal position have since been undermined; indeed they were never entirely secure. We no longer accept the Malthusian view of population — rather do we rush to the other extreme and argue that birth-rates tend to fall as living standards are raised, in itself a doubtful proposition if we consider the recent experience of the United States. In any case, we question the unique relation traced by Malthusians between population and living standards, particularly with the widespread increase in birth-control.

The second support is also insecure. The assumption behind the Classical argument was that the amount of saving undertaken by the community determined the rate of capital accumulation. The more saved, the lower would be the charge on borrowed funds and the higher would be the level of investment in plant and machinery. The modern revolt against this view was led by one of the greatest Liberals of our age, John Maynard Keynes. Keynesians hold that it is the level of the community's expenditure on all kinds of goods and services, and thus the prospective profits of business, which determine the amount of investment undertaken by industry and not the terms on which industry can borrow. Saving, according to this argument, has a rather negative part to play in regulating economic growth. It acts rather as a check to consumption than as a stimulus to investment, but this check need not operate unless the level of consumption-expenditure rises so high that it encourages rises in prices rather than increases in productivity and so causes inflation.

The striking paradox of this change in our economic reasoning is best illustrated if we assume that there is a long-run tendency for the economy to operate at much less than full stretch so that there is always a considerable part of the labour force unemployed. If this were so, it would be the task of the Government to stimulate consumption in order to encourage industry to expand output and absorb the unemployed. One obvious method of doing this would be to increase the Government's own expenditure, for example on social services, and another would be to put money in the hands of those who would spend it readily, for example the unemployed themselves.[1] The argument of the earlier political economists has been stood on its head. Redistribution from rich to poor, far from reducing the level of investment, would be a positive method of encouraging it. Having been led to expect, by the great discussions on reconstruction towards the end of the War, that slump conditions would haunt us again within a few years, it is not surprising that the British public have found it difficult to rid themselves of the great illusion of our times, that there is practically no limit to the amount of social services we can have.

Thus the re-definition of the Liberal attitude to social services requires no modification of the general aims laid down by the earlier Liberal philosophers. We may be less averse to State intervention in order to remove inequalities of wealth and income, partly because our experience of social services belies the forecasts of our forbears and partly because we believe that their logic was not entirely secure. But if we have come to accept more State intervention than they would have tolerated, let no one believe that the problem which worried them most, the conflict between progress and security, has been solved. More important still, the acceptance of State intervention for purposes of social policy does not imply that Liberals must be indifferent to the *form* of intervention or to its *extent*. It is probably in regard to this last question that Liberal social policy differs most markedly from that of the Socialists.

2. THE PRINCIPLES OF A LIBERAL SOCIAL POLICY

In a Liberal society the basis of any policy regarding social policy is the belief that all persons should live in reasonable com-

[1] 'The Plan for Social Security set out in my Report on Social Insurance and Allied Services . . . will . . . help materially towards the maintenance of employment by expanding and maintaining private consumption outlay' (William H. Beveridge, *Full Employment in a Free Society* (1944), pp. 159–160).

fort within the limits imposed by the state of development of the economy, and that no person's opportunities to develop his particular gifts should be frustrated by material circumstances. But a Liberal society is primarily concerned with the freedom of the individual, which obliges us to consider carefully to what extent we must assume that such a social policy be accompanied by State provision of social services.

Let us assume that we are dissatisfied with the way in which the private-enterprise system distributes income and wealth because it does not allow everybody to live in reasonable comfort. This state of affairs would require that we adjust the tax system or the system of family allowance payments so that our social policy could be achieved. Two important points follow from this attempt to implement a Liberal social policy. The first is that redistribution of income and wealth is merely a means to an end. If a society existed which was able to prevent great inequalities of income and wealth within the free-enterprise system, it could logically dispense with this form of State intervention. It follows from this that Liberal support for such measures as progressive taxation does not rest on the utilitarian belief that an extra pound is more 'valuable' or will 'afford a greater utility' to a poor man than to a rich man. It rests on a positive dislike of gross inequality. But if the extremes of inequality are not there, then progressive taxation is not necessary; other grounds, if there are any, must be sought for its continuance in such circumstances. We can be fairly certain that a Liberal social policy would require something more than the adjustment of taxes financing traditional functions of government, law and order and defence, in order to exempt the poor. For one thing, these items may not always be large enough to enable the taxes to finance them to exercise a powerful discrimination in favour of the poor; for another, tax exemption for poor persons only produces the desired effect so long as those we wish to benefit are earning incomes. It provides no protection for the able-bodied unemployed or the old. This brings home to us the second important point. A Liberal social policy designed to maintain minimum standards of comfort may require us to intervene positively in the system of public finance in order to redistribute income, but it justifies no other form of social services other than those which involve *transfers of income*. Other arguments must be found in order to justify State intervention in order to 'produce' particular services, such as education and health, which could be provided by private individuals. While there is no doubt that the basic principle of a Liberal social policy is that of ensuring an equitable distribution of income, such a policy also embodies the principle that the community must devote enough of its resources to provide social services, particularly health and education, in order to fulfil the second aim — the provision of more equal opportunity. In a Liberal Utopia, where the distribution of income would be 'equitable' and all parents were responsible and far-sighted individuals, there would be no need to remind citizens where their duty lay. But this state of affairs can only represent a goal to work for. It is hardly the starting-point for a realistic Liberal social policy. We must assume that the minimum standards of education and health we should require cannot be attained by private individuals buying for themselves the services of educators and healers in the open market.

It is very easy at this stage of the argument to assume that the case for nationalized services has been made. But nationalization is not by any means the sole method by which compulsory consumption can be enforced. Consider education as an example. Minimum standards of education could be laid down by the Government for private institutions, and parents could then choose to meet State requirements as they pleased. If it were thought necessary to combine compulsory education with redistributive measures then, as Professor Milton Friedman has suggested, parents who showed that the minimum standards had been met could receive vouchers redeemable for a specified maximum sum per child.[1] The only Liberal case for a nationalization of education services would be if education were a natural monopoly, that is to say if the economical size of education unit were so large that

[1] Milton Friedman, 'The Role of the Government in Education', in *Economics and the Public Interest*, ed. Robert Solo (New Brunswick, 1955), p. 127.

WELFARE IN THE LIBERAL STATE

competition between schools is bound to be eliminated in the end. This seems to fit only the village-school case. The last-ditch argument of those who seek grounds for nationalization within a Liberal programme is usually that nationalization makes the imposition of minimum standards easier, but the logical conclusion of this argument is that we should have no private education at all — a proposition which Liberals are surely bound to deny.

The 'natural monopoly' argument may have much more force when we consider health services. It may well be that the most efficient provision of minimum standards of sanitation and protection against epidemics is a local monopoly which is publicly controlled. Moreover, the argument for public provision is strengthened by the fact that it may be difficult to devise a system of charging which exactly reflects the costs of health services for particular individuals. The natural monopoly argument could be extended to hospitals. It wears rather thin, perhaps, when applied to all health services, including routine medical attention and dental services. It is rare that one finds justification for free services for this sort which does not confuse the argument for State provision and the argument for redistributing income. Moreover, as it stands, the natural monopoly argument is not by any means an argument for *centralized* services. That must rest on separate criteria, such as the presumption that central control is in some sense more 'efficient' than local control.

Now it must certainly be agreed that a policy which requires income redistribution but which at the same time makes the individual responsible for the fulfilment of these minimum conditions imposed by society implies a high standard of social conduct. In any society there will be people who will prefer beer and skittles to bread and butter. Free education and health services, subsidized food and housing, all compulsorily financed through taxation with standards laid down by professional administrators and specialists — these are one way round the problem of social irresponsibility. But this attitude is fundamentally illiberal. It is one thing to introduce such measures in war-time emergency; it is another to

perpetuate conditions under which individuals have no opportunities for exercising social responsibility for themselves.

3. LIBERAL PRINCIPLES AND
THE BRITISH WELFARE STATE

The fundamental question we have to answer is how much
income redistribution should we have; or what proportion of our
resources should be devoted to social services.

Before we can answer, we must make some assumptions about
the economic environment of social policy in the years to come.
We shall assume that it is possible to maintain a high level of employment and that our national productivity will increase at something like its present rate.[1] What can we say about a Liberal social
policy under such conditions? We shall consider each important
group of social sercives in turn.

i. *National Insurance and Assistance*

A successful employment policy would obviously provide a
useful corrective to any tendencies towards income inequality, as
is evident from our recent experience. The opportunity for continuous uninterrupted earning provides a favourable environment
for one's own protection against poverty by saving for old age and
for periods of sickness. Given these conditions in the years to
come, will there really be any need for elaborate social security
schemes? Does not the guarantee of high employment meet in full
the Liberal aim?

If one thinks exclusively in terms of today and the immediate
future, then the obvious answer seems to be No. While we have
full employment and the prospect of its continuance, we still have

[1] While fully aware of the technical difficulties encountered in maintaining
a high level of employment in a country like the United Kingdom whose level
of output depends so much on foreign demand, at least it can be said that not
only is this policy accepted by all Parties, but that it is accepted by the major
industrial countries as a policy requiring international co-operation. Moreover, there is a large measure of agreement about the methods which can be
used to achieve this objective, although they have not been fully tested.

one section of the population whose poverty is established beyond any reasonable doubt — the old. Many are living at the margin of subsistence, a large proportion of them are not able to earn their livelihood and, even if they do so, receive ample discouragement through the operation of a system of National Insurance which discriminates against those who earn more than £2 a week. The removal of the earnings limit would do something to solve the problem. But the obvious answer seems to be to pay all those above a certain age an adequate pension without enquiry into means. We have all been made aware of the consequences of this type of policy. The ageing of our population will mean that the pensions burden will rise much faster than the growth in our output, and it will also require a growth in redistributive taxation; the young would be taxed in order to support the old. This conclusion assumes that the family is no longer the main unit of support for the old, and that the old of the future have no means of supporting themselves unless they are forced to save through a compulsory National Insurance scheme.

Now there is good reason to believe that the poverty of the old may be a transitory phenomenon. The retired people of today were the wage-earners of the depression years whose opportunities to save were marred by long periods of unemployment. The old of the future are the wage-earners who have experienced few years of unemployment and who at least have the guarantee that a high level of employment will be the object of Government policy. Quite apart from the opportunities which high employment offers, there is a good deal of evidence that saving for old age is on the increase through the growing number of industrial pension schemes, which are officially encouraged by generous tax-reliefs. It is true that these schemes are generally compulsory and that they have only recently been extended to cover wage-earners, but they indicate a significant trend in provision for retirement. In short, the opportunities of full employment together with the extension of coverage of industrial schemes lead one to question the desirability of continuing the present National Insurance system.

What does a Liberal policy of protection against this kind of poverty demand? If the distributional problem is solved by the presence of high employment and by discriminatory taxation in order to finance the basic services of defence and law and order, then the extreme position would be to leave individuals to insure themselves. But this presupposes certain standards of behaviour which will only be approximately realized. Obviously there will be people who through no fault of their own are unable to work or become incapacitated during their working life. There will always be people who are feckless and irresponsible. The nearest approximation to the ideal Liberal situation would be to make retirement provision compulsory, and perhaps to make the amount of contributions depend on income. There are many examples of cases where individuals are compelled to incur costs for the benefit of society, such as compulsory accident insurance for motorists. But this is no argument for requiring the individual to insure with a particular company or to be a member of a particular scheme. The Liberal position must lead logically to the view that both industrial and State retirement schemes are poor approximations to the Liberal ideal, although they have obvious administrative advantages.

It is not our purpose to consider in detail how a Liberal scheme of retirement provision could be instituted, nor to deny that administrative questions are not to be neglected in considering the logic of the Liberal position. Obviously administration involves economic costs, and if compulsion could only be enforced by inquisitorial methods then the means would not justify the ends in view. However, there seems no reason why the matter should not be considered rather than dismissed because of the risks of altering existing institutions.

On the assumption that it would be impracticable to scrap industrial and State retirement schemes, certain modifications can be suggested which would bring them more into line with the broad objectives of Liberal social and economic policy. In regard to industrial schemes, some method must be sought to make pension rights transferable so that the mobility of labour is not impeded, and some of the anomalies must be removed by which self-employed persons receive much less generous tax-reliefs than the employed. While the National Insurance scheme does have the advantage associated with transferability, there seems a strong case, given the continuance of high employment conditions, for the payment of a limited retirement pension of a fixed amount without a means test taxable as earned income. Given this 'floor', then any supplement would come from private saving or industrial schemes. Any further State supplement would involve a means test. Under conditions of reasonable prosperity there seems no case for guaranteeing a subsistence minimum for all retired persons for the sake of covering the few who cannot provide for themselves.

This last suggestion would involve a complete change in the thinking of Liberals, who have so far supported the amalgamation of social security and income-tax along the lines originally suggested by Lady Rhys Williams.[1] This scheme rested on the assumption that the means test was a bad thing; therefore the only way to provide adequate subsistence for all without enquiry into means was to provide a weekly allowance, payable like the family allowances, whether the employed person was in work or not. While the scheme had the attraction of simplicity and stimulated interesting discussion which led to a better understanding of social policy, for us it rests on a false premise. The real objection to the pre-war means test was not the principle involved but the method by which the principle was applied. There is no reason why enquiry into means cannot be conducted with sympathy and tact as it is done today by the National Assistance Board. Anyone who objects to a means test on principle must ask himself whether he objects to claiming allowances under income-tax.

It must be realized that the growing burden of the old is quite independent of the method of finance which is adopted. The retired population will exercise a relatively greater claim on national output, whether they can provide for themselves out of their own savings or whether they are cared for by the State. But the

[1] See her *Taxation and Incentives* (1952), and the discussion of these proposals by A. T. Peacock, *Economics of National Insurance* (1952).

importance of voluntary saving for old age lies in the fact that, apart from being an element in the Liberal idea of social policy, retired persons would lay claim to part of the national output without involving the community in a compulsory transfer of claims by taxation from the earning to the retired population. Given present trends in the growth of public expenditure, including the growth in retirement pensions, such taxation might discourage production.

It would be possible to extend the above argument at least to sickness benefit, but there is a strong case for making society bear at least most of the burden of poverty caused by unemployment and family allowances. With a full employment policy, poverty caused by cyclical unemployment should be exterminated, but unemployment caused by incapacity seems best dealt with by a State scheme of workmen's compensation as at present. Again, family allowances to prevent poverty caused by large families seem a desirable provision. As the amounts involved in the payment of the latter are not likely to be large in relation to the whole budget, it seems simpler to pay family allowances to all as at present and to continue to regard them as part of taxable income.

ii. *Food and Housing Subsidies*

Our argument so far has laid stress on the Liberal principle that the form which income redistribution takes is as important as its extent. We have paid particular attention to the problem of old-age provision because of its contemporary significance. It is to be noted, however, that the argument applies *a fortiori* to the case of food and housing subsidies. There is no place in a Liberal philosophy for their retention unless one is completely sceptical of the sense of responsibility of the general public. If it is thought that any move towards their removal must mean that large families and those in the lowest income groups would be hard hit, then tax and transfer adjustment should be made. Thus the objections on distributional grounds to the removal of rent restriction can be met by an adjustment of family allowances and by the alteration of income-tax exemption limits. Besides, there are strong economic arguments against such subsidies and restrictions. Rent restriction, by reducing the private supply of house-room, has been a main contributory cause of the post-war housing shortage. If rent restriction had been removed some years ago, with appropriate adjustments in taxation and transfers, the pace of the housing programme could have been reduced and the pressure on our resources might have been considerably eased without penalizing those in lower income groups.

iii. *Education and Health Services*

It is when we turn to the nationalized social services, health and education, that Liberals may demand most changes in structure. As we have contended, the distributional argument for social services is quite a separate one from the argument for nationalized services. We have seen that there are three criteria for State provision of these services. The first is that State provision may be the only way of instituting a community service because no voluntary system of charging can be introduced. The second is that if a 'natural monopoly' is likely to grow up because of restricted local demand, then it is better that the State administer it.[1] The third is that State provision is more 'efficient' in the sense that it uses fewer resources in order to produce the same 'output' of (say) education or health.

In Britain we have nationalized education and health, both services being largely controlled from the centre. The National Health Service, with certain minor exceptions, is primarily the responsibility of central government. While Local Authorities administer school education and some further education, they receive 65% of their funds from central government grants. What is a Liberal to think of this form of provision in the light of these criteria?

So far as education is concerned, the first two criteria do not

---

[1] Strictly speaking, even this argument is a little thin. Recognition of the fact that a natural monopoly, e.g. water supply, may develop is an argument for regulating the monopoly's activities, but this does not prove that the State must *own* it.

hold. We have no reason to suppose that, once given the distribution problem as solved, a system of charging could not be introduced; nor does the natural monopoly argument apply. Applying the third criterion is more difficult. How is one to measure educational output? How can one discern the connection between employing (say) additional teachers and some definite 'return'? What we can say is that once the market system does not govern the amount of resources devoted to education, then financial control is obviously difficult, because it is never clear what precisely is being controlled. Would educational provision not be more efficient, then, once the distributional objective is given, if schools were left to compete against one another, and parents were forced to provide a minimum of education for their children? The usual reply of supporters of State education is that the quality of education would suffer, to which the obvious reply is that this is an argument for State regulation by inspection and not for State ownership. The onus of proof is on the supporters of State education to show that a system of inspection would not work.

In applying these criteria to the National Health Service, a case can be argued for State provision of hospital services, and more obviously for public health. The case for routine medical attention and dental services is a very shaky one. Here there is a parallel with the case of education. Some enforcement of standards is essential and some method of ensuring that individuals 'buy' the requisite amount of medical and dental attention. Providing these things free virtually means that there is no limit to the resources which might be used in the provision of health. It is difficult to think of a short-term solution to this problem, but in the long run education seems the answer. There seems a strong case here for maintaining compulsory medical and dental attention in schools not merely because of their immediate benefits but also because of their educative value.

Once granted that health and education services should be provided at least in part by the State, the question remains whether they should be provided centrally or locally. The overwhelming influence on the structure of nationalized social services has been the desire to maintain uniformity in the standards of provision on the one hand and 'equity' in the finance of these services on the other. The result has been a very considerable decline in the importance of Local Authorities. Uniformity in provision has meant centralized administration, control of the National Health Service and centrally controlled (although locally administered) education. 'Equity' in the finance of these services has meant financing them from taxes raised at the centre rather than by the regressive local rate. As has been pointed out, educational services, although locally administered, receive the greater part of their funds from central government.

These developments must disturb Liberals who see devolution as one of the principal methods by which experience of democratic government can be diffused and faith in democratic methods preserved. But devolution cannot be a reality unless much more power is given to Local Authorities over the type of *expenditure* they undertake; and, as it is impossible to contemplate the running of defence services at the local level, the social services are the only remaining major items of expenditure which remain.

The problem of increasing local autonomy is that of devising a method of doing so without increasing the level of taxation and expenditure of both central and local government combined, for there will obviously be strong resistance (which Liberals will support) for increasing tax burdens much further. One way of meeting this problem without altering the level of expenditure of the combined public authorities or the level of their taxation would be to finance education services by local and not by central taxation disbursed in the form of grants. The Ministry of Education would still be responsible for the enforcing of minimum standards, and poorer authorities could still be given subsidies based on a needs formula, although not necessarily of the form exemplified by the present Exchequer Equalization Grant. In this way the Liberal desire for the reform of social policy could be linked to the desire for more local autonomy. The problem would then remain which central government taxes should be reduced and which local taxes should take their place. This large question cannot be treated here. It is raised in order to show that no reform of this sort can be considered in isolation. We confine ourselves to pointing out that we are not obliged to assume that the sole method of local taxation need be a local rate. In fact, the logic of the Liberal position would demand that if the distribution of income is 'correct' then local education provision should be financed by fees. Where consumption of education services is compulsory, then fees would in effect be taxes. It might be simpler to raise an education tax, and partial exemptions could be granted to those who bought private education services which measured up to the minimum standards laid down by the Ministry of Education.

We have argued that there is a good Liberal case for State hospital services. But should they be administered locally? This is not an easy question to answer. The Guillebaud Committee[1] have argued that, even if Local Authority finance were reorganized, this would not be sufficient to improve the efficiency of administration. Their argument is essentially a practical one, namely that they believe that many Local Authorities would not be willing to undertake the responsibilities of administering hospitals, that the medical profession are in general opposed to the idea and, most telling of all, that the most efficient administrative unit is the region, an area which is greater than the Local Authority area of administration. There is much force in these arguments, but they are only relevant if we define efficiency of administration in the narrow sense of the cost of providing a 'unit' of health. If it were thought that greater local autonomy in social services were desirable, then the word efficiency has a different connotation. It might be considered worth while sacrificing some efficiency in the narrow sense of the term for the sake of preserving interest and experience in democratic government. It is impossible to be dogmatic in this matter. Many Liberals would probably be satisfied with the transfer of responsibility for education to Local Authorities. As we shall suggest in the next chapter, some sort of regional government might be an effective compromise.

[1] Report of the Committee of Enquiry into the Cost of the National Health Service, Cmd. 9663 (1956), especially paras. 117–29.

There is one counter-argument which Liberals must watch very closely. It has been argued by Socialist writers that the reorganized health and education services give ample opportunity for democratic experience through local committees, such as the Executive Councils of the National Health Services and the various hospital committees. But it must be remembered that these committees are usually executive and not legislative bodies. The Liberal must ask himself: (*a*) are these bodies periodically elected? (*b*) do they have revenue-raising powers? and (*c*) do they have legislative powers? These are the essential elements of democratic government.

4. CONCLUSION

The purpose of this chapter has been to examine the *logic* of the Liberal position about social policy, because at this stage of the debate it is important to know what precisely are the arguments which justify some given amount and pattern of social services. We have seen that an important distinction has to be made between the distributional objectives of Liberal policy and social provision itself. We have also tried to show that one cannot be dogmatic about some forms of provision either because of logical difficulties, such as those which govern the measurement of 'efficiency' in social provision, or because of lack of evidence about contemporary social conditions and uncertainty about future events. Nothing but a very radical reform in the existing structure of social services would make them conform to Liberal requirements, but there are a number of individual changes which could form part of a present-day Liberal programme of reform. These are:

(*a*) A full-scale investigation of the present and future economic condition of the aged with a view to reforming the existing structure of pensions.

(*b*) Notwithstanding (*a*), the immediate abolition of the earnings limit for retirement pensions and widows benefits.

(*c*) Measures to increase the transferability of pension rights. (One method would be to remove the tax privileges

E

afforded to these schemes from those which are financed
solely by an employer's contribution.)

(d) The abolition of all food and housing subsidies.

(e) The introduction of some form of tax relief to those who
choose to educate children privately, related perhaps to the
direct cost per child educated in State institutions.

The reader may well doubt the possibility of applying our
logic to a realistic policy of social reform. This scepticism is well
founded. It is a measure of the extent to which our society has
turned its back on Liberal philosophy. But this is not the whole
story. Our judgment of any institution is based as much on those
who administer it as on the institution itself, and there is much
evidence that social policy, particularly education, has been conducted with sagacity and discretion. Any policy recommendations
based on this logic must obviously be considered in terms of
modifying existing institutions if they are to be politically realistic.
This is no compromise in the Liberal position but merely a recognition of the fact that Liberal ideals have to be worked for.

Nevertheless, as Keynes once remarked, 'in the field of action
reformers will not be successful until they can steadily pursue a
clear and definite object with their intellects and their feelings in
tune.'[1] The ultimate object of a Liberal society is surely to persuade individuals to recognize their social responsibilities and to
carry them out themselves. A social policy which accepts it as
axiomatic that individuals are totally unfit to live up to these ideals
is adopting what must always appear to Liberals a counsel of
despair.

A. T. P.

[1] J. M. Keynes, *Essays in Persuasion* (1931), p. 321.

CHAPTER VI

THE GEOGRAPHY OF
LIBERTY

I. THE THREAT OF MEGALOPOLIS

LEONARDO DA VINCI set the tone of most subsequent political thinking on the objectives of what we now call Town and Country Planning when he asked the Duke of Milan to 'separate this great congregation of people who herd together like goats on top of another, filling each place with foul odour and sowing seeds of pestilence and death'. Although men like Ebenezer Howard and Lewis Mumford have had a wider vision their views have percolated down to the Radical politicians, with a very few exceptions, stripped of all but their materialist elements. Few intent on outlining political programmes have considered Town and Country Planning and Local Government reform as a means of securing the environment, both physical and moral, necessary to foster a humane and liberal society. Where, for example, regionalism has been advocated the general effect has been to accept the geographical distribution of the population much as it is, reformers being generally content to set out the blueprint, and the means to attain it, for more decentralized political institutions. The geographical *status quo* has been almost sacrosanct. One cannot regard a few satellite 'new towns' as a fundamental change. Hardly any politician ever considers whether large and congested cities are compatible with political liberty and a society which will continue to respect the individual or whether they will ultimately produce 'other-directed men', as David Riesman has called them, worshipping the mass.[1]

---

[1] G. D. H. Cole's *Local and Regional Government* (1947), is a good example

The great error has been for intellectuals to assume that a society geographically organized to suit their own needs will be the one to provide the ideal environment for the great majority of men who do not breathe rarefied intellectual air. Since most people will spend two-thirds of their waking life away from paid employment at home and in recreation and since their lasting interests will be parochial[1] the institutions and ordering of the local societies, or what passes for societies, will probably be the most powerful single influence on their political and social attitudes and the most effective single means of providing them with a full and liberal life. Accordingly, we unashamedly assert that Town and Country Planning, the sizes of towns and their situations should be in the forefront of Liberal policy-making and that geographical distributism and regionalism must be among our first objectives.

In Chapter I we have already stressed 'personalism' and a sense of community as essentials of liberty. Yet the size of our cities, large conurbations and metropolitan encephalitis restrict feelings of true fellowship and respect for an individual as a unique person. The people of the congested urban mass are 'the lonely crowd'; they have 'the faces in the crowd'; relationships become depersonalized and over-rationalized. Customs, tastes, cultures and the Press are dominated by the metropolitan mass-mind; the diversity which is an essential element in a liberal society is greatly diminished, if not destroyed. Civic and national duties have become more and more abstract and obscure since the effects of one's views and behaviour on others are less evident than in the less sophisticated social organization of small towns and villages. The late Lord Lindsay diagnosed accurately, writing in 1924: 'The distance

of such blinkered analysis. The Socialist Union statement, *Twentieth Century Socialism* (1956), makes a sincere effort to banish materialism as a political doctrine yet fails to consider the question of geographical decentralization, notwithstanding an early and most apposite quotation from Robert Blatchford's *Merrie England*.

[1] The word is in no way used in a derogatory sense. It is testimony to the intellectual treason of our times that 'parochial' and 'provincial' normally carry derogatory overtones.

which imagination has to travel from the isolated industrial to the public cause in any great Society is too vast unless it is mediated by companionship in a small Society. All devotion to public good implies a common life inspired by and inspiring that devotion, and a real common life can only be lived in a small circle.' Earlier societies have recognized the importance of spontaneous and self-disciplined group co-operation and realized that it needed careful fostering; yet since the Industrial Revolution, if not the Renaissance, democrats have been content with *laissez-faire* in these matters, irrespective of political creed.

It is understandable why the incidence of crime and prostitution tends to increase with size of town; why there is an inverse relationship between the population of boroughs and the proportion of registered voters using the suffrage in municipal elections;[1] why the Communists, refusing to regard the individual as any more than a living instrument, favour the congregation of the masses into large towns. The Communist dictatorships, like the Fascist ones, have another reason for favouring large towns: large towns mean tall blocks of flats; flats need door and lift attendants; attendants can be, and often are, police spies.

The need for status and function is one of the most fundamental human requirements. This should be common sense yet it is too often ignored. But is it common sense; why else do we employ rodent-officers and not rat-catchers? Even assuming that only a minority are concerned with this search for status, that minority comprises the politically and socially active, those who can make or break a liberal society. The demand for personal status is something different from simple individual responsibility: it can generally only be achieved by being the member of a social group with its own achievable, evident and self-evident objectives, by being an obvious and necessary contributor to securing the agreed end. For a few people, usually intellectuals, such effective and recognized groups will not be greatly limited by the distances between

[1] A similar tendency exists for consumer co-operative societies. The larger the membership of a society the smaller the proportion of members attending its meetings.

individual members; but for most such opportunities will be found at the regional, municipal or parochial level and will be greater in small communities than in large.

Take an example which is typical of many men, that of a man with a single talent. Suppose he is a reasonably skilled cricketer. In either a large or small town he can become a member, even the captain, of a local team. In the large town his talents and achievements are recognized only by the few with whom he plays; in the small one a large part of the inhabitants will be aware and in some degree interested in his doings. There must be more satisfaction for the man if his team is a distinct unit in the social life of a relatively small community than if it is undistinguishably merged in the impersonal and multitudinous week-end activities of a great conurbation.

Again, large cities and centralized government, like other large organizations, offer greater scope to the few for personal aggrandizement; but in the process many must be placed in situations they regard as servile. Add to this the *apartheid* of the large city: this is not a society in which different social groups can mix with mutual respect; they separate into housing estates clearly defined by income levels and educational attainment.

We can now detail more fully the damaging effects of excess urbanization. As we have it today, it must, by destroying or restricting status and hence causing a sense of insecurity, not only remove some of the physical checks against dictatorship but, as Lewis Mumford recognized, provide a breeding ground for it. The Communists know this very well.

In much the same way urbanization is a major factor promoting the furious and futile materialism that dominates the Western world. This is not an attack on higher material standards — they are generally the pre-requisite of other worthy objectives and deplorable only when they become the sole end in themselves. Materialism is exalted in an attempt to find a substitute for the loss of status and sense of community which so many seem to feel. Yet to find lasting satisfaction simply by achieving a material one-upmanship will prove impossible and undesirable. By definition this denies the element of fellowship which is so often a prerequisite of status. Success is precarious, since the Joneses may jump ahead again. Excessive urbanization leads to the worship of false and deceitful gods.

The charge-sheet is not yet finished. There is a strong and growing body of opinion which associates much of the incidence of psychosomatic illnesses with the depersonalization of relationships in large industrial organizations, where discipline is not self-imposed but comes from 'them', and with the demotion of primary working groups to an insignificant rôle in the planning of operations. The symptoms are abundantly clear. Industrial dermatitis has been described as a 'disorder of the personality'. The Acton Society Trust report, *Size and Morale* (1953), shows how generally accepted signs of stress and dissatisfaction, absenteeism and accident rates, increase with the size of the working group and of chemical factory or coal mine. Professor Revens has recently extended this evidence.[1] As early as 1869 it was found that the percentage of deaths after the amputation of a limb rose rapidly with the size of hospital where the operation was carried out. (Of course the smaller hospitals *might* have had the healthier patients.)

One of the scarcest of all human talents is the ability to organize and manage men in the mass for whatever purpose, while maintaining both technical efficiency and civilized human relationships in the fullest sense. Considerable personal frustration and discontent are incurable results of 'bigness', with the probable by-product of ill health.

So we can fairly argue from analogy. What the big factory can cause the big town can cause as well, for exactly the same reasons. To separate out the effects of each individually would be almost impossible, especially as most big factories and occupations involving mental strain are found in large towns. At least we can say that largish factories in smallish towns will probably produce less stress illness than similar factories in big towns. These stresses

[1] *Political Quarterly*, July–September 1956.
The illnesses with partly psychological origins grow more numerous almost daily. Even tuberculosis is in the list and there is some evidence to suggest that the incidence of this disease increases with the size of the factory.

will take several forms — peptic ulcers, mental illnesses, perversions and instability leading to suicides.[1] Congested and depersonalized environment is obviously not the only cause of such troubles but it is certainly at least the straw which breaks the camel's back.

Anyone who remains sceptical of the argument so far should consider one other non-economic reason for geographical decentralization — the virtual elimination of live Local Government and the evolution of a one-tier system of national Government. This is an inevitable result of metropolitan encephalitis. Even if London were not relatively favoured by the range of jobs it can offer it would still remain as the almost all-powerful magnet for the talented by virtue of its cultural and other amenities. Thus the provinces lose, by a process of selective migration, many of those best capable of providing the voluntary service on which an effective local government is to be based. Nor is their loss completely London's gain; many of the true social leaders who go there are forced into inactivity since the worth-while positions of real and ultimate responsibility, being centralized, are insufficient to use fully the talents available. Accordingly a necessary condition of establishing good local government, and of promoting the regional government proposed later, will be to bring the cultural, shopping and recreational amenities throughout the greater

[1] According to the *Manchester Guardian* (1 February 1954) a survey (reported in that day's issue of *The Practitioner*) concluded that 'about 20 % of the patients seen on any day in a medical practice in a town are suffering from "stress" disorders. In the country the proportion is from 10–15%'. Despite the wording the contrast here is between London and small country towns, since four of the six practices surveyed were in London — two in Bermondsey — and the other two were at Wootton Bassett in Wiltshire and Grange-over-Sands in Lancashire. In July the same newspaper reported on a conference of the British Medical Association where was emphasized the vulnerability of the man between 35 and 65 and living in a city to such diseases as coronary thrombosis and the duodenal ulcer. They had apparently a 3% chance of 'admission at least once to a mental asylum'. In *Suicide in London* (1956), Dr P. Sainsbury shows that high suicide rates are associated with the social isolation and mobility of a district and not with poverty, slum conditions and unemployment.

part of the country much closer to the standard of those in London. With the cinema at least as good an art form as the living stage and with the development of high frequency broadcasting and television and, one day, of better roads and long-distance electric trains, differences between provincial and metropolitan standards should no longer enable London to exercise its present magnetic effect. But the most striking differences must be eliminated and this means more people for the provinces. Fortunately, by comparing London with several European capitals, it seems certain that London's population could fall considerably without changing the quality, range or cost of the attractions it provides.

2. THE ECONOMIC PRICE OF CONCENTRATION

But can we afford dispersion from the great wens? For once the pursuit of the economic and the non-economic follow the same path. Most economists and those Civil Servants concerned with problems of industrial location have too readily assumed that the present geographical distribution of industries and towns has developed, generally speaking, in the most economic way. This is entirely false.

The large and densely-settled towns incur heavy costs which are thrown on to society as a whole and which are not in consequence sufficiently reckoned in the costs of the businesses located there. The possibilities in respect to stress illnesses has been shown already: more obvious are those with primarily physical causes, especially carciogenic ones. Cancer of the lung has a sharply rising incidence with size and population density of town[1] which cannot be explained solely by locational differences in the extent of

[1] See Percy Stocks in the *Journal of the Faculty of Radiologists*, January 1955, and Richard Doll in the *British Medical Journal*, 5 and 12 September 1955. A recent comparison between the incidences of this disease in native-born New Zealanders and in immigrants from the United Kingdom, much higher for the latter, strongly supports the view that urbanization is a major cause of it. See D. F. Eastcott in the *Lancet*, 7 January 1956. Over the last 50 years tobacco consumption has been greater in New Zealand than in the United Kingdom.

tobacco consumption. The Beaver Report on atmospheric pollution found that the chance of dying of respiratory diseases was 10
to 50 times greater in Britain than in Scandinavia. The problem of
ill health in the large city is underlined by the fact that in 1949–50
the L.C.C. spent £921 per thousand people on health services
compared with an average expenditure in county boroughs of
£620 per thousand and in England and Wales of £677. True,
London has many teaching hospitals which to some extent serve
national needs but this fact can hardly explain all the differences in
costs, especially as the age structure of its population should favour
low sickness rates. Another important example is the cost of atmospheric pollution, estimated in 1954 by the Beaver Report as costing £250 m. Four-fifths is due to domestic fires, the source of
pollution the least easy to control by 'smokeless zone' legislation.

The wastes of the large towns and congested regions are enormous, but they are either paid through subsidies by the whole
nation or met by the local inhabitants, businesses and factories so
indirectly that these have neither inducement nor pressure to move
to the less overblown and congested parts of the country. We
may quote August Lösch, whose book, *The Economics of Location*
(1943), is the most recent and authoritative analysis available of the
relevant issues: 'There is an optimum point beyond which con-
finement to a town tends to raise costs. The growth of towns is
slowed on the one hand by the increasing disadvantages and costs
of crowding . . . and on the other by the increasing disadvantages
and costs of distance from places of work and from sellers of
agricultural and buyers of industrial products. These costs . . .
have been shifted in part to the general public: for example, in the
case of expensive railway terminals in metropolitan centres and of
the expensive supply installations of suburban settlements, but
also through the prevention of speculation in land.'

The London tubes are not an economic proposition[1] yet the pro-

---

[1] 'The earnings of a Tube railway, even under favourable circumstances,
are not sufficient to provide the interest and the sinking fund upon the capital
invested . . .' (Mr Frank Pick, Vice-Chairman of the London Passenger
Transport Board, in 1938).

posal is to extend them to cope with the growing number of office workers in central districts. The whole of the London railway system almost certainly receives a heavy subsidy, hidden away in the general accounts of British Railways. Expensive road tunnels are proposed for London but much of the cost will be carried by the central Exchequer. The same procedure applies to much of the expenditure required to cope with congestion in any town. In 1949 the Ministry of Transport paid 75% of the cost of construction and improvement of Class 1 roads which are often by-passes for congested towns, 60% for Class 2 roads, 50% for Class 3 roads, 50% for road safety measures and 60% of the costs of installing and maintaining traffic light signals. The percentage grant is an unfailing subsidy to economic inefficiency.

The grossest waste of all is the heavy subsidies paid by the Exchequer to make tolerable, both to Local Authorities and to the occupants, the costs of building flats, rather than houses, in order to shorten the journey to work. Broadly speaking five houses can be built for the cost of three flats, each dwelling accommodating four people. The economic rent per house would be thirty-three shillings a week and a pound extra for the flat. On most expensive sites the economic rent for a similar flat would be sixty-three shillings. Taking into account the two subsidies, the ordinary differential one on flats and the more restricted one to cover the extra site costs on expensive land, the excess subsidy paid per flat over that on a house has a present capitalized value varying between some £1,200 to £1,900.[1]

The unavoidable conclusion is that, as Sir Frederic Osborn puts it, 'we have drifted into a practice of encouraging financially, out of taxes collected from the whole nation, the maintenance of overgrown and over-concentrated urban fabrics and, in the case

[1] These statistics are taken from Sir Frederic Osborn's article, 'How Subsidies Distort Housing Development', in *Lloyd's Bank Review*, April 1955. The writer is the Executive Chairman of the Town and Country Planning Association and was Estate Manager at Welwyn Garden City from 1919 to 1936.

of large cities still growing, the continuance of a fundamentally uneconomic growth.'

One reason why the diseconomies of extreme concentration of population is overlooked is probably the more blatant economic (and social) disadvantages of many of the scarcely populated and relatively underdeveloped regions of the country; mid and north Wales, the northern Pennine country and many parts of Scotland are extreme cases, but even relatively prosperous parts such as East Anglia are handicapped by lack of people. The large conurbations suffer the disadvantages of large scale and many other parts of the country those of small scale, so that there is obvious economic advantage in peopling the latter at the expense of the former. There is no substantial statistical evidence where the balance of advantage lies but it seems reasonable to expect that a region the size of Wiltshire with half a million people (particularly if it has several middling sized towns) secures most of the economic advantages of concentration while densely settled conurbations of more than one to one and half millions (raised somewhat for the metropolitan conurbation) incur great economic waste. It is probably the Oxfordshires and Nottinghamshires or the semi-industrial and contiguous parts of Somerset, Wiltshire and Gloucestershire which underwrite the present locational disadvantages of the marginal farming areas and the purely agricultural counties on the one hand and the large towns and conurbations on the other.

The free market has not proved efficient in securing the economically best geographical distribution of population. To a large degree this is because the social costs described earlier have not been paid directly by those responsible for them and because, to a lesser extent, restrictions have recently been placed on the operation of a free market in land. Much can be done by charging social costs directly to those who incur them. This involves many radical changes which would have to be implemented slowly, such as the removal of the differential subsidies in favour of flats, and would involve a revaluation in the assessment of State contributions to local finances. In addition and better still would be to require Local Authorities to be more self-reliant for finance for administration, public works and housing and to allow them the means of raising it.

Yet, with even these improvements, there are many grounds for thinking the free market would prove unsatisfactory by itself. One reason for the over-expansion of large towns, which would still apply under the régime outlined in the preceeding paragraph, is that the additional costs incurred when a town expands beyond a given size cannot be attributed directly to the persons or organizations responsible or benefiting from the expansion. Services are charged on the basis of their average cost while the unit cost of their extension to meet the expansion of the town is often above this average cost. Again, many organizations needing large quantities of labour are not subject to any recognized test of economic efficiency, so that they can choose expensive locations with impunity. The headquarters of the National Farmers' Union and of the National Coal Board are examples. The Civil Service is the chief offender where in many cases one suspects the only reason for location in or near Whitehall is that the administrative élite wishes to be near the social and intellectual facilities of London. For example, it is hard to understand why most of the Ministry of Agriculture and Food must be in London while the Ministry of Labour can satisfactorily operate from Watford, or the Ministry of Health from Newcastle-upon-Tyne. The price-leading firms in many oligopolistic industries are largely immune to the increased competition which can come from a rival in a more favourable site; the near-monopolists even more so.

Other factors restrict economically justified shifts of population. These can occur without special public planning, as the growth of Coventry or Slough shows, or where a very large firm has the resources itself to effect or ensure all necessary measures for such a move, as shown by Ford's transfer to Dagenham from Manchester. But more often they are handicapped because there is lacking an organization with the powers to effect all the administrative co-ordination involved. For example, if one proposal of this chapter were accepted (to double the population of East Anglia) no other body but the State (or an appropriate regional

Government) would have the means of co-ordinating the various interests or be prepared to finance many of the extremely long-term investments required. Private, profit-seeking enterprise is not generally interested in developing even a new town, a much simpler task, although perhaps it would do so if given less public opposition to speculation on rising land values.[1] J. S. Mill was justified in arguing that colonization would generally need to be planned by public authority. Finally, many firms stick to a location which is the more favourable to them in the short run. If left to themselves they would not choose the site which ultimately would prove more economical.

At most times population tends to distribute itself so that a clearly defined hierarchy of towns is created according to size. The characteristics of any one hierarchy are not necessarily those of another established under different circumstances, but the tendency itself is a fact, whether we are considering England in 1086 or 1377, France in the eighteenth century or any modern country. 'Big fleas have little fleas.' But no hierarchy is sacrosanct. Indeed, the object of our present proposals is to replace the existing highly centralized hierarchy with another in which the small towns and those of moderate size are more numerous. Experience suggests that *some* hierarchy must be established. Otherwise the geographical pattern would be internally inconsistent and extra and unnecessary planning would be needed to maintain a system which is 'against nature' or to bring order into the pattern.

Dispersion from a few large conurbations means not only that more small towns should be established or substantially enlarged but that some relatively large town of about 100,000 people should be created or developed around existing centres to fill the upper ranks of the new hierarchy. Such towns are needed to help revive the life of the provinces.

[1] The articles of association of the company which founded Letchworth were *intended* to ensure that all appreciation in site values accrued to the town's population, not to the shareholders. Recent events have shown that the draftsmen failed.

3. FROM TOWN-AND-COUNTRY-PLANNING TO REGIONALISM

Briefly, our aim is to ensure that over the years a much larger proportion of the nation comes to live in small towns and that the populations of the great conurbations should be greatly reduced. The gradual shifts of population required should be influenced so that provincial regions can be made alive and effective by being adequately peopled. The reform and revitalizing of Local Government must be linked with these plans; in fact, only on the basis of regionalism can it be satisfactorily strengthened against the powers of the central bureaucracy.

Current town-and-country and location-of-industries policies are clearly inadequate. They are excessively preoccupied with the Development Areas. Most of the New Towns are simply satellites of London, instead of being placed much further afield. The Town Development Act of 1949, intended to assist financially the transfer of 'overspill' from the larger to the smaller towns, has been a virtual failure. In the place of this inadequate hotchpotch the following proposals provide the outlines of an immediate and long-term programme for geographical and administrative decentralization.

First of all we need geographical decentralization. A new hierarchy of towns must be ultimately created in which the large centres are reduced greatly in size and very many more people come to live in towns of between 10,000 and 100,000 people each. It is not too much to hope that the net effect would be ultimately to reduce by some five millions the total population in the conurbations of London, Birmingham, Glasgow, Liverpool and Manchester and to halt the expansion of other towns with more than some 100,000 inhabitants.

Geographical decentralization is more likely to be effective if accompanied by administrative decentralization. Each reinforces the other and each is desirable for its own sake. In particular we need, as will be shown, infinitely many administrative measures to ensure geographical dispersal. Political weight and enthusiasm must be put behind these, and this can only be achieved by devolving a number of hitherto centralized administrative functions to newly constituted regional authorities. In advocating regionalism it cannot be too strongly emphasized that we see in it a way of removing power from the centre, not of further drawing the life-blood of Local Authorities. The reform of these bodies — inseparable with the creation of regions — is beyond our scope here.

Accordingly the second and ultimate objective must be the evolution of resilient regional government and regions which for the great majority of people will be more socially attractive than the large conurbations. This cannot be secured simply by a fiat giving specially created regional authorities greater administrative and more independent powers than are now exercised by Local Authorities, since in most cases their regions would not have the necessary population and regional income to remain socially viable. Regionalism implies substantial geographical shifts in population and inducements and administrative machinery to effect these changes as smoothly and quickly as possible. We by no means envisage a spread-eagle development of factories scattered over the country in rural semi-isolation, but the relatively compact development which would be secured, for example, if there were a little 'infilling' in the already semi-industrial area of the contiguous parts of Somerset, Wiltshire and Gloucestershire. A set of regions would need to be defined, recognizing both present geographical realities and the need to achieve reasonably economic siting of industries,[1] and subsequent developments would be required to foster and not frustrate their evolution. Among many proposed systems for England and Wales probably the most suitable would be that of Professor Gilbert. Apart from

[1] It so happens, as this chapter has shown, that unless one attempted to move many industries to such inaccessible parts as central Wales, almost any shift would increase the overall efficiency of the economy. In any case, with a few obvious and major exceptions, location is now an unimportant determinant of economic progress in manufacturing industries. What matters is the economic costs of towns and regions, and these depend mostly on the number of inhabitants, not on location.

Scotland, this would give fifteen regions, one being Wales, and has the great merit that it does not involve too much changing of county boundaries.[1] Counties still count for something in many people's minds, and not only for cricket. Such boundary revision as is required should not disrupt existing Local Authority boundaries. Many of the existing administrative and economic anomalies arising from local boundary problems, such as the present division of Oxford from its hinterland, would prove more amenable to treatment given regional government; proposals to change Local-Authority boundaries would be most controversial; in any case the available evidence suggests there are no significant economies to be secured by amalgamating Local Authorities into larger units for the functions which they at present perform.[2] Regional government is a process of devolution from the centre and not of absorption from the periphery.

Among ways and means the first step would be to enable the free market to do more adequately the job for which it is theoretically intended, by ensuring that the social costs of congestion and conurbation are paid by the people and organizations benefiting from the amenities of the 'big city'. The differential subsidies in favour of flats should be ended; the employer's contribution to National Insurance should be varied from district to district, being higher the more unhealthy the district is considered to be; a tax on fuel, especially the types used for domestic purposes, should be imposed, varying from town to town according to the intensity of atmospheric pollution.

Equally important are financial inducements to move from the congested areas and direct planning to overcome the frictions, inertia and administrative complications which otherwise greatly

[1] One more change would perhaps be necessary to those proposed by Professor Gilbert. Northumbrian Tweedside would be better administered as part of the whole Tweed and Teviot valleys, already considerably industrialized, than from Newcastle. The outlines of Professor Gilbert's proposals can be found in R. E. Dickinson, *City Region and Regionalism* (1947), p. 281.

[2] See the West Midland Group's *Local Government and Central Control* (1956), p. 170.

slow down this movement. The main weapons already exist, the New Towns Act and the Town Development Act. The first needs to be used more often and imaginatively, especially as some of the New Towns already created since the war are beginning to show a profit. The second needs to be made more effective, particularly by the central Government showing a greater willingness to bear the apparent financial uncertainties which deter many small towns from becoming reception points for 'overspill' population. New Towns, a few larger than the 60,000 inhabitants limit usually accepted, need to be built, particularly in those regions which are now relatively underdeveloped, well away from the main conurbations yet highly suitable to receive a large population inflow, such as East Anglia, the Welsh Marches, the East Riding of Yorkshire and the Tweed and Teviot valleys. For example, the last named area has a population of 135,000 and an established industrial base and would benefit from a doubling of its population. This would require a new regional centre, namely a new town at the village of St Boswells, as proposed in the *Regional Plan for Central and South-East Scotland* (1948). Both to individuals and to firms grants towards the cost of transfer to approved districts should be available. The building of standard-design factories in advance of demand, which has proved so successful both before the War and since in guiding the location of industry, needs to be used—in fact all the techniques which have been applied to the Development Areas.

Policies in other matters bearing on administrative or geographical decentralization, unless there are important reasons to the contrary, should be fashioned to be consistent with the aims of this chapter. They must avoid reinforcing the social and economic failure of excessive geographical concentration of power and peoples. For example, if the University Grants Committee decides to establish a new university college it should not accept Brighton's tempting bait but should offer the inducements necessary to establish one in East Anglia. An illustration of what should not be done is given in the 1954 Railway Development Plan. This proposes substantial electrification of lines including the main northerly lines to Manchester, Liverpool and Leeds but not any further north nor any connecting routes, such as Birmingham to Nottingham, between these two main routes. Resources are insufficient. Yet the lines into the Isle of Thanet and to Ipswich and its nearby ports are to be electrified. This is merely the economics of the tidy mind or of megalopolitan greed.[1] Analysis of proposed expenditure on roads would reveal a similar unbalance.

The process of devolution cannot be examined in detail here. The first step would be to appoint regional planning commissions to do much the same sort of survey work as is now undertaken by the County Planning Authorities, the appointment of members being made mostly by the Local Authorities embraced by the various regions. These commissions would become elected bodies on being given administrative functions, which would be as soon as their work had made clear the regional problems and had encouraged those who were previously interested in local government to think regionally. Devolution of powers and revenue-raising would be on a functional basis, as the occasion arose. The first step might be to give the regions control of the present Regional Hospital Boards and Gas Councils.

Some regions would catch the local imagination in the course of time, especially Wales and Scotland. They would acquire greater power by private Acts of Parliament. At the other extreme a few regions, especially near London, might move no further forward than to exercise the powers handed to them. Yet these powers would be considerable. The probable contrasts in regional enthusiasms do not prove regions are unnecessary but simply that we must avoid uniform and rigid plans for them.

G. A.

[1] A brief summary of the plan is given in the *Journal of the Town Planning Institute*, March 1955.

CHAPTER VII

EDUCATION

I. THE DEMANDS OF THE STATE

THE Welfare State, as we have seen, commits itself to maintaining the economic liberty of its citizens even to the point of curtailing some cherished liberties of the individual. In theory such curtailments are acceptable to educationists; in practice they are repugnant if they assail such ideals as the post-war shibboleth that every child has a born right to be educated in proportion to his 'aptitudes and abilities'.

For a Minister of Education this situation is one of constant dilemma. He knows what the educationists believe — he may even sympathize with them — but he also knows that slogans like 'education for a free society', however welcome on the hustings, will be frowned upon by his colleagues in the Cabinet (assuming he has been strong enough to gain a seat there) if the educational system allows the country to lag behind its rivals in some technical respect. So he searches diligently for a compromise. He is opposed, and rightly, to using his power directly to influence curricula and hesitates to say outright what the educationists must forgo. Instead, he reminds them from time to time that the State must have an economic return from its vast educational expenditure and that, in a far from tranquil world, ideals are heavily handicapped by needs.

Twelve years ago, in a passage of the 1944 Act, it was stated amidst educational rejoicing:

'The schools available for an area shall not be deemed to be sufficient unless they are sufficient in number, character and equipment to afford for all pupils opportunities for education offering such variety of instruction and training as may be desirable in view of their different ages, abilities and aptitudes. . . .'

In the event this has proved too rosy a picture. Jobs cannot always be found to fit the varying aptitudes and abilities of children and often it is the children who must be reshaped to fit an economic mould. Just now what the State needs most urgently are young men and women capable of making the best use of technological developments in many spheres. It cannot be put off by arguments about aptitudes, the demand must be met by a sufficient supply, even if some children are guided away from what they wish to do into a direction where a living can be earned. If this suggests a restriction on liberty it is one neither as severe nor as novel as some educationists suppose. Occupations have always been largely determined by the nature of work available and this restriction to personal liberty is less grave than incapacity to play a useful part in society.

The State's other main demand from its educational system is that it should serve the cause of political stability. Over the years it is the object of the State to justify the introduction of universal suffrage, but to do this it must first ensure that the individual can think and act for himself. It does not occur to the State — chiefly because a solution would be too expensive — that it cannot achieve its object so long as most children are allowed to leave school at 15 without provision for further education. It is the oddest thing, if one cares to contemplate it, that most children end their formal and expensive education just at the point when, by continuing it, they might begin permanently to benefit from it. In a liberal society the individual's concern for the State is as much a duty as the State's concern for the individual; but this is a concept beyond the grasp of schoolchildren and the State cannot be surprised that in this direction the schools fail to satisfy its demand.

2. THE AGENTS OF THE SYSTEM

The educational system is operated by three classes of persons: the parents (who, as a class, are the least coherent of the three), the

Local Authorities and the teachers. All may be well-meaning, but they lack a common object and common assumptions.

i. *The Parents*

Because of an honourable mention in the 1944 Act which gave some of them exalted and, in the event, erroneous ideas concerning their function in the system, parents are difficult to instruct in the virtues of State education. In education the term 'parents' is practically synonymous with mothers and, broadly, their idea of liberty is to have their say. They think naturally in terms of individuals and their opinions often seem reactionary and unreasonable. But they do ask questions that reveal weaknesses and at times stubbornly resist the decrees of administrative convenience. At present their function in the service of liberty is to jolt the complacency of others by insisting that merit is not always to be acquired by a readiness to conform. The vocal section is in fact very small and within it the number thinking other than selfishly smaller still; but the position, helped by the useful parent-teacher associations, shows such an improvement on that of twenty years ago that the State has some reason to feel complacent on this score.

ii. *Local Authorities*

Well as some of them perform their duties, Local Authorities, in their present financial position, are not ideal bodies to control education. They are often niggardly, through no fault of their own, and they operate their control through two groups of people, councillors and officials, handicapped on the one hand by too little learning and, on the other, by minds conditioned by the restrictive practices that are the inescapable companions of bureaucracy. The councillors, though often taking an intense pride in a school as managers and governors, dwell tediously on manners and the elementary skills; the officials are inclined to boss and to demand from teachers the qualities which are their own. Indeed, the officials might at times be thought to be without interest in freedom were it not for an animated display when faced with the demands and pressures of Whitehall.

But one cannot blame the Local Authorities for wishing to keep education, which is expensive in any case, as cheap as possible. All councillors are aware that in spite of rate-payers' lip-service to the ideal of good schools no one wishes to pay for them. Moreover, it is hard for officials to associate the word 'liberty' with the day-to-day routine of administering schools; they like things to be tidy, as they could not be if dozens of schools were going their own way, and they are not perturbed by visions of head teachers wasting their time and abilities on administration and in supplying, as they believe, essential details on forms.

The reform of Local Government is long overdue and if it is to survive in small units it is time for the authorities to appreciate that liberty does not necessarily lie in objecting to more financial aid. For example, an agreement that the State should pay the whole bill for teachers' salaries would immediately remove a stumbling block to co-operation between the schools and the authorities. At present, when salary disputes arise, as they do with monotonous regularity, teachers and Local Authorities are inevitably on opposite sides. Although not necessarily opposed to the teachers' claims, the Local Authorities think first of the effect of an increase upon the rates; the State, on the other hand, though deeply concerned with the financial aspect of an increase, is able to take a broader view which, whatever it is, will not spoil the relationship between authorities and schools.

One gesture to favour educational liberty, which could be made at once, would be for Local Authorities to decide to place more power in the hands of managers and governors. If this were done, and the Local Authorities were less afraid than they are of appointing more than a minority of managers and governors from outside the council, a few State schools (more accurately county schools in the State system) would quickly build up reputations analogous to those of the better public schools. Backed by a worthy body of managers or governors, made competent for the purpose by being concerned as a body in administering only one school, head teachers would thrive and with them the staffs and children under them. Officials insist that competent persons other

than council members are difficult to find for this service, but this
is a view sustained only by the trouble of seeking them out and
instructing them. Given worth-while tasks, with decisions to be
taken without reference to higher authority, many would be glad
to serve. Even the smallest primary school now has old pupils who
have prospered sufficiently to warrant invitations to join in looking after their old school.

Finally, Local Authorities are wise, as most of them are, to
avoid political scares. A situation may arise compelling a particular council to take steps to remove a teacher because of his or her
insistence on indoctrinating children with subversive political
views. If it does it should be treated on its merits as an individual
case and not used as an excuse for witch-hunts, or for loyalty tests
before appointment. In a free country, licence to believe what one
likes is an essential personal liberty only to be curtailed when
it threatens the personal liberties of others or the country's
safety.

iii. *The Teachers*

Teachers like to think that the schools are theirs, that they
alone really know what is best for children and that much of the
control and advice they receive from others, particularly from the
Local Authorities, are other names for interference. But for three-
quarters of a century the State teachers' ideas on freedom have
been confused with ideas about personal salaries and status — an
understandable misunderstanding of their own interests which, as
the Drapier relates, 'is every man's principal study.' One result of
these preoccupations has been that, in spite of fine individual
qualities and a devotion to duty which should be the admiration
of all, teachers have failed to present themselves in a sympathetic
light. Worse, the charge is made, and can be supported, that they
have neglected to give sufficient attention to the big educational
issues of their times. The difference of their attitude to that of
members of other professions is revealed by an examination of
their debates in conference.

There is the dilemma. Teachers, particularly head teachers,

need more freedom of action in their own schools. Yet who, on present evidence, would claim that the removal of the need to account for pettifogging detail to an official of the Local Authority would release a more ebullient spirit and a wealth of sensible experimentation overnight? Teachers are not very remarkable people; great head masters and mistresses, even in the public schools, do not abound. Mostly, in the State system, they are fairly average products of conventional middle-class homes, not very brave, not very original or thoughtful, often disillusioned and even bored, though as individuals surprisingly attached to the children — which attachment, it is pleasant to relate, is the chief reason for their presence in the teaching profession. Sir Eric James in his *Essay on the Content of Education* (1949) has gone so far as to say that 'one of the most alarming features in contemporary English education is the fear of freedom and responsibility on the part of many teachers. Instead of struggling to take over new responsibilities which are properly theirs and which are still enjoyed by many schools fortunately placed under good Local Authorities, or safeguarded by good governors, we can see every evidence of teachers actually asking that administrators should remove from them the privilege and temptations of decision.'

Clearly the solutions are to give more responsibility and to expect more, for liberty cannot be taught by those who do not enjoy it. Something, too, must be done to improve the training of teachers and to sustain their morale over the working years. A bright sign has been the better relationship which now exists between teachers and inspectors, but the real problem lies in recruitment. Can the State expect to recruit for teaching a body of men and women, 300,000 strong, enough of whom have the spirit as well as the talent and the love that the children require to give the profession as a whole the inspiring lead it needs? Only, one suspects, if it goes about the task with a financial structure which will attract the ambitious and reward teaching merit, and with an imaginative programme for progress over the years such as the big commercial firms provide.

3. THE REFORM OF THE SYSTEM

i. *The Size of Class*

Teachers want to teach the individual child. Nothing more insidiously undermines the teacher's spirit than the knowledge, in over-large classes, that no personal contact is being made. The child, too, is looking for this intimate relationship; good, bad or middling, he wants to show teacher what he has done. He is right in this instinct, for apart from his willingness to learn being dependent on encouragement, his personal liberty is cradled in a just appreciation of himself as an individual working within a society whose lives are interdependent. This is one of the great lessons that a child may learn at school, but he cannot do so unless the monstrous size of many classes is reduced to a maximum of about thirty throughout the whole State system. As it is, in the urban primary schools at least, the teacher has no chance. Already the 11-plus examination looms ahead, yet he, or more often she, is responsible for seeing that the best is made of forty or more children's abilities, remembering that some will be wanted for the grammar schools and some, by way of the modern schools for skilled trades, while all the time there are the less able and the backward to be spurred and helped. Placed in this situation the teacher probably will not attempt to give equal attention to all. Instead he will concentrate on doing his best for the more academic children and, because his heart is often the strongest part of his equipment, he will distribute what remains of his emotional energy on the dull. The big block in the middle — the Jacks and Jills on whose disciplined efforts eventually the State's welfare greatly depends — apart from those individuals who have especially endearing qualities for teacher, will receive routine attention but not enough more to draw out their latent powers or to suggest personal lines of approach.

To reduce the size of classes will be costly in manpower, in salaries and in buildings, but the essential nature of this advance is beyond doubt. The tiny classes of the recognized private preparatory schools produce successful candidates for common entrance to the public schools, often from Jack and Jill material. They do it easily, without teachers of outstanding merit and without sacrificing an individual's personal development. More important, however, is the evidence of the Jacks and Jills themselves when they get to the secondary modern schools. Here the best of them, relieved from the frustrating competition of those now in the grammar schools, advance at a rapid rate. They become capable of accepting responsibilities and of reaching a standard of work, often higher than that of some 'C' streams in grammar schools — to judge by results in the Ordinary Level of the General Certificate of Education at the modern schools where G.C.E. is taken. Most children enjoy being one of a herd and will not ask to be taken out, but they will respond to more individual treatment when it comes. Children, too, normally flourish when their importance is established in their community, an argument for the retention of a variety of smaller schools for secondary education in preference to the multilateral or comprehensive establishments.

ii. *The Developing Individual*

A child's second demand from his school is liberty to develop at his own pace. Montaigne said that the symptoms of children's 'inclinations in that tender age are so obscure, and the promises so uncertain and fallacious, that it is very hard to establish any solid judgment or conjecture upon them'. Yet solid judgment is passed on them every day. The child who is unready or has been ill-taught so as to be unable to enter a grammar school at 11-plus has often lost his chance of ever doing so. If the child at the grammar school lags behind his fellows and fails to pass satisfactorily the Ordinary Level of G.C.E. in his sixteenth year he severely handicaps himself for the university race. No thought that he might be the tortoise who will beat the hare enters the official mind; or, if it does, no provision is made for later development. And this is strange, for all know that the order of merit at school stands in disarray forty years on.

The Liberal Report on Education, *Looking Ahead* (1955), has dealt with one aspect of this problem. The proposals there were

mindful that a variety of schools is essential if children are to have
the opportunity to grow in a favourable environment. It saw no
reason to delay after 11 the selection for grammar schools of the
ablest children whose success was assured; it suggested that the
remainder should all go from primary to secondary modern
schools where at 13 all should have a second opportunity to transfer to grammar schools if their progress by that date suggested
that later they would be capable of reaching the standard of Advanced Level in G.C.E. Some others below that standard were to
remain at the secondary modern school after 15 to take ordinary
level of G.C.E. at 16 or later and then to graduate, if the term be
permitted, by apprenticeship courses not only to skilled work but,
if sufficiently able, to professions. All the rest should receive a
leaving certificate stating their useful but lesser attainments.

The objects of these proposals were to preserve for the child
the liberty to advance at any time and to guarantee to the State a
maximum return for its educational expenditure. If the 'A' road
was missed at 11-plus and the 'B' one at 13 there still were minor
roads leading to the same goal though by longer routes. No child,
said the Report, was to think himself a failure; there was always
another chance if development came later and for the weakest a
written assurance that he, too, had a contribution to make.

This is not sentimentality but sense. There can be no liberty in
the educational system, or in the State, if the bell tolls for most at
11-plus. In many fields already the apprenticeship course, revealing to the adolescent through practice the need for theory, has
discovered in the apprentice an intellectual capacity that was dor-
mant. A much wider use of such courses should be made if valuable material is not to be abandoned or ill-used.

ii. *The Humanities*

To draw from the child the most he has to offer economically is
a relatively easy matter compared with educating him in thought
and judgment. To read great plays, to learn noble passages by
heart, to study history is to make a beginning but no more. Hardly
anything will come of it unless these lessons are repeated in

maturer years and the teachers have the humanities in mind and heart. 'Education', as Sir Richard Livingstone has said, 'is atmosphere as well as instruction,' and unless it is intended to jettison the most valuable part of the educational cargo determined efforts must be made to ensure that it is the humanities and not the sciences that dominate the environment of schools. But this is only part of the task; the other is to ensure, through county colleges and other means of further education, that the whole population lacking the benefits of university training gets its opportunity to study the humanities at a time when experience of life comes to their aid in developing their understanding. Probably the best period of life for most men to embrace for the first time since school a course of study in the humanities would be between the ages of 35 and 45. That such a course would be difficult to organize should not deter the universities from examining ways and means for making it possible for men of commercial and industrial experience to have this chance. The benefits to them and to the country at large could be far-reaching. Power to affect the well-being of society lies today in many hands; a knowledge of the humanities can no longer influence society if confined to a small group.

If this belief leads us to the conclusion that the time is ripe for the universities to reconsider their position in society it is no more than the situation demands. In the last fifty years great strides have been made in educating large numbers at the preparatory stage for a society that offers many more jobs requiring educational attainments and intelligently applied skills. But at 15, when most leave school, and even at 18, a boy and girl are insufficiently advanced to benefit much from a study of the humanities and it is rare for them to return to study without encouragement and without organized opportunities. The universities are making little progress towards fitting themselves for new tasks. Non-resident universities have little chance to fulfil the supreme function of a university to bring together the students of the various faculties; so-called residential universities, where more than half the students are living out of college, watch, complacently it seems, the fragmentation of their society. The students of arts subjects, potentially so important to the bigger society just beyond the walls, limit their opportunities for serving that greater society by failing to fit themselves for managerial or executive positions in commerce or industry; insufficient courses are provided to help them to do so. If the university students of arts subjects are not to be condemned to worldly incompetence outside the narrow confines of a few professions a determined attack will need to be made on the citadels of business and industry where graduates in arts rarely gain secure footholds. As it is, when they do stray they are in danger of being exploited as cheap labour, almost the only kind of labour during the years 1945–55 of which supply outstripped demand.

The universities will never succeed in convincing modern technological society of the importance of the humanities unless they can demonstrate the value of the humanities on three fronts. First, they must put their own house in order. A university should be a microcosm of the society in which it believes. The barriers, so high today, to communication and association between the members of the different faculties should be broken down; and if this implies a first-year general course for all undergraduates and the demand for a wider range of subjects from university entrants, these are changes that should be made. Secondly, when arts and science undergraduates have learned to live and talk together at the universities means should be sought to enable them to work together in fruitful collaboration. Thirdly, the universities should turn their attention to the organization, through efficient extramural departments, of a further educational system that will meet the needs of a vital society whose educational development, except in technical subjects, was arrested at some point between the ages of 15 and 18.

J. A.

BOOK THREE

THE ECONOMICS OF
LIBERTY

VIII
The Dynamics of Progress

IX
Relations in Industry

X
Monopoly

XI
Agriculture

CHAPTER VIII

THE DYNAMICS OF
PROGRESS

THE greatest achievement of Liberals, first in Britain and then abroad, was the liberation of the creative talents of individuals and associations. This liberation arose in a society that had little belief in, or even aspiration towards, economic equality. It began to appear in Britain before Rousseau's emphasis on the three irreconcilable absolutes of liberty, equality and fraternity. It had its prodigious achievements, in a purely material sense, between 1815 and 1885 — a period of grievous though lessening hardship for the mass of the British people. This period of pioneering, abstinence, austerity and inhumanity produced a phenomenal amount of productive capital of all kinds all over the globe, but particularly in the country of its origin, Britain: the fastest communications since the post-highways of the Roman empire, in ports, steamships, new highways, the telegraph and cable, machines power-driven for repetitive performance, and the beginnings of mass-production and the vast and swift exploitation of the earth's resources. The consumption of more than two generations was held back while this capital was built up. Liberals everywhere improved social conditions and foretold better times from the fruits of capital. Then, at varying dates after 1850, the material consumption of ordinary people began to rise fast in all industrialized nations, and in Britain, naturally, first.

In 1890 the consumption standards, productive efficiency, and capital and horse-power per head in Britain and the United States were roughly equal. Since then, in less than sixty years, the American worker and his family — originating from the average of most European stocks — have pushed their consumption and productive powers to more than double those of the British. This astonishing material advance in America has not been due to the sinews or skills of the average American workman, but to the development of mechanization of production and of the skills and techniques of management. It has also been due, and emphasis must be laid here at the outset, to the *mores*, human and material values and general attitude to life of the American people. That Britain's lag in this material respect cannot merely be due to the effects of two World Wars may be gauged from the astounding material achievements of Hitlerite Germany in a few years, of imperialist Japan, of Russia since 1945, and of Western Germany since 1948.

I. THE CREATION OF CAPITAL

We do not know what combination of factors makes a people, a race, a society, a company or a political Party progressive or decadent. We know that is is seldom, if ever, one isolable factor; and economists know[1] that economic factors alone do not suffice to explain it. A nation today might justifiably decide that the threat of atomic war was so imminent, the efforts of imagination and organization required to build up capital for a higher standard of life so troublesome, and the social and political implications of a progressive material economy so inimical to a quiet life, that they preferred to decay gently and easily while others bore the brunt of forging ahead in the world. A people can decay easily because it wants to, or because it is ignorant and incompetent, and yet it need not do so for economic reasons. It can on the other hand rapidly build up productive capital under a totalitarian system (Hitler's Germany, Russia in large part, pre-war Japan) for aggressive-defensive purposes, or for peaceful ends under a democratic one (Switzerland, Sweden, pre-war America) and to that

[1] Cf. the conference report, *Capital Formation and Economic Growth* (Princeton, 1955) and W. Arthur Lewis, *The Theory of Economic Growth* (1955).

extent be 'dynamic' and materially progressive under either of these opposed systems. Moreover a society may materially progress, though more slowly, if its capital remains roughly the same in value or volume, but technical progress renders it more productive year by year, as the old is replaced by the new.

The important fact is that capital matters. The ends which capital serves are legion and not mutually exclusive: war or peace, consumers' welfare or much more capital for much later welfare, individually-decided welfare or State-decided-and-distributed welfare, apparatus and consumers' goods for the State or for ultimate consumers. But everywhere, at all times, the *means* of the most rapid material progress have been capital goods, from the days of the first hunter's weapon.

Creating capital means saving resources which could otherwise be consumed and making tools out of them. A modern industrial democracy is built on freedoms; and as it already possesses much capital, it naturally tends to leave the saving for the upkeep and growth of its capital to persons and corporate bodies as a voluntary act. But the leading industrial democracies have reached a critical stage in the capital-creating process. In America, the richest of all in capital per head, the tendency *not* to save more as real income rises is now established. In all industrialized democracies, with full adult suffrage, social trends have put premiums on personal consumption up to the hilt, rather than on personal saving; in inflation, brim-full employment, and other policies which also leave the bulk of the saving necessary for growth to corporate bodies — companies (profits not distributed), the State (Budget surpluses from taxes), State agencies (surpluses). Liberals must emphasize here the dangers that, if the old ways of freedom and voluntary action no longer work, the familiar democratic State, to secure growth, may have to become less and less familiarly democratic and more and more authoritarian. There is clearly at the heart of democracies and authoritarian states today much the same *economic* problem: namely, how to keep up and expand capital most quickly. If persons can or will no longer do the job freely in democracies, the latter — if they are to grow or be dynamic at all — must either permit conditions which allow free corporate enterprises to do it (as in America) or use the State's power to make persons and companies do it (by way of taxes). The job will only be done in this latter way if surplus tax-proceeds (Budget surpluses) are earmarked, ahead of receipt, *for capital purposes*, both public and private; and not, as in post-war Britain, used to further current consumption.

We cannot enter more into fiscal details here, beyond emphasizing this paradox at the heart of a modern industrial democracy: if the State forces all the saving through its own channels, it will be tempted to take on itself decisions about production, consumption and developments for everyone and everything — an illiberal end to liberal beginnings. It might of course impose taxes heavy enough to secure the Budget surplus (saving) and then redeem public debt with it; thus putting the forced savings back into the free capital market. Or it could keep some of the forced saving for its own capital purposes (roads, railways, State Boards and agencies, housing, education, health, etc.) and let the rest go back into the capital market to be 'higgled for'. But Liberals must admit, from British post-war experience of the State's behaviour with its revenues and Budget surpluses (under both Socialists and Conservatives), that to make *all* net saving a State activity would either bode ill for our future economic growth (it would tend to go on consumers' services) or render the entire State far less democratic and liberal than it still is.

Thus, if a modern industrial mass-democracy wants to be dynamic and progressive, wants to grow materially as fast as possible and wants most rapidly to raise its people's standards of consumption, it faces one problem — it may yet prove the mortal dilemma of democracy everywhere — which the authoritarian State does not face. It is whether a democracy of personal and corporate freedoms can *voluntarily* conserve current resources and convert them, *at the required rate*, into productive capital; or whether, to do so, it must undemocratize and illiberalize itself to a degree rendering it scarcely distinguishable from an authoritarian State. No Liberal could justify or wish for material progress purchased at such a cost to individuals and their free associational life. Yet it would be idle to deny that both of the major political Parties in Britain since war ended have paid, and continue to pay, lip-service to familiar freedoms in our democracy, without making clear that the British people can only rapidly raise their consumption if, for a preparatory period, they permit much more voluntary saving to be made and converted into productive capital (which means taking less of personal incomes and undistributed company profits, through taxes, for our current consumption); or if, on the other hand, they become citizens of a much less liberal State which forces and canalizes saving for them.

A Liberal cannot deny the existence of this problem, for the failure of all post-war governments to face, proclaim and solve it has been manifested in our lagging in the international capital race. But no Liberal, either, would admit that the problem is insoluble in a democracy and by democratic methods. Its solution, however, demands three clear-cut qualities: leadership, programme and response. Knowledge of the facts, however uncomfortable; the will and programme to put them to rights; and popular readiness to face facts, learn and change wrong courses — these are the indispensable conditions for a democratic and dynamic society. Failing them, democracy will fail. Without them, an authoritarian society can be dynamic, but not worth living in.

2. THE CHALLENGE OF CONSUMPTION

The British people meanwhile have made one thing clear: in their great mass — that is, the three-quarters of them who are wage and lower salary earners and their dependents — they decidedly *want*, even if they do not yet possess the economic means of *demanding*, all the constituents of a much higher material standard of life. This higher standard of material life becomes more and more like that enjoyed at present by Americans. It is important for liberal-minded men not to commit the intellectual's fallacy — it may even be treason — here: that of disdaining the tastes of the masses, and so tending to become dictators of their

culture and values. Some Liberals may regret the onrush, everywhere on earth, of what may be called a juke-box, feverish, enter-
tainment-ridden materialism — the worst of the West conquering
the best of the East, the best of the old western Christian Socialism and Liberalism and Conservatism going down before an
undistinguished, indecent scramble for broken meats. Yet the
Liberal must reckon many things: that moral, cultural, artistic and
intellectual progress is painfully slow for more than nine-tenths of
humanity in any one lifetime; that the $2\frac{1}{2}\%$ or 5% or 10%
minority of builders, creators, reformers and helpers of that
human mass dare not take a short cut (like Communists, 'totalitarian democrats' among Socialists and reactionaries of the Right)
without incurring the risks of set-backs, counter-revolutions and
revolts by the deepest instincts of individual human beings; and
that the material betterment of individual human lives, even if it
first take the form of juke-boxes to fill otherwise empty hours of
unaccustomed leisure, is the pre-requisite of that human dissatisfaction with one's own life which leads to thought, aspiration (for
one's children if not for one's self), and a slow jerky rise towards
the fuller life of the mind. Though the Liberal tries to raise the
general level as rapidly as he can, he must never, as a Scots divine
put it, commit the flaming heresy of believing he can put God's
work 'right' within one man's lifetime; to explode in impatience
with the slowness and crassness of the mass of humanity and clap
them under imposed standards for their own good; to love 'equality' so much as to impose a standardized version of it on the infinite
variety of human kind, to the damage of a precious minority and
making 'liberty' and 'fraternity' mere terms in newspeak.

Unless a society is pulling together; unless it believes in a
worth-while future for its social units (families); unless it is well
led by the 'clerks' who are at most about $2\frac{1}{2}\%$ to 5% of it, and they
do not betray their calling as leaders; unless its sum of leaders of
all kinds — perhaps 10% of it — possess a common ground of
values and beliefs and practices (what Calhoun in early American
society called 'the doctrine of the concurrent majority'); unless it
has, as an aggregate, some sense of achievement, advance and ad-

venture — then it will hardly avoid degeneration. And the Liberal cannot conceive of these desiderata being met without individual freedoms to differ in ways of life and expressions; without differential material *incomes*[1] and ways of spending them, to a demonstrably productive extent; and without a pervading sense of building for the better future of a rewarding and encouraging society.

British society since 1945 has been far from dynamic in material economic terms. Most of the average 20% increase in the material consumption of three-quarters of the people in the country, compared with 1938, has come, not from extra output per worker, but from a mere *re*distribution of the national dividend — the output available for consumption and capital-creation in Britain. That is mainly because the position of the nation in world affairs is worse. It had in 1938 overseas investments that bought it (at lower world prices then, relative to the prices of its exports of manufactures) one-fifth of its huge imports, but today they buy it only one-twenty-fifth. It has become the biggest debtor in the world, mainly to its associates in the Commonwealth and sterling area; and most heavily to the darker-skinned denizens of its own remaining colonies, from whom it has borrowed heavily since 1945 out of the fruits of their toil. Its defence burden is more than double what it was, in manpower and real economic burden. A rapidly-developing world has turned the terms of trade against it, so that it has to make and send out more manufactures to buy the same quantity of imports as before. Finally, it has to provide new capital to develop the resources of underdeveloped peoples associated with it. All of this builds up to a formidable demand upon the exporting ability of the British people, in a world more competitive than before, more industrialized than before, with newer needs than it had and developing economically more swiftly than ever in history. Accordingly

(*a*) what is left over for consumption or capital-creation in

[1] See Ch. IV above for the distinction between differential incomes and a more equal distribution of capital (property).

Britain is now less, as a proportion of all our output, than
ever before; we work more for foreigners;

(b) we need much more capital, mainly of a productive kind,
especially for our basic network of roads and railways (not
improved for 25 years), alternative fuels to coal or new
ways of getting and using coal, our ports and their equipment, the up-dating of our private enterprises' equipment
(flogged during the war, and only spasmodically built up
since), etc., etc.;

(c) this implies a much higher amount of savings, in a country
which has had the biggest defence burden in the free world
since war ended, but one of the lowest savings ratios; and

(d) this in turn, implies either

(1) a reversal of the decade-long propensity to consume
up to the hilt, or to put much of the available capital
into the durable consumers' goods of houses, social
service equipment, etc.; or

(2) a substantial rise in productivity (productive efficiency of all factors, in all occupations) so that the real
national income rises quickly and appreciably, and
more saving gets made and invested without consumption falling.

The greatest single economic factor militating against our requirements had been the pace and extent of inflation since 1945.
No Government has stopped or even controlled it. Its progress
has been the swiftest in British or American history. The pound
has lost almost half its purchasing-power since war ended, and the
rate of that loss has been as great under Conservative as under
Labour Governments. A period of such rapid inflation permits
'paper' profits, and some 'real' profits, in lines to which the general
rush to spend depreciating money brings prosperity. But it
certainly does not encourage personal saving, which, on balance,
has scarcely been a positive quantity since 1946. It encourages the
'saving' of paper profits by companies enormously; but all
Governments then cheerfully milk more and more of them away

as profits taxes, for current governmental expenditure (consumption). These circumstances of our British inflation have combined to slow down the cumulation of *real* productive capital. A premium is put on a spending spree (even on the cost-side of companies). There is a general flight from money into goods, an undue stocking-up or unproductive expenditure of companies, the odd buying-up of a picture or antique by one private individual from another who consumes the proceeds. Those with fixed incomes, the retired, pensioned and those on whom the highest rate of surtax falls, cannot increase their real incomes, which are thereby slowly eroded and redistributed (not only by tax but by the effect of inflation) in favour of trade unionists, workers in lower income-brackets, and any workers who can still push up money income to match depreciation of the money. So property and incomes alike become redistributed — not by taxes and due process of law, with safeguards of justice and equity, but by blind monetary processes which militate against all real and productive saving. Social and political tensions, jealousies, envies and hatreds multiply. Worse, capital itself, already existing, tends to be worn out, not replaced properly, consumed or 'made-do and mended' instead of being replaced with ever-more-costly but ever-more-efficient equipment. The mainsprings of a modern economy — the capital-formation sector — tend to run down. Compared with the Russian, West German, American, Swiss and Canadian economies, this is what has been happening in Britain. It has not — yet — become perilous; but it has steadily been getting more perilous as the world has become more competitive, the sterling area (a somewhat 'shielded' trading area for Britain) harder to control, and technological advances have been made more rapidly abroad.

The people of Britain, in all their Parties or in none, might snap their fingers at 'the dynamic society', at the need for more saving, at the need for more productive (rather than consumers' durable) investment, at technological advances, and at the whole world outside, if they were not 51,000,000 souls penned in vulnerable islands, dependent 50% *more* than they were in 1938 on foreign trading, and composed of a rapidly ageing population with a still-rapidly-falling birthrate. (Even France has a rising birthrate, and the American population is rising more than that of Russia or India.) This is a dangerous laboratory wherein to experiment with social statics, lotus-eating, capital-consumption, and olde-worlde easygoingness. The fact is that, unless we sell and go on selling *double* the quantity (and more, if the terms of trade worsen) of exports we sold in 1938, we must reduce our consumption accordingly or reorganize our work so that we can make good the loss of imports. And the latter will be very hard in a country so poor in natural resources.

For a country so dependent on world trading, for the banking centre of a currency system on which one-third of international trade is done, the maintenance of the purchasing-power of that currency is vital. It has had to be devalued three times in the last 25 years; and the respite gained by the 1949 devaluation had worn out by 1956, when a similar crisis hit Britain and the sterling area. Thus, a vital need of capital up-dating and formation coincides with another vital need of foreign trade on a competitive basis. Both needs can only adequately be met by overcoming a disastrously rapid inflation, which has rendered them imperative. Hence, in the regular two-year economic crises afflicting post-war Britain under both Party Governments, the identical and recurrent pleas for more exports, more saving, and 'restraint'. True, the monetary income and material consumption of three-quarters of the people go on rising in and after each such crisis. But they rise, like an inexperienced climber, to the most dangerous razor-edge on which the risk of disaster is greatest. And they rise at the expense of the remaining quarter, whose incomes are steadily depressed by inflation.

It should be said here that 'sound money'— that is, the monetary system and practice which do not frighten firms and savers from the currency into goods but instil a sense of security in the future value of the currency — does *not* imply that real wages, money wages or even retail prices must not go up or that unem-

ployment must be rife.[1] 'Sound money' to a Liberal connotes such
a system of monetary supply and control that renders fairly long-
term contracts fairly secure in real terms; that encourages and
matches, reasonably closely, the year-to-year rise in the nation's
productivity; and that responds easily and quickly to needs expressed in the various markets for money (short- and long-term).
Thus, *average* money wages could rise regularly with *national*
productivity, while some wages rose faster than others (to attract
labour where most needed); yet prices need not go up, if the rise
in productivity were faster; they might even stay stable on average or come down slightly. Then *real* incomes would be rising.
An unsound money in a runaway inflation should not be used as
an argument for fixed or stable prices. Indeed, prices are more
likely to rise in decades to come, though gradually, as a result of a
combination of democracy with full employment. As long as productivity rises, however, *real* incomes can rise even with rising
wages and prices.

The trouble in post-war Britain has been rapid and uninterrupted inflation, causing over-full (brim-full) employment, a
chaos of wage-rates and disappearing 'differentials' and the
rigidity in the economic system. Lord Beveridge and his helpers
calculated for 'full employment' a revolving number of unemployed, for short periods, amounting to 3% of the working
population.[2] The annual average figure for Britain from 1948 to
1956 has been half that ($1\frac{1}{2}$%), and from 1952 to 1956 it has been
around one-third (1%), while the *total employed* has risen steadily.
In America, the total employed has risen in the post-war decade
by over 6 millions (to 65 m.), yet the 'revolving fund' of unemployed has averaged about 3 to 4%, and none of them out of work
for more than a few weeks. The West German, French, Dutch and
Scandinavian figures are nearer the American, on average, than
the British. A rise in the British unemployed monthly count to
2% — the average figure from 1947 to 1952 — provided the

[1] See Ch. IX below for a discussion of the theory of sound money in relation to wage claims.
[2] Based on the Nuffield College calculations and definition.

overwhelming majority were 'in and out' within a few weeks, would be an economic gain to the country in flexibility, efficiency and competitiveness. Nor need the unemployed themselves suffer. The vast Unemployment Fund, to which the record numbers of fully-employed contribute, is bursting at the seams after ten years of unemployment at unforeseen low levels. Its benefits could be up-graded for claimants, thus easing the transfers of labour so necessary. It is a confession of political and intellectual bankruptcy that declares Britain's 1946–56 inflation to be the inescapable condition precedent for 'full employment'. On the contrary, it has concealed unemployment (labour-hoarding), wasted our skills, run down capital and savings, produced grievous social injustices and run us into four post-war economic crises on international account.

3. THE TRADE UNIONS

American economists studying capital formation and the economic growth of societies have declared that what makes the British economy so static today is the inheritance of old capital equipment, the nation-wide prevalence of old-fashioned ideas and methods and the lack of reward for applying any new ideas or methods. There is something in it. The biggest surge forward made by the bulk of the British economy — which is still in the hands of private enterprise and supplies 100% of our exports — was made when the last Labour Government began to remove controls and restrictions from consumers and producers alike, and when the succeeding Conservative Government rigorously carried on the work of freeing the economy. But a damning inheritance of old-fashioned ideas, practices and methods remains — in the State-owned as in private enterprises, and on the part of managements as well as that of trade unions. The growing similarity — identity is not too strong a word — between the attitudes of British managements and trade union leaders to tariffs, restrictive practices, restraints on trade, evasions of competition and competitiveness and demands for 'security first' has been striking since the beginning of this century, when Britain began to feel the full force of international competition and to lose her first industrial preeminence. It is so shared by what are (inaccurately but usually) termed 'both sides of industry' in Britain that one can justifiably call it a national characteristic, a popular attitude and a social aim. It is obviously antithetical to any dynamic in society. That means that what the overwhelming mass of the British people *want*, what their leaders agree in promising them and what is technically feasible in a truly dynamic economy — namely, the doubling of the material average standard of life of the people in a generation — can never be achieved by the aims, policies, attitudes and leaderships of British society as it is and has been for many decades past, 'on both sides of industry' and 'on both sides of the House'.

It has recently become matter of public comment in Britain that there is 'no difference between Conservative and Labour Governments'. Both of the major political parties in the past decade seem to have slid into a convenient set of expedients rather than to have planned and adopted any constructive policies for the nation as a whole. These expedients consist in 'charging what the traffic will bear' in the shape of taxation of all kinds and on all payers of it, in order to pay away as much as possible through the Budget (i.e. State-decided consumption) to as large as possible a sector of the electoral masses, in order to continue to enjoy a majority of the franchises of those masses and so continue in power. In that process, constructive minorities have been ignored or penalized. There has been no Conservative 'shape' to British society for the past decade; and, even more odd, to the chagrin of many Socialists, there has been no recognizably Socialist shape to it either. For a critical decade, which might have been better used for reconstruction after war (as Germany, Holland and Belgium showed), Conservatives and Socialists in Britain vied with each other in pursuing expedients aimed at the biggest possible redistribution of earned income and of power to consume, the lowest degree of personal saving and productive investment and the greatest amount of State-distributed welfare — as though we were all back in the poverty-ridden, but rapidly capital-forming, Britain of more than a century ago.

The damaging inflation of sterling is in large measure an inevitable by-product of this steering-by-expediency, this unanimous tenderness to every kind of pressure-group and vested interest of organized labour and private and public enterprises alike. The outcome has been economic arthritis. The once flexible limbs and organs of the British economy have become ossified. Rigidities have become vested interests, and therefore left frozen. Adaptability, initiative, enterprise, mobility and resourcefulness have all gone into the discard with thrift, prudence and the nice calculation of comparative values. And a wild prodigality, in consumption and production, in both public and private life, has sent money careering ever more swiftly around a more and more standardized national pattern of consumers' behaviour.

So diagnosing, the Liberal must take account of the inescapable facts of Britain's position in the world today: her straitened resources and ageing population, the old-fashioned out-of-date shackles that bind her economy and ossify her limbs, and the tradition-mindedness of *all* her people which renders them well-nigh immune to new ideas and new methods. This is no country sufficient unto itself, which can take time out for a transitional decade or century, wherein its leaders can afford to experiment with methods calculated to bring about an order of society hitherto unknown among men. On the other hand, it is a country which will become increasingly static and economically decadent — perhaps, if it becomes increasingly materialistic as it becomes impoverished, it will become morally decadent too — unless its managements and trade unionists (and many more besides) become more performance-conscious and productive; unless they are willing to install and use to its fullest extent (which means much more shift-work) much more productive capital equipment; unless they do the same with the old equipment now merely 'babied along'; unless, therefore, Governments and the people as a whole agree on the primary needs for more saving, more productive investment, better *methods* of work and considerable changes in everyone's habits of thought and behaviour.

That the British people can and do unconsciously change these habits very quickly is obvious from a superficial look at what three-quarters of our people now think and do, as compared with what they thought and did in 1938. The trouble seems to be that neither of the major Parties has given any leadership since war ended comparable with what they both gave in the War for the inspiration, informing and invigoration of our people. A too-narrow concentration on marginal expedients, ways and means, and infinitesimal variations between Parties is not calculated to inspire a people which notoriously, throughout a millennium and more, has always wanted inspirers and not once failed to follow them, even in a cause that seemed hopeless.

It may, however, be said here: 'How then do your Liberals differ from the Communist or Socialist? You are all variants of materialism, and damned by it! You are all lowering your eyes to the trough and how to fill it. Humanity, and the British bit of it at the least, deserve better than that.' There is force in the stricture; but the Liberal's withers need not be wrung. Humility about the infinite variety of the human individual's talents and potentiality, not the arrogance that wants to clap all individuals under the same treatment, underlies the Liberal's approach to society, and particularly lies behind his concept of a truly dynamic, creative, liberating and constructive society. True equality of opportunity — but not victimization or holding-back of any outstanding talents; reform of the abuse of inherited wealth; differential real rewards (as in Russia and America) for proven skills and responsibilities, sufficient to elicit and reward saving out of income; careers open to the talents, no matter what the social origin in a class-conscious (but no longer class-ridden) society; eradication of the vested economic interests that stifle initiative and competition; due safeguards by the State for the pains and penalties of transition, mobility and flexibility demanded by a dynamic society — these seem to be the minimal requirements of a Liberal approach to Britain's present, pressing and repetitive economic problems.

The more skilled, responsible and productive 20% of Britain's working population is the most highly *directly* taxed group of people (income-*plus*-surtax) in the world. The net incomes left with it are, for the top one-fifth of the spectrum of incomes, less than one-half those in the top one-fifth of the American income-range; and the *indirect* burden of taxation, after paying these direct taxes, is the heaviest, save only that of France (where direct taxes are neither so heavy nor so generally paid). Indeed, the burden of direct taxes in Britain on higher-paid individuals and on businesses — it has slightly risen in *real* terms since 1951 for individuals, and also for businesses — is crushing. It leads to legal avoidance wherever possible, and more often than before the war it leads to evasion and fraud upon the Revenue. That this should be so in a Britain formerly famed for honesty, and still relatively honest, compels the reflection that the burdens must have become excessive — in the same sense in which the ancient Romans said, 'Multiply laws, and you multiply lawyers and criminals.' If to this be added the insidious and disincentive effect of a too-rapid inflation, which pushes earners into higher income-brackets where more income is eroded, the explanation of the differential-working disincentive on the more responsible, more skilled elements in our working people is not far to seek. Trade unionists, for instance, can raise a 1946 annual earning of £325 for a relatively unskilled man to £550 or £650 by 1956; but the skilled man's and foreman's rises have been hit by income-tax, thus narrowing their 'differentials'; and if a manager, technician or other skilled executive earned £1,000 in 1946 and £2,000 in 1956, his purchasing power would only have risen by about one-third to one half of the rise in purchasing power of the less skilled trade unionist. This is, of course, the same erosion of rewards for skill, as in the trade union world is criticized, opposed and combated to the point of strikes in the sacred name of 'differentials'. Nor has the Labour Party, in its statement *Towards Equality* (1956), denied the dependence of our economy for progress on such differential rewards for differential contributions to the national well-being. How could it, when four-fifths of its annual income, and six-sevenths of its funds in an election year, come from trade unionists?

Yet generations of propaganda about the evil of private property in the means of production, about the 'immorality' of
private profit and about the need to equalize everyone above you
downwards (but not anyone below you upwards) have left perhaps as many as half the electorate in Britain with a stock of moral,
political and economic myths and slogans derived from emotional
thinking in harder times. These myths and slogans bemuse even
Conservatives and create a kind of guilt-complex about private
property (whether in the means of production or not), or profits
(even as an indicator of economies), or substantial 'differentials'
for the skilled and trained and responsible workpeople in our
productive system. Britain has passed a dismal decade in the mist
of these out-of-date, unprogressive and hampering myths and
slogans. They must be shaken off by those who, never subjecting
them to critical analysis in the modern world, have unworthily
used them to mislead their followers and promise things which the
economy was incapable of performing. Happily, there is some
evidence — despite *Towards Equality* and the Conservatives'
post-war policy of 'me-too-ism' in State expenditure on consumers' services — that responsible trade union leaders, Socialist
economists (e.g. Professor Lewis, Mr Gaitskell, Mr Crosland,
Mr Harold Wilson and others) and younger Conservative thinkers
are swinging towards the Liberal viewpoint: namely, that to put
premiums on consumption up to the hilt, to penalize skill and
responsibility, and render a real increase in saving impossible or
not worth while, is to subsidize inefficiency.

It can be held that, in the Welfare State, the rôle of trade unions
is over: that the State will equalize welfare and iron-out 'differentials', preserve good working conditions, etc. In a Socialist State,
as in Russia, the trade unions do not fulfil much of a rôle beyond
that of rudimentary organization of workers at factory level. But
in Britain this result is not likely to come about for a long time, if
ever. Accordingly, Liberals must repose great hopes on the trade
union movement as a whole, and its leaders in particular. These,
themselves insufficiently rewarded, must in turn reorganize their

administration to equip their responsible officers for the co-operative task of pulling together with managements (in public and
private enterprise alike). This implies much more education and
training; much more discipline in the unions themselves for due
attendance at meetings; much more selection and promotion of
union officers on merit, training and skill, and less on seniority. If
(as is shown in Chapter X below) Liberals require the leaders of
management to give the fullest information to their workpeople's
representatives, and to make more provision for the sharing of the
extra fruits of a rising efficiency and productivity, they must also
require unions and *their* leaders and members to fulfil much more
of the urgent national task of bringing home to workpeople the
basic, inescapable facts of progressive industrial life. Union members can still vote as they please; but for political Party purposes
they ought not to do violence to these basic facts, supporting one
major Party out of no greater conviction than that of class-loyalty
and thereby implicating themselves, their Party and their country
in disastrous and recurrent dilemmas.

British trade unionism could copy, with great advantage to itself and the country, the training, educational and civic functions
discharged by many of the Scandinavian, Swiss, American and
Canadian unions. It is not enough for the best British trade unionists to deplore in private the lack of so many things in British trade
unionism in comparison with unionism abroad, yet in public perpetuate out-of-date slogans, dogmas and myths irrelevant to our
national situation today. It is no wonder that the nation-wide
shop-stewards' movement, at a shop-floor level, has made such
inroads into the domain once the preserve of the various union
executives — to the grave detriment of union discipline, of the
general awareness by union members of national facts and issues
and of practical common sense. No true and fruitful co-operation
with skilled, fair and enlightened managements (either in a Socialist Britain or in a 'mixed economy' like that we possess) can come
from self-depreciatory, apathetic, ill-equipped, semi-educated trade
unionists, led by poorly-paid leaders who are fearful about unofficial misleaders. There is enormous, little-tapped goodwill and

talent in the ranks of British trade unionism. But to develop and channel it for its members', and the nation's, benefit will take time, much energy and more brains in the trade union movement itself, and a lot of help from outside it.

The Liberal view of all this is that many of the pettinesses, inadequacies and inconsistencies of British trade unionism arise from a false contrast between 'two sides of industry': that such a concept should be impossible to hold: and that freer association of responsible and trained union personnel with management should be urged, fostered and induced by every means in our power, publicly and privately.

4. MANAGEMENT

No country can be dynamic or materially progressive with bad management of its publicly and privately owned productive or service units. Modern management is composed of many technical skills, trainable in places of formal instruction as well as (though not instead of) 'on the site'. This the Americans, Swiss, Scandinavians, Dutch, Germans and others highly competitive in the international field discovered and developed early this century. Nepotism, the ease of business derived from a privileged place in the world, and the masking of our imports bill by a large unearned income before the second World War, have combined to render the average and bulk of British management too easy-going, old-fashioned, uncompetitive and unenterprising. The buffers and cushions of 'soft options' in a still-controlled sterling area, of 'unrequited exports' paid for out of Britain's new oversea debts and of inflation at home, have combined since the war to mask the urgent need for a higher average and bulk level of managerial skill. And there is still far too much of the old attitudes of British management towards workpeople. It is arguable that this is partly, though oddly, due to the preoccupation of Socialists with nationalization of anything and everything: to the over-provision of welfare services under State aegis, instead of (as in America, Scandinavia and elsewhere) under the aegis of particular agreements on many welfare benefits between unions and managements in particular industries, services, etc., whether State or privately owned. For example, much of the cost of pensions and benefits other than unemployment or accident insurance could have been — indeed, could still be — borne under such particular agreements industry by industry. If so, taxes could be reduced, and more mobility in our economy might be gained by making certain progressive lines more attractive. The securing of transferable 'seniority rights', 'pension rights', etc., is not an insuperable problem. A Liberal cannot view the distressing rigidity of the British economy today — with premiums put on occupation of an artificially-subsidized house, and other 'social fixtures' — without wishing to introduce many more *real* incentives to mobility, transfer and attractiveness of jobs.

In all this go-ahead managements, amounting to some 5% of the whole, have been pursuing new methods, but their example has not been often followed. It is the same story with the components of rapidly rising productivity — work study, economy in fuels and transport and materials, training schemes, supply of vital information to employees, etc. The average and bulk of British managements remain in quality distressingly low compared with the average and bulk of those of our chief competitors in foreign markets. But before the general level can be raised, real 'differentials' must be offered to the managerial grades, just as skilled trade unionists expect them. Britain has lost, and is still losing, younger men of outstanding technical ability, in all grades of potential or actual prowess, for no other reason than the fact that the combined effects of penal taxation and inflation render the rearing of a family and the accumulation of a little capital (both of them in the ways men would like) virtually impossible of legal achievement in Britain. It is idle to spend much more public money — as is needed — on the institutions and training of technically qualified young men and women if, when so qualified, they are driven abroad in sufficient numbers to keep the country's requirement of managerial talent where it was, or even to lower the level of what is left.

In a nation which has so flagrantly failed to find and develop both managerial and trade union talents for leadership, organization and enterprising initiative — more obviously in the newer State Boards and services, but almost as much (if less obviously) in private businesses — there is a natural, and dangerous, tendency to assume that the problem is insoluble *because of* mere bigness. It is not so. There are vast potential economies in large-scale design, standardization, simplification of output and models, assembly and production. There are vast potential benefits in more mechanization and shift-working; for instance, higher wage- and salary-payments, shorter hours of work, better working conditions, elimination of inferior kinds of human handiwork, etc. And there are vast potential increases in real standards of living in big-scale operations. But all of this is the raw material of those studies by which modern managers and trade union officers should be trained. It is a problem of human potentialities, and of how quickly they can be realized.

We have also shown, as a nation, a deplorable and retrogressive tendency to assume that any and every production or service run by the State or local government is *ipso facto* (and, as some Socialist economists have declared, *should* be) beyond the normal criteria of efficiency in business: i.e. beyond the obligation to cover its real costs and pay its way. Public services do not need to make a 'private profit'. But they should be run *as if* they did; that is, should be run with an all-pervading sense of the national need to keep costs down and economize resources, so that a 'surplus' on their budgets can arise and progress can be most economically financed in that way. The old-fashioned 'Treasury view' — born in days when a national Budget allocated a sum and all of it had to be spent or else it would go back into the Exchequer — has pervaded too much of our public, and latterly even our business, life. If the nation in Parliament, or that part of it in local governments, decides to run a service at a loss — which is in some cases sensible — that service should be run at *the minimum loss* consonant with quality of service. And to cover costs, or keep them to a minimum, the criteria are the same everywhere — in Russia as in America — namely, continuous review of each item of cost, against standards

(or budgets), with the aim of keeping it to its minimum. It is significant that the leading industrial consultants in America, Britain
and elsewhere follow principles and practices closely akin to those
of 'examiners' in the big Russian enterprises and services. Their
expert skills take a long time to learn. Here again, the combined
effect of penal taxation and rapid inflation in Britain has made
managements less economy- or cost-conscious than they ought to
have been; and in our public services, too, there has been all too little
evidence of an overriding concern to keep unit-costs to a minimum,
and charge such prices as the services are 'worth'. Lackadaisical-
ness of this sort, brought about by so many influences in the
past decade and more, is no recipe for dynamic progressivism.

Much of our adult population goes on in an easy, unquestion-
ing, 'couldn't-care-less' way. It is easy for an economist or student
of social affairs to point to this or that element in the life of the
nation and say, 'Here, and here, such-and-such needs to be recti-
fied.' It is much harder to change the attitudes to everyday life of
a whole people. Yet that people cannot have altered, biologically
or psychologically, since less than a score of years ago it rose like
a wave and took foes and friends by surprise. The same people are
now in trade unions, managements, politics and public administration. Yet they seem to have relapsed into that fatal peace-time
drift in British affairs, punctuated by crises and wars. In these,
alone, the British seem to awake convulsively and show their
talents. Clearly, piecemeal improvements — in political Parties,
managements, trade unions and administration — will help to
render us, as a nation, more productive, efficient and dynamic. But
something bigger than piecemeal improvements is required; and it
is hard to resist the impression that a change in the entire social
environment, 'the climate of opinion,' the nation's way of thinking and feeling, is needed.

5. SOME PROPOSALS

Those who write on these subjects are naturally criticized for
being so critical. 'And what, pray, would you do if *you* were in

power?' is the right and proper query with which they are invariably met by Socialists and Conservatives. In the light of the foregoing, it may be helpful if we set forth the main outlines of some possibilities in the fiscal field which alone would go far towards changing the social environment and 'climate of opinion' in Britain and render it more favourable to swift economic progress. These outlines stem from a concern to increase saving and investment in productive capital, to increase real rewards for skills and responsibilities and to increase the general awareness of comparative values, costs, economies and competitiveness.

The national Budget can now and then be pruned by reduction in costs of defence. If so, such reduction should not be 'given away' in reduced taxes. It should be kept, for State capital purposes, as explained earlier. Moreover, a significant part of the Budget — certainly as much as £500 m. — *can* be put on shoulders well able to bear it directly, in a nation fully-employed and living as well as the mass of the earning population of Britain now lives. This sum of £500 m. can be found under various heads in 'welfare services', subsidizing the National Health Service and other services. There is no reason why — as with house-rents for half the dwellings in Britain which are still controlled — well-paid *households* (there are 1·7 pay-packets per week for the 14½ m. *households* in Britain on average) should not pay economic rents and the economic contributions required on their cards to make most of the social services solvent, without subsidies from taxes. That would mean a rise of some shillings per week per card, shared between employers, employed and to a smaller extent the State (which might then quite properly readjust its own and other contributions to prevent injustices).

The shocked cry 'This will raise the cost of living' will be made. It is not true. Direct and indirect taxes could then be reduced by some £500 m. The price of goods and services need not alter significantly. That a man and his employer should pay the proper rates for the present degree of State welfare does not alter the cost of living; but it may make both of them wonder whether that amount of 'welfare' through State hands is worth the contributions.

At present, the cost of this welfare is masked by budgetary subsidies *to 'rich' and 'poor'*, those in need and those much more numerous who are in no need at all. A long-overdue financial overhaul of rent-subsidies and rent-controls coupled with a simultaneous overhaul of our ramshackle methods of financing the Welfare State need not increase the cost of living, would reduce burdens on rates and taxes (both direct and indirect), would lead to greater efficiency in the administration of many welfare services, would show up those really in need (who could then have proper legislation and administration for their needs) and would also show up the real costs of State welfare. The costs to businesses, employers and self-employed would rise, but marginally in most businesses, and only significantly for the self-employed — for whom, however, benefits would accrue elsewhere. The rise in family budgets under the heading of 'rent' and reduction in income due to (say) a half-a-crown a week more going to the State for health and insurance stamps, would be offset by reductions in taxes both direct and indirect.

Reduction in these taxes should then be made in such a way as to lower the fiercely progressive rates of income-tax from £750 p.a. upwards, to extend the practice of exempting savings and insurance premiums, and to reduce or abolish such indirect taxes as are cumbrous, costly to administer or (for various economic reasons) capable of allowing demand to rise without danger to our resources. Taxation on company profits should be unified (as recommended by the Royal Commission) and reduced. This would force investment (within the firm or in other firms indirectly), or reduced selling prices. There is no reason in equity why the commencing of surtax for *earned* incomes (which are three-quarters of surtaxed incomes anyway) should not be at £3,000 or £4,000 p.a., since it has stayed at £2,000 p.a. for over 30 years.

It is worth noting that *all* surtax (on both unearned and earned incomes) only brings in about $2\frac{1}{2}\%$ of all public revenue, and that if we collared *every £1 of income over £2,000 p.a.*, we would only net an extra $1\frac{1}{2}\%$ of revenue in the first year — and nothing there-

after, as everyone would take good care not to get any income
over £2,000. Indeed, the massive contributions to income-tax and
surtax come from incomes between £750 p.a. and £3,000 p.a. —
i.e. just those which begin with foremen and end with managers,
or begin with public servants just taking responsibility and end
with those at the head of our Civil and other services. It is a crying commentary on the present state of knowledge about real
rewards for services in Britain that Socialists should demand
further penalization of skill and effort, Conservatives should put
out premium bonds, 'capital gains' should be viewed as a potential
source of new revenue, and the capital gains (and losses) of pools
and gambling among 15 m. adults should all be viewed as natural
developments having nothing to do with taxation.

The old Liberal principles of rewarding differential contributions, building a 'floor' of welfare below which no one in the
nation could sink, providing State or public subsidies only on
proof of need and then in clear totals publicly accounted-for, and
removing evils, ills and distresses where they arise are still good
guiding principles. Our Welfare State was conceived on those
principles early in this century. But its development, at other than
Liberal hands, has introduced many confusing, unnecessary, uneconomical and inefficient (though in many cases deliberate)
features, whereby the well-to-do receive exactly what 'the poor'
receive, administrative costs are raised and the productive and
creative contributors to the national welfare are penalized for being
so. This is not only illiberal: it is absurd, uneconomic and
the reverse of dynamic. It produces a regressive, bewildering,
bumbling and futile-feeling State, wherein the honest, skilled,
fruitful worker gains no more than the scrimshanker, the lowest
boy in the class and the lawbreaker. Indeed, the persistence of law-
breaking for money (the latter as rife among the spare-time
workers at one end of the income-spectrum as among the 'rich' at
the other) eleven years after the end of the war should make all
citizens wonder whether British legislation in fiscal matters has
not already run counter to deep-laid human emotions. It has certainly, and swiftly, run counter to what were once deep-laid

British acquired characteristics of honesty and integrity, both in private and public life.

The British people have borne heavier burdens than any other in the free world in the past eleven years. They still bear them. But the burdens were, and still are, borne very differentially as between income-groups, family conditions and 'ways of living' (to avoid the odious and inaccurate word 'classes'). The British economy is still sound. But it is old, and its newer elements have gone ahead after the war at the cost of its older elements — communications, textiles, shipbuilding, etc. It has great need of more personal and corporate saving to make it up-to-date and more flexible. But, more than any detailed economic item, its people have great need of more freedom — to gain differentials of income, to express themselves and to venture in business or management or trade-union life. A democratic dynamic society can only be built upon this freedom. An undemocratic one can always be built without it. Politics, not economics, ultimately decides.

G. H.

CHAPTER IX

RELATIONS IN INDUSTRY

THE root of Liberalism is belief in the intrinsic value of the individual. From this belief springs the demand for freedom and the fear of concentration of power, since this concentration is seen to lead to an inevitable limitation of opportunities for the individual to make responsible choices and to the probable abuse of power, with wanton restrictions on individual freedom.

In applying these principles to industrial affairs, Liberals normally favour the system of free enterprise with a large number of competing firms, and oppose the growth of State-owned industry and of private monopolies. Free enterprise gives a wider range of choice to the consumer, enabling him to spend his money as he sees fit; greater scope for the entrepreneur to develop his ideas, his capital and his energies to the best advantage; and greater opportunity for the worker to choose his employer and his job. But while we must logically be supporters of free enterprise we do not deny that the State has rights and duties in the economic and industrial sphere, and it will be a major problem for the Liberal society of the future to decide what action the State should take to ensure that relationships within industry, and between industry and the State, are in accordance with Liberal ideas.

I. THE CASE FOR CO-OWNERSHIP

Half a century ago Liberals were fighting to improve the position of the industrial worker. The second World War, vigorous trade-union action, full employment and the growth of the Welfare State have altered the situation beyond all recognition. Today the Liberal critic no longer complains that the worker is exploited, unprotected and underpaid, but that industrial life is so organized that little opportunity is given him for real responsibility and involvement and that insufficient demands are made on him as a person. Nor is it only the Liberal who is aware that the focal point has shifted. It is fashionable in many quarters to assert that the basic issue in industrial relations today is the problem of status, and there is no doubt a good deal of truth in this statement, though it is probably nearer the mark to suggest that for many people the real trouble is a lack of any sense of significance in their work. They are unable to feel that so far as work is concerned they count for anything, or that the work to which they contribute matters to the community. Indeed, many people take it for granted, as one writer recently put it, that 'work means earning money, leisure means spending it'. It may be that the reiterated demand for enhanced status springs from an inarticulate but profound sense of futility and personal insignificance in industry. Liberal industrial policy attempts to face these related problems of status and significance.

In the post-war period considerable changes have taken place in the distribution of income from industry, but the ownership of industry itself, like the ownership of property in general, is still in the hands of a tiny minority, while industrial power is confined to a still smaller number of large owners of industrial capital and a small and highly influential group of managers. This power is limited by the authority the State has assumed over capital investment and industrial location, and by the trade unions, whose vast influence is exerted both directly in the industrial field, particularly in wage questions, and indirectly through political action. The important point is that both those who exercise power and those who limit its use tend to be relatively few in number, to work in London or, more rarely, in one of the larger industrial centres, and to be remote from the great mass of people in industry, both workers and executives. This situation may make for peace; it does not make for vitality or for a sense of personal responsibility. Moreover, while it is true that over the years unions and employers have worked out a code of behaviour to which both sides commonly conform, the deep conviction remains that industry is divided into two sides and that this division must continue for all time. Yet though it cannot be denied that there are matters over which the various groups in industry will continue to come into conflict, any attempt to deal with the problems of status and significance are severely handicapped so long as the belief in two sides persists.

In these circumstances we recognize that if industry is to become more liberal then the place where changes must start is the individual firm. For thirty years Liberals have been pressing for the introduction of schemes of co-partnership, or *co-ownership* as it has been called since 1948. Experiments of this type have taken many forms,[1] and few people today would argue dogmatically in favour of any particular system of co-ownership. But whatever form a scheme may take, if a new and liberal wind is to blow through industry all engaged in most undertakings must be ensured of four things: a share in profits; a share, through consultation, in the management of the concern; a share in ownership through some system of employee-shareholding; and a share in policy-making through some form of representation at board level. In certain circumstances the share in policy-making might eventually be achieved by the normal exercise of shareholders' rights, which would arise out of the development of employee-shareholding. Clearly, the nature and scale of these schemes will vary considerably. As with all other developments in industrial relations, methods must be tailor-made to fit each individual concern. But whatever form may be adopted, the threefold purpose of the scheme remains the same: to contribute towards the wide distribution of private property which characterizes a Liberal Society; to blur the distinction between the 'two sides' in industry, each with its sharply contrasting status, by creating a situation in which wage-earners are also owners, and personally interested in profits; and to make the fortunes of the company a matter of direct personal concern to everyone in it.

[1] See especially the article 'Profit-Sharing and Co-Partnership Schemes,' *Ministry of Labour Gazette*, May 1956.

Experience over the last generation has shown that exhortation and propaganda alone will not lead to a widespread development of co-ownership. On the other hand, the great variety in the nature of industrial enterprises and lack of experience in the working of different types of schemes make legislation in this field difficult. Moreover co-ownership, to succeed, needs the enthusiastic support of the leaders of all sections in the firm concerned, and compulsion might well mean that many schemes were launched in an unfavourable climate. In these circumstances it seems desirable, as a first step, to remove the obstacles to the introduction of co-ownership which spring from the present system of taxation — a system which makes it relatively easy to introduce a limited profit-sharing scheme but which hampers the development of the more fundamental changes which co-ownership involves.

In pressing for the introduction of co-ownership schemes we are not deaf to the criticisms which can be levelled at these plans, and which may well prove justified unless proper safeguards are provided. Industrial relationships extend beyond the relations of employer and employed, and the position of investors and consumers must be brought into balance. In a society requiring more investment, adequate inducements and security must be offered to capital, particularly to risk captial, and the position of the investor must not be undermined by a lavish distribution of profits to employee-shareholders.

It must also be made clear that the right of employees to representation at board level does not imply a right to interfere with the proper tasks of management. The vital national need to maintain and increase industrial efficiency requires the appointment of competent managers who must be given full scope. Such evidence as exists suggests, however, that the more employees stand to benefit from the success of the firm, the more they appreciate the need for efficient and experienced management and the conditions necessary for a manager to do his work.

So far as the consumer is concerned, the greater the identification of interest between employer and employed, the more the position of the consumer could be threatened by monopoly industry, where employer and employed could form a united front against the consumer. Co-ownership is appropriate to a Liberal society only if there is genuine competition or, where monopoly is inevitable, if there is really adequate protection for consumers.

Even for employees, who stand to benefit most directly and immediately by co-ownership, certain types of scheme could become a drag on the worker rather than a means of greater freedom. Co-ownership must not become a device for tying a worker to a single company against his true interest, by making it impossible for him to change employment without a considerable sacrifice. There is no doubt that pension schemes have frequently had this effect — a state of affairs with which, incidentally, Liberals will have to deal. Co-ownership must be so developed that this mistake is not repeated, and it is probable that in many cases this will be best achieved by making the position of the employee-shareholder as like that of the ordinary shareholder as circumstances permit. This point assumes even greater importance as it becomes clear that the speed of technical change is likely to be intensified by the introduction of automatic machinery and new forms of power, and by sheer economic necessity. In these conditions it would clearly be the height of folly to devise a system which hampered mobility of labour by penalizing the man prepared to move from one firm to another. When co-ownership was first adopted as a Liberal policy emphasis was laid primarily on the importance of the worker having a stake in his own firm. This purpose remains, but must be seen in the perspective of changing industrial activity. It is becoming increasingly important to stress the different but essential purpose of encouraging wage-earners to invest in industry, and not exclusively in the industry in which they themselves are employed. This requires a change of attitude on the part of the great majority of people, and in this direction co-ownership may have a considerable educational effect.

It would be foolish to imagine that the introduction of co-ownership will by itself provide a cure for the basic ills of industry. The problem of status is clearly related to opportunities for promotion. For many people, immediate status is less important than the possibility of future advancement, and the knowledge that the way up is blocked is a source of the bitterest resentment and is a potent element in bad industrial relations. The Liberal society cannot be an egalitarian society, since freedom includes the freedom to make headway or to fall back, and Liberals cannot agree to restrict the energetic in the interest of the leisurely. On the contrary we should try to ensure equality of opportunity, accepting the implication that those who seize opportunities will go faster and farther than those who do not.

But if equality of opportunity means anything it means generous and imaginative schemes for education, including all forms of adult education. Educational plans for the future must be so devised that a double challenge is adequately met. In the interest both of individuals and of the community, no one of ability should be prevented from developing his powers through lack of money or because of the poor quality of schools in a particular area. The 1944 Education Act must be regarded as a brave beginning rather than a final answer.

The educational problem is not, however, merely a question of providing opportunities for promising students. These opportunities must in fact be the most appropriate that can be devised for the industrial society in which we shall all be living. For those who are to work in industry, the education they receive must enable them both to live as responsible and perceptive human beings and to carry satisfactorily whatever job in industry they have to tackle. It has recently come home with great force to many people in this country that we are not in fact providing the kind of education and training that will enable us to have an adequate corps of technically qualified people. That we do need more technologists and technicians, and shall need a larger number in the future, no one can deny, and schools and colleges must be developed to give the kind of teaching that is needed. At the same time, in a Liberal society industrial success is a means and not an end in itself. To encourage technical education at the expense of humane studies would not be likely to bring about a society rich in the quality of its living as well as in material possessions. To get this kind of society we have to be prepared to spend more time and money to equip people with the knowledge and the judgment to live effect-tively in a world in which new and complicated discoveries are continually being made.

Nor must it be assumed the study of technology by itself will adequately prepare a man for responsible positions in industry. Over the last ten years, in this country and in the U.S.A., increas-ing attention has been given to the training and education of supervisors and managers, as it is realized that the leadership managers have to give calls for a kind of understanding and skill which a young man cannot be expected to pick up as a side-line while acquiring technical knowledge or practical know-how. Training for management, in addition to technical training, is seen to be part of the essential equipment of the manager. While it is highly improbable that any one limited method of entry into management positions will be developed, this acceptance of the need for management training makes it likely that increasingly jobs will be given only to those properly qualified to hold them. A country as dependent on its industry as Great Britain cannot afford any managers except the best, and while this cannot be brought about by direct legislation every encouragement could be given to the development of high standards of management, every discouragement to systems of promotion based on nepotism and jobs-for-the-boys.

2. THE RÔLE OF THE TRADE UNIONS

The development of co-ownership will bring certain funda-mental alterations in industrial relationships, and it has been sug-gested that once these changes have taken place the function of the trade unions will be drastically altered and perhaps considerably reduced. We must, therefore, clarify the Liberal attitude towards trade unionism and suggest the kind of rôle the trade unions will play in an industrial system based on co-ownership.

In the days when trade unions were struggling for recognition Liberals fought to enable them to obtain their rightful position,

G

and it is no accident that most of the important legislation which
has established the legal rights of unions, in particular the Trade
Disputes Act of 1906 and the Trade Union Act of 1913, were the
work of Liberal Governments. Moreover, a Liberal society must
essentially be a society in which voluntary associations of all kinds
can flourish. Men do and should develop loyalties to many different institutions, and it is for the individual to choose the voluntary
associations which seem valuable to him and to solve such problems of conflicting loyalties as may in certain cases arise. In the
modern industrial world, the place of work is for many people far
more important than the place in which they live and many of the
relationships and experiences that matter most to individuals are
connected with work. This being so, Liberals would expect and
encourage the further development of the various organizations
that spring up to meet the needs of men at work, including all
types of professional associations and trade unions. It is also clear
that professional associations and trade unions, like any other voluntary associations, have a right to make appropriate rules and
regulations and to run their own affairs without interference from
the State. The right of the State to intervene in the internal matters
of any voluntary association is limited to circumstances in which
the voluntary association is behaving in a way which conflicts
with law, or in a manner which denies fundamental freedom to
an individual. Mere inconvenience or the interruption of some
public plan is not in itself sufficient to justify State action against a
voluntary association. Very considerable public loss may in fact
be preferable to State interference. For example, we recognize that
without freedom to strike the right of free association can become
an empty phrase, and in a Liberal society the freedom to strike
must normally be upheld.

A distinction must, however, be made between strike action
against an employer or employers in the free enterprise sector,
and a strike in an essential industry under public ownership.
Strikes in public enterprise of this type are strikes against the
community as a whole, in conditions in which the community is
powerless to protect itself. Liberals are entitled to point out that

this is one of the undesirable results of nationalization we have always foreseen and one of the reasons why we have regarded nationalization as a last resort. But in the situation that now exists it may well be that in the nationalized sector the much greater strength of organized producers can only be appropriately balanced by a greater limitation of their freedom than would be permissible in the free sector. Wage contracts in nationalized industries might be agreed for a fixed period of time, and unions be made liable for damages in the event of a strike against the contract within the agreed period. In the event of unofficial action, the union would still be liable unless they could show they had done everything in their power to prevent the strike. In such a case some method could be devised for penalizing those who had broken the agreement against the orders of their union.[1] Similarly, it is significant that the Liberal Trade Union Commission of 1949 held that a different attitude should be adopted towards the enforcement of the 'closed shop' in nationalized industry and in the private sector. While deploring the system of a 'closed shop' in any part of industry, the Commission recognized that there were important historical reasons why this practice had developed and it did not consider that the threat to the individual resulting from a 'closed shop' in private industry was sufficient to warrant State interference, since it was still usually possible for the individual worker who opposed the 'closed shop' to move to another employer. 'The case against the Closed Shop', the Commission states 'is far stronger in connection with the nationalized industries than elsewhere. The worker in such an industry who for any reason is unwilling to join, or remain in the recognized union can be wholly debarred from any other employment in his trade. Moreover, the combination of the power of the State as employer, and the power of a great union recognized as the only appropriate union for a

[1] It is of course true that the community may be as much threatened by a large-scale strike in an important industry in the private sector as by a strike in an essential nationalized industry. But it would be intolerable to restrict strike action in an industry in which the direction and the profit remained in private hands.

certain category of workers, is so great as to menace freedom. To a lesser extent the same is true of local and other public authorities.' In view of this, the Commission recommended that special 'closed shop' agreements should be prohibited in the nationalized industries and in all other forms of public employment. It is difficult to see what other policy is possible for Liberals seeking to oppose concentration of power and to protect the individual.

For the same reasons we cannot approve attempts to prevent the formation of new associations. There can never be a final and unchangeable pattern of organization, and freedom to associate implies freedom to dissociate and to form fresh groups. The right of association is, after all, vested in the individual and cannot be bartered for any particular union card. It is on the foundation of this right that trade unions came into existence, and it is on this right that their claim to wield considerable power is justly based. To deny it, merely because existing unions disapprove of the use to which it is put, is in fact to deny the very corner-stone of the whole movement. Moreover, so long as men are free to leave their union and to form a fresh association, a powerful safeguard for the individual member remains. Much has been heard in recent years of the need to protect individual workers against the actions of a strong union. Whatever other protection may be given, the right to leave and if need be to form a new union remains an essential bulwark of individual freedom.

What further protection needs to be provided for individuals who consider themselves wronged by their unions it is by no means easy to say. Any voluntary body is entitled to enforce its rules against workers who have accepted these rules on entering the association. If members do not like the way the union is run it is still possible, if difficult, to bring about changes by persistence and hard work. It seems probable that in trade unions, as in other democratic organizations, many grievances go unredressed because nobody cares enough to do the work that is necessary to get wrongs righted. But this is the common dilemma of democracy, not the original sin of trade unions. Where unions fail to give individual members their due, or to honour their undertakings, it is of course right that the aggrieved worker should have access to the courts, as in the case of *Harkness* v. *the E.T.U.* (1956). The protection of individuals against injustice within the union is probably best safeguarded by the development of case law of this type and by the alertness of members themselves.

While the rights of individual members of the union must in large measure remain an internal union matter, there are certain trade-union practices which closely affect not only the individual member but also the community as a whole. Practices such as rigid rules governing apprenticeship are inevitably a matter of concern to the community, since industrial efficiency is greatly in-fluenced by them. In deciding what attitude a Liberal society should take to such union rules it is important to recognize that frequently, as in the case of apprenticeship, they are based on long-established custom, and to recognize the important function of custom in British industrial relations. The relative freedom we enjoy in industrial matters, and the fact that we have been able to avoid the development of any elaborate legal code governing in-dustrial relations, is closely associated with the general realization of the importance of maintaining recognized custom. It is an essential lubricant, not lightly to be discarded. This does not mean, however, that custom can never be challenged and modi-fied. Employers and managements, whose job it is to be con-tinuously active in pursuit of industrial efficiency, should take the initiative through the ordinary channels of negotiation to revise customs which have become out of date.

It may well be, however, that such customs have outlived their usefulness not merely as a result of alterations in industrial methods, but because of broader social and economic changes. Many restrictive practices were developed at a time when little protection was given to the industrial worker, when he was poli-tically under-privileged and when economic conditions weighted the scales against him. But in a Welfare State in which organized labour is of the greatest political importance, and in which the maintenance of full employment is pledged by every political party, the purpose and the justification for many of these practices has passed. Where it can be shown that they are no longer needed to provide reasonable protection, are hampering the development of the economy and are maintained solely to support the vested interest of a privileged group at the expense of the community as a whole, then Parliament is entitled to take action, as against any other unjustified monopolistic practice. These considerations clearly apply with equal force whether the restrictions have been introduced in a trade union or in a professional association. In this regard there is no fundamental difference between the Sheet Metal Workers Union and the British Medical Association, if we are really to apply the doctrine of equality of opportunity consistently.

3. WAGES AND INFLATION

While Liberals continue to recognize and support the fundamental rights of trade unions as legitimate voluntary associations, it is apparent that certain aspects of trade-union activity are of great moment to the Government and to the country. In particular the union attitude towards wages may profoundly influence economic development. Many feel that under conditions of full employment the trade unions' power to force up the wages of one section of the community through collective bargaining leads inevitably to inflation and to an unfair distribution of national income. So strongly is this view held that the suggestion has been put forward that collective bargaining has outlived its usefulness, and that wages should be determined by a National Wages Board acting according to an agreed national wages policy. Only in this way, it has been argued, can inflation be avoided, manpower distributed where it is most needed in the national interest and wages paid on an equitable basis.

This argument has for many people a considerable attraction. But Liberals cannot logically accept the idea that wages ought in no way to respond to changes in supply and demand. It is by such fluctuations that men and women are encouraged to equip themselves for new types of work and to move into occupations and industries which are meeting the changing demands of consumers. We cannot, for example, share the view put forward by Professor Barbara Wootton in *The Social Foundations of Wage Policy* (1955), where she states that wages must either be determined on a basis of supply and demand or alternatively are to be fixed according to some ethical principle. Liberals do not agree that a choice has to be made between these two approaches, or that there is no ethical justification for allowing the forces of supply and demand to influence wage rates. This is not to say that we hold that considerations of supply and demand should be the only factor in determining wages; it was, after all, a Liberal Government which passed the Trade Boards Act of 1909 to fix a floor in the most poorly paid trades. But if the supply of labour is to respond to the needs of the consumer it must be recognized and accepted that the laws of supply and demand have and should have a considerable part to play. If this idea is abandoned, then the value attached to a job must be determined by a small group of people, probably Civil Servants, trade unionists, employers' representatives and economists — 'a hugger-mugger of invisible experts', as a distinguished Liberal once dubbed them — who will decide how consumers *ought* to value work and not how they in fact do value it. In rejecting the idea of a national wages policy we recognize that as long as wages are allowed to respond to changes in supply and demand there cannot be one universal and eternal rate for the job, and apparently irrational discrepancies in wages will continue. We also accept collective bargaining as the most effective way in which the relationship between wages and the supply and demand of labour can be effected in competitive industry.

But if Liberals continue to uphold collective bargaining as the normal method of determining wages, have they no contribution to make to one of our most serious dilemmas, the problem of avoiding inflation under conditions of full employment, combined with the system of free collective bargaining?

The real issue is to find a way to ensure that the proper attempt by all sections of the community to push up the standard of living is not pursued in such a way that it is accompanied by a continuous rise in prices and a fall in the value of money. The task is to make certain that additional consumption and investment, both public and private, does not outstrip additional production, assuming that the terms of trade remain steady. As a first step towards a solution of this problem we must distinguish between the rôle of Government and the rôle of industry. It is easy for Liberals, but less easy perhaps for others, to realize that a confusion of ideas at this point may make any solution of this problem in a free society well-nigh impossible.

In a liberal representative democracy the first responsibility of government in the economic sphere is the maintenance of 'a sound money'. Without this, all else sooner or later crumbles in ruins. By 'a sound money' is not necessarily meant a rigid fixity of prices. Prices could rise slowly, on average, or stay stable. But individual prices *must* vary among themselves in a progressive, flexible economy, reflecting advances or relative declines in different sectors.[1] Nor does a *gradual, long-run* rise in the price-level, spread over a generation or more during which productivity also steadily rises, rule out 'a sound money'. But in a big country crucially dependent on world trade, a monetary unit losing its domestic purchasing power at the rate of 4% to 6% per annum — i.e. losing nearly half its purchasing power every 8 years — which is what happened in Britain between 1947 and 1956, cannot be described as 'a sound money'. Such a rapid inflation, unparalleled in our history, creates more than full employment as defined by Lord Beveridge and his experts, or by the economists of our various post-war international institutions. They defined 'full employment' as employment over a period of time (say a year) of around 97% of the available working population, leaving a 're-volving fund' of temporarily unemployed in transition between jobs on any day of the count of around 3%.

Governments now have overwhelming economic power in the fields of the Budget (including 'below the line' about 35% of the nation's expenditure in a year), taxation, contributions for the Welfare State, the supply of money and credit, control of invest-

[1] See Ch. VIII above.

ment, promotion of saving, etc. 'A sound money', meaning a financial and fiscal policy that secures say a full employment a $97\frac{1}{2}\%$ on average with avoidance of repetitive inflationary crises, demands in the first place a regulation by the Government itself of its own spending and investment policy so that it is not continuously borrowing from the banking system and thus swelling the credit-base of that system. It demands, first of all, a trimming of coats to cloth on the governmental plane. Otherwise the inflation due to expansion of credit and money supply, primarily for the Government's account, produces over-full employment (more vacancies than workers), a perilous import surplus, currency troubles, dangers of devaluation and demands for such illiberal concepts as State controls over wages, jobs, investment, prices and rationing — all the stigmata of authoritarian States. All this stems from governmental inability or unwillingness to set conditions for a sound money and a progressive economy.

Governments *can* secure 'a sound money' and full employment, but it demands political courage to take the necessary economic steps, information of the public (which includes supporters of Oppositions as well as Governments) and conditions for a progressive economy. (It is obviously impossible to secure full employment in a declining economy without inflation; and such an inflation, in such an economy, will lead more rapidly to ruin.) In a progressive economy productivity should be steadily rising; so steady full employment, combined with steady $2\frac{1}{2}\%$ transfers of labour, should secure the required adaptability and flexibility. This kind of transfer unemployment, where the individual is confident of obtaining work soon, is different not in degree but in kind from the indefinite and hopeless unemployment of the thirties. The State's unemployment fund in such a situation would be 'swelling visibly' (as it has in Britain since 1947), and it could therefore be used to offer adequate 'transfer benefits' for limited periods of unemployment (say six weeks) over and above benefits which would accrue if unemployment of the individual persisted beyond six weeks. In addition, governmental measures to secure rising productivity could be linked with technical, educational and re-train-

G2

ing schemes to foster voluntary, or ease involuntary, transfers between jobs. In such a setting for a progressive economy with a
sound money, other social and economic measures could more
easily be taken to encourage and control productive investment
(both private and public), particularly in that field which has been
vulgarly and vaguely called 'automation', with the due safeguards
for workers making transfers between jobs and undergoing re-
training.

Government, in fact, should be charged with the task of maintaining stable prices and promoting flexibility and high productivity in industry. The determination of the level of wages would
remain the function of industry and would be settled by the
traditional method of collective bargaining. But since the objective
is to ensure that the attempted rise in the standard of living does
not outstrip the increase in productivity, the more closely wage
increases are related to productivity the greater the chance that
this policy can succeed with a minimum of friction. One of the
weaknesses of our present system of collective bargaining is that
as our wage rates are normally negotiated for an industry as a
whole, the connection between increased output and higher wages
is often extremely remote. It is not suggested that the practice of
industry-wide bargaining should be totally abandoned, but certain adjustments should be made to reflect what are in fact the
realities of the situation today. It is usually only the minimum
wage that is negotiated for the whole industry. Even today, firm
by firm, a wage structure, with varying methods of wage payment, is established to suit the needs and to match the capacity of
each particular enterprise. It is in this way that, despite a common
minimum wage throughout an industry, earnings vary greatly in
different firms within the same industry, according to the prosperity of the particular concern, the local labour supply position,
or the success of local trade union efforts in attempting to improve the lot of their members. By means of these local arrangements, negotiated by the local trade union officials, trade union activity is to some extent decentralized and vitality returns to local
branches. With the development of co-ownership, this trend might

be greatly strengthened. The industry-wide agreement could then provide a floor to guarantee a reasonable minimum standard. Above this standard, each company could fix its wage rates for different grades of job with the local trade union representatives. In companies in which productivity increased, local unions might press for an increase in rates. On the other hand, it might be agreed to keep the rates steady, thereby strengthening the selling position of the organization, and to rely on the benefits of co-ownership to secure to all those in the undertaking a share in its increased profits. In these circumstances — and this is indeed a revolutionary proposal — an increase in the basic minimum wage rate for the industry as a whole should apply only to those workers who were in fact receiving only the minimum rate for agreed hours. Those above the minimum would not benefit by changes in the industry-wide level of basic pay, but would improve their relative position by local action. In this way an adequate level of wages could be maintained to ensure reasonable standards for the lowest paid worker, without the inflationary consequences of a wage increase applied throughout the entire industry, irrespective either of productivity or of need. Above this minimum figure wages would vary according to the success of particular concerns and the demand for particular types of labour. Such a change would, of course, require a fundamental alteration of outlook on the part not only of trade unions but also of employers' associations. But it is no part of the purpose of this book to pretend that the Liberal society can be achieved without radical changes in existing institutions and attitudes.

There is no reason to suppose that even in a Liberal society with widespread co-ownership, collective bargaining would never break down, and provision has to be continued for conciliation and arbitration in cases in which unions and employers fail to reach agreement. Traditionally, arbitration in this country has been voluntary and it is one of the achievements of the British system of industrial relations that voluntary arbitration has on the whole worked remarkably well, and that arbitration awards, once accepted, have been honoured by both unions and employers, despite the absence of legal compulsion. During and since the second World War, however, an element of compulsion has crept in as it is now possible for either side in a dispute to be compelled unwillingly to go to arbitration and to be forced to accept the award of the tribunal. This innovation appears to have worked quite satisfactorily, but it has certain dangers. With compulsory arbitration in the background, there is always a temptation to avoid the blood, sweat and tears which is the inescapable price of free collective bargaining and to push difficult cases too easily on to the arbitrators. But if a high proportion of disputed wage claims are settled as a result of arbitration, it in fact means that wage-levels in this country are largely determined by arbitration decisions; and the tribunal becomes something very near to a National Wages Board, but a National Wages Board acting on no clear national wages policy, uncontrolled by Parliament and subject to none of the normal safeguards of a court of law. In a Liberal society there clearly could be no intention to create a National Wages Board, either covertly or openly. If, however, it were accepted that industry-wide wage increases applied only to those receiving the minimum rate, then in dealing with disputes arising over claims to an increase in the minimum wage compulsory arbitration could be used, since these decisions would not be the most important fact in determining the actual wages paid throughout the country. But where negotiations broke down in claims for wages above the minimum, voluntary arbitration only would be available. Broadly speaking, compulsory arbitration would be used to lay down a reasonable minimum, having regard to the cost of living and to practice in comparable industries, while disputes dealing with claims based on the capacity of firms to pay above the minimum would be dealt with by negotiation, supplemented by voluntary arbitration only.

4. THE NATIONALIZED INDUSTRIES

Where an industry is producing goods which are exposed to foreign competition, or for which substitutes can easily be produced, a limit is set to the wages that can be exacted by collective bargaining by fear of being priced out of the market. Liberal anti-monopoly legislation and the freeing of our trade would greatly extend the range of industries in which consumer interests are protected in this way, but the problem of wages in the State monopolies will remain. In Britain all the industries and services now nationalized, except the air-lines, are monopolies or near-monopolies producing essential goods and services, and the consumer is almost powerless to resist demands for wage increases by refusing to buy if prices are outrageously increased. The political power of unions in nationalized industries is also great — any Government may well dread a strike in a vital national service. It is no secret that post-war Governments, anxious to maintain the peace, have intervened over the heads of the Boards of nationalized industries to see that wage increases are granted and strife averted. This situation is good neither for the consumer, the Government nor the efficient conduct of the industry. If Government is to override the authority of the Boards, it cannot properly ask them to be responsible for the efficient and economic direction of the public corporations. Arbitrary emergency intervention by Government can have no place in the proper running of nationalized industry. Either the Government must accept full responsibility for these industries, as it does for the Post Office, or it must leave the Boards free to deal with all questions, including wage claims, which affect the efficient management of their corporations. In that case the consumer could only be adequately protected if jobs in nationalized industries were paid on the same level as similar jobs in private enterprise. In addition, employees in nationalized industries should be able to qualify for additional payments as a result of increased efficiency to compensate them for the benefits received under co-ownership by employees in the private sector.

A Liberal society is essentially dynamic, and there can be no rigid uniformity in its industrial life. It is a society which accepts the inevitability of change and allows growth to take place flexibly and with a minimum of conflict. It hates and will defeat poverty, but it is not suspicious of success. In its industrial affairs the State has an active part to play, but not by attempting to do industry's work for it. The essential task of the State is to create the conditions in which industry can most effectively perform its function of producing goods and services, of using with economy the invested wealth of the community, and of providing jobs in which men are not diminished but may grow in wealth, in control over their destinies and in personal significance.

N. S.

CHAPTER X

MONOPOLY

IT is a belief widely acknowledged that economic monopoly is an evil which should be controlled, restricted or eliminated. But like so many axioms of political faith, the more closely it is examined the more complex it becomes. Our purpose here is to suggest that if the word *monopoly* were not exclusively used in a derogatory sense it would be easier to work out a policy for controlling the exercise of economic power. We must think out the issues again before assessing the merits of various methods of controlling or eliminating monopoly practices. It is precisely because in Britain today the cart has been put before the horse that progress since the passing of the Monopolies and Restrictive Practices Act has appeared exasperatingly slow.

I. DEFINING MONOPOLY

Monopoly is a word which covers a multitude of economic practices and institutions, and even when it has been established that monopoly power exists it may not be easy to determine how the pattern of production or distribution has been affected, or whether it has been affected for better or worse. Moreover, to assess implications on purely economic grounds is to narrow the problem unjustifiably, for the exercise of monopoly power may involve political, social and even ethical considerations. Whatever the economic considerations, it is undesirable that private courts of justice should be operated, or that individuals should be driven out of their chosen trade, or that the consumer should be forced to take a particular type of article. Although the Monopolies Act defined the public interest in a purely economic sense, the Commission has clearly stepped outside these limits, for instance in condemnation of Trade Association Tribunals.

How can monopoly best be defined? A wide definition is probably a better point of departure than a narrow one, since it enables the widest possible field of economic activity to be scrutinized. Once emotion has been drained from the word there is no danger in labelling a situation as monopolistic, particularly if the distinction between the possibility of exercising monopoly power, its actual exercise and the implications for the public interest of this exercise is always borne in mind.

Monopoly is henceforward taken to mean the existence of effective control by an individual or group of individuals acting in concert over the production, distribution or sale of any good or service. Effective control is defined as control which is recognized to exist by outside parties, either in potentiality or in the actual exercise, and is such as to prevent them from freely choosing what to produce, how to produce, how to sell, to whom to sell, where to buy, etc. 'A good or service' may cover a group with a number of variant types which can still be recognized as meeting some distinct need for which there is no substitute readily available.

With such a wide definition it is clear that monopoly cannot be condemned out of hand but only recognized and assessed. The real issues become those of determining the public interest and deciding how monopolistic practice affects it. But at least the recognition that today most current business activity and practice involves an element of monopoly should clear away the prejudice of the word and make control simpler. Once it is recognized that the existence of monopoly is neither good nor bad and that its exercise may well be in the public interest, it should not be difficult to win acceptance for the view that there must exist a means of assessing its performance in the light of public interest. It follows that the public interest must be assessed on principles which are generally acceptable. As long as the vague idea is still entertained that all monopoly is an evil to be rooted out, business men will hotly deny that they are monopolists. They may, indeed, go further than this, and argue that since all mono-

poly is bad, and since they are not monopolists, their conduct
must be good.

2. THE HISTORICAL BACKGROUND

It must be confessed that political economists are largely to
blame that the simple dichotomy between 'monopoly, bad: competition, good' has come to be so generally accepted. The fact is
that since the repeal of the Corn Laws till recently the problem has
not appeared intellectually or practically important. It was Adam
Smith who launched a campaign against monopoly and spread the
belief that competition, untrammelled by State or private control,
would produce both the best allocation of economic resources and
the maximum of personal liberty. The doctrines of *laissez-faire*
and free competition came to be linked together, and the fantastic
growth of prosperity in the second half of the nineteenth century
was seen as their justification in practice. Liberal economists further elaborated on the competitive system and produced the perfect competition theory, showing how under the spur of individual profit resources were adjusted to give the consumers exactly
what they wanted as cheaply as possible. Thus a generation ago
there was neither theoretical nor practical interest in the problem
of monopoly in Britain. Where it was inevitable, it was regarded
as an excrescence which must be strictly controlled on the smooth
working of a competitive market economy. In practice, except for
an outburst of interest during the reconstruction period after
World War I, mostly directed against the evils of profiteering, the
existence of monopolistic practices seemed a small issue compared
with unemployment, the efforts to increase the pace of British
economic advance or the struggle to regain export markets. Indeed
the trend was towards a greater concentration of economic control. In the 1920's there was the call for 'rationalization', a vague
and never explicitly defined ideal that always implied concentration into fewer or more efficient units of control; there was the call
for 'self-government in industry' which meant more co-operation
and co-ordination. In the 1930's the State embarked on a confused

policy of what may be called State Cartelization. Some note-worthy examples of this were the setting up of the London Passenger Transport Board (1930), the Milk Marketing Board (1931), the creation of the Iron and Steel Federation (1935) and the passing of the Coal Mines Act and Cotton Spinners Act (1938). These measures tended to limit competition and reduce the number of competing units.

Socialists were quite content with this development of monopoly capitalism as representing a fulfilment of Marxist prophecy, and believed that large units would be far easier to place under national control, while government departments always found it easier to deal with the representatives of industry rather than with the confusion of a competitive system. No wonder that as controls proliferated business men were content to hand over some of their sovereignty to trade associations, staffed by lawyers and public relations officers able to argue their case in private and state it convincingly in public.

The post-war situation has seen an abrupt reversal of this trend. There has been such growth of general interest in monopoly and in what are called monopolistic and restrictive practices that a statutory body was set up in 1948 to investigate and suggest remedies for such practices as are 'against the public interest', although there is so much intellectual confusion on the subject that there is still no agreement on what exactly is and what is not 'in the public interest'.

It is this confusion rather than the pace of investigation that has delayed results, but one cannot for that reason condemn the confusion as 'muddled thinking' and necessarily harmful. In such a matter a simple diagnosis and an easy panacea are more likely to be devastatingly wrong than nearly right.

3. THEORETICAL REAPPRAISAL

It is essential to reconsider the view that free enterprise, working in conditions that economists have called perfect competition, produces the best allocation of productive resources. This does

not, of course, dispose of the problems of how far reality differs
from this theoretical perfection, or what steps would be necessary
to square reality with the ideal. These issues are not unconnected,
since the more practice differs from precept the more certain must
we be of our standard in order to justify widespread interference
and coercion.

Under what assumptions does a system of perfect competition
produce the best allocation of economic resources? Broadly these
assumptions are:

(i) that there is a given state of technical knowledge;[1]
(ii) that there is a given state of income distribution;
(iii) that there are a large number of units of economic decision;
(iv) that the goods produced are of a standard quality and that
the public knows where these goods may be obtained;
(v) that the factors of production can move freely between individual producers and different types of production; and
(vi) finally, that all parties act rationally, in their own self-
interest, and in particular that producers are actuated solely
by the desire to maximize their profits.

Given these assumptions it can be shown that an optimum will
be achieved in the sense that once equilibrium has been reached
(this represents a situation from which no one wishes to move) no
movement of factors would lead to any increase in the total value
of total production.

Moreover, through the exercise of competition, no factor of
production, including enterprise, receives more than is required
to ensure its continuance in economic use, which means that for
enterprise the level of profit covers the wages of management and

[1] This phrase, which has become part of the accepted jargon of economists,
is as so often with ritualistic incantations a stumbling-block to laymen. Briefly,
the assumption made is that technical progress plays *no* part in establishing
market equilibrium. There may be technical progress, but it is not the result of
competition between firms, and when it happens its results are available to all
firms. The highly unrealistic nature of this assumption is clearly laid bare
when it is expanded.

maintenance of capital and no more. As consumers' needs change, so the pattern of production alters; the consumer is sovereign, and through the ballot of the market is the arbiter of production. Though increased demand may at first lead to higher prices and higher profits, soon the entry of new capital and new firms will expand production and reduce prices, and profits will fall to their old level.

It is easy to see why this system appeals so powerfully to Liberals, for both economic and social reasons. The social reasons, which will be discussed more fully later, spring from the fact that the system appears to operate most successfully with the greatest amount of freedom for producer and consumer alike, because it appears to solve the problem of economic power and because it envisages an economic society where the individual, given the will, can always better himself, and where vested interest is always called upon to justify its existence in the verdict of the market.

Its economic attractions are obvious, given the assumptions. Here is a system which realistically accepts man's self-interestedness, and shows how it is turned to social advantage. No one has improved on Adam Smith's language in stating this: 'Man has almost constant occasion for the help of his brethren, and it is vain for him to expect it from their benevolence only. He would be more likely to prevail if he can interest their self-love in his favour, or show them it is for their own advantage to do for him what he requires of them. . . . It is not from the benevolence of the butcher, the brewer or the baker that we expect our dinner, but from their regard to their own interest. We address ourselves, not to their humanity, but to their self-love, and never talk to them of our own necessities, but of their advantages.'[1]

Besides, as the nineteenth century progressed and profits came under the lash of Socialist thinkers, it was an attraction of the system that though profits were the main-spring of endeavour, they themselves were continually being reduced as each man took from the economy to the extent to which he contributed to it.

Only some of the assumptions of perfect competition have a

[1] *The Wealth of Nations* (1776), II, i.

direct bearing on the problem of monopoly; these can be conveniently grouped under two broad headings: (i) the nature of the competitive process, and (ii) the requirements of a progressive economy.

(i) The implications of the doctrine of profit-maximization when combined with a free flow of productive factors and the existence of unrestricted competition. It is asserted that under free competition the very striving after profits effects their elimination, and that the greatest social benefit is gained through the blind self-interest of individuals. Not only are business men selfish, but they ought to be so, for if they take into account wider considerations than those of the balance-sheet the effectiveness of the system will be reduced. But the maximization of profit is only socially desirable under the stringent conditions of perfect market competition; profits must be not engrossed through twisting the economic system out of true; business men must either voluntarily play the rules of the game or be made to do so.

At this point it would be as well to emphasize how unrealistic this assumption as to the nature of business behaviour and motivation has become. Briefly, business motivation is in fact a complex of many elements, among them:

(a) the desire to achieve a level of profits sufficient to provide some desired standard of living, or to satisfy shareholders, or to secure funds for fresh capital expansion.

(b) the desire to consolidate and secure the position of the firm for the future by building up the good-will of customers and so reducing the prospect of too much competition.

(c) such personal motives, in endless variety, as the desire for success, social advancement, natural combativeness, professional pride in the job, loyalty to colleagues and to the firm.

The emergence of the joint-stock company has further complicated the issue, both because it is a deathless institution and because of the division which often occurs between financial ownership and operational control. To say that business men operate only under the lure of profit is not only to oversimplify the problem but to neglect the rôle of intelligent individual self-interest.

The function of profit under the competitive system is twofold: to provide an incentive to enterprise and to ensure the correct allocation of resources. However, as has been shown, it is an incentive which is continually being dulled by realization, and the emphasis is therefore on the allocative function. The rôle of the business man is reduced to that of the professional organizer of production, and as such he scarcely deserves the title of *entrepreneur*. In a progressive economy profits have the entirely different task of luring the business man out of the well-tried methods of production and the sale of goods that are known to be safe and steady lines. This was the thesis that Schumpeter has so notably developed.[1] Moreover, profits are often the sources of expansion and development, because the capital market, even when well organized, is far from perfect, largely because of the existence of lenders' and borrowers' risk. Lenders' risk is that associated with lending money to another for capital development, over and above the normal risk of the enterprise, and demands a premium to overcome this personal uncertainty. Borrowers' risk represents the loss that a borrower incurs through becoming indebted to another for finance capital, and covers the loss of control which follows from this and the disadvantage which may spring from having to make fixed payments of interest, possibly at awkward times. For both these reasons, firms prefer to expand with their own money, being prepared both to lend more cheaply and to borrow more dearly from themselves than from an outsider. Another factor which increases the imperfection of the capital market is that real capital is usually highly specific and immobile. Unless some guarantee of a fair return over the period of life of plant can be assured business men may well hesitate to embark on highly capitalized projects, but would rather content themselves with projects which though theoretically less profitable involve less loss of liquidity. Here is the problem of how far illiquidity is a

[1] J. A. Schumpeter, *The Theory of Economic Development* (Cambridge, Mass., 1934) and *Capitalism, Socialism and Democracy* (1943).

genuine economic cost, to overcome which some premium should be paid; for in many cases it is clearly not a social cost but only an aspect of the imperfection of the capital market. A competitive system which tended to eliminate profit too quickly might well slow down the pace of capital development.

The word *competition*, too, is used in a rather restricted sense, for it is not competition of one business man against another, but of the business man against the general market conditions. To take a parallel from the running-track, each business man is a runner racing against a standard time who gets points to the extent to which he betters this time and who is not immediately concerned with the performance of other runners. However, the general level of performance will itself determine the standard time, for if the standard is set at too low a performance, more competitors will come into that event and the time will be gradually cut. Now this is a very restricted form of racing: most competition will be of the direct personal kind with each striving to beat his neighbour, and often the race would be run differently with a different type of competitor. Here-there is recognition that each man's actions will have repercussions on those of his rival. This may lead either to an intensification of competition and bitter expression of it, such as tripping up rivals, or alternatively an explicit or implicit agreement not to set too hot a pace and so keep the standard of performance low. In this way personal competition may in business lead to intensification of effort (greater efficiency), or to unfair competition or to collusive action restricting competition. Thus, once again, it is clear that in either sense the desirability of competition cannot be accepted without qualification.

(ii) As for the requirements of a progressive society, it has already been suggested that the over-rapid elimination of profit might be undesirable as penalizing the progressive firm who may have sunk considerable capital in research and development. It is probably the greatest weakness of the perfect competition model that it makes no provision for the problem of the development of new ideas and techniques, that it is essentially static in its conception. How an economic society provides for an increase in its stock of capital and how techniques may be modified and advanced are vital questions, and it is a justification of the private enterprise system that it does provide a mechanism for effective progress. It is ironical that perfect competition, which was originally conceived of as providing a justification for private enterprise, has come to be regarded as proving that it is both inefficient and unnecessary.

Faith in perfect competition (and therefore in private enterprise) was greatly weakened in the 1930's by the development of theories of imperfect competition which claimed to have more relevance to current business practice. These demonstrated that even under the influence of competitive forces, largely because of market imperfections, a final position would be reached where products would be sold at higher prices and of an inferior quality, with uneconomic expenditure on sales promotion and the uneconomical use of productive factors, than would be the case under conditions of perfect competition. Not even the business man would be making a good thing of this, as his profits would be no higher than before; in fact everyone would be worse off.

This inevitably led to the development of what might be termed 'market Socialism', where the rôle of the business men was to be taken by paid managers whose duty it was to act as if they were business men, operating in perfect markets, because they would be equally capable of organizing production and of adjusting themselves to the mechanical forces of the market. It might have been more profitable to consider whether the deficiency was not in business men but in the analysis which had assigned to them so mechanical a rôle.

4. THE LIMITS OF COMPETITION

The conclusion must be that *perfect* competition can be accepted as a standard against which economic practice can be compared only over a limited field of activity — probably the routine production of articles of known type where change and innovation are not of great importance — and that elsewhere competition can never be perfect. The apparent loss in abandoning one standard will be more than compensated for by a growth in realism. We do not mean that market competition should not be accepted as a desirable factor, but it should not be the sole criterion. The recognition of this situation will release Liberals from their dilemma of having to advocate widespread interference with business activities in order to create artificially the conditions of perfect competition.

What should our positive policy be? First, there should be a clear recognition that market situations are essentially diversified and that no norm exists. A number of basic principles should be established upon which a progressive liberal society should operate; these principles should be generally recognized and accepted not only by the general public but also by the business community. There should be a mechanism for establishing the evidence regarding the actual working of business practice, and finally a means of assessing how far this practice is in conformity with the principles of a healthy society.

First, the economy must be as *efficient* as possible, by which is meant that existing resources must be used to the fullest extent in a manner which provides a maximum of satisfaction to the community. However, efficiency cannot be judged by mere physical output, since in a developed society choice itself is an economic good, besides providing an opportunity for development and change. There is no absolute standard for judging economic efficiency, and intelligent choice by consumers represents a continual check on the operation of the economy; the production of other countries, too, should provide external standards of quality and cheapness. Restrictive schemes must always be regarded as suspect unless they can be justified on other principles. The issue of standardization versus diversification is not an easy one, but usually common sense will show when variety is an economic good. The consumer should always be given an opportunity of knowing what the cost of variety is; often it is clear that the consumer cares little for the variety of choice offered; which indeed, may be a disadvantage to him, as in the case of electric-light fittings. One possible solution lies in the standardization of components while allowing for variety of end-products.

Secondly, the economy must be *progressive*, that is, it must be continually adding to its stock of capital equipment and ready to develop new products and new methods of production; it must, in fact, be adaptable and venturesome. Competition is one of the great engines of change, particularly competition from new men and new firms and since we must accept the large firm as a feature of the modern economy, from old firms branching into new lines of business. Schemes to restrict competition and demarcate markets and agreements, often unwritten, to stick to certain lines of production must inevitably lessen the force of competitive change. Existing firms, however efficient and well intentioned, represent vested interests and must not be allowed to be the sole judges of who is to operate in their field of business. Profits, if earned by adventurous productive methods, should not be regarded as evil but as the reward for enterprise. Complaints that competition is unfair and uneconomic must always be regarded with scepticism and its curtailment is only justified after an independent body has been satisfied that it is operating against the public interest.

Can there be too much competition? Can some forms of competition be economically undesirable? It is certain that competition can be so intense that it leads to an uneconomic state of affairs; either because resources are wasted or because over-competition inhibits capital and technological development by so reducing profits that capital cannot be maintained at an efficient level or the expectation of profit to a level which will encourage the venturing of risk capital. Here is a real dilemma between competition which stimulates enterprise and that which inhibits it. Somehow there must be a balance between a level of profits which encourages innovation and is sufficient to maintain old capital and attract new without sapping initiative and drive.

Certainly the value of competition will vary between expanding and contracting situations. In expansion it seems doubtful whether there is much danger of there being too much competition, though even here it may lead to a profligate use of resources such as soil mining and exploitation of only the best coal seams. In a contracting situation competition may well have many undesirable effects and perpetuate conditions within an industry until they become chronic as, for example, in the British cotton industry.

Competition which is often styled 'unfair' from the consumer's angle should usually be examined on strictly economic grounds. The two examples most often discussed are deceptive practices such as the concealed deterioration of a product and practices designed to eliminate rival competition with a view to establishing a monopoly position from which to exploit the consumer in the future. Producers make play of these dangers, but the remedy does not necessarily lie in an indiscriminate ban on competition, but rather in establishing methods whereby standards can be checked by independent bodies and the exploitation of a monopoly position made impossible. In general it is better to leave to the consumer himself the task of deciding how he gets value for money.

Of the so-called wastes of competition the most usually cited are unnecessary excess capacity and advertising. The former may be a necessary price to pay for variety and competitive development. Advertising, however, presents more complexities, though it too is usually associated in its most blatant forms with fierce oligopoly competition, and the public may gain more, in terms of the technological development that goes with this rivalry, than it loses through the resources devoted to advertising, e.g. in the present 'detergent-war' between Unilever's and Hedley's. There are in fact two quite separate issues: (i) the economic loss in terms of resources devoted to advertising; and (ii) the actual results of advertising, for on the latter advertising may be classified as beneficial, neutral or positively harmful. If informative or educative advertising performs a service in acquainting the consumer what he can buy, and where, and why he should buy it, it may be justifiable in terms of its cost. If it is merely harmless it provides no social benefit except that of subsidizing our newspapers. But some advertising is completely unjustifiable and of course the measure of harm is not only economic, in the sense of persuading individuals to buy the wrong goods, for it may play on people's morbid fear of not being accepted or teach them to be discontented with their possessions.

Thirdly, an economy, however progressive, must be reasonably *stable*. Generally, it will be the rôle of Government to ensure that where change is necessary it will not violently disrupt the lives of individuals. Firms, especially when they are large, can themselves do much to ensure maintenance of full employment, to counteract inflation and to promote export markets. Even where the Government will tend to use indirect controls of a fiscal and financial nature it is inevitable that direct controls will be necessary from time to time. Government departments naturally prefer to deal with as few bodies as possible and so direct controls foster the growth of trade associations. It is useless to ignore this awkward fact, and not surprising that business men resent a situation where the Government on the one hand is encouraging collective action and on the other denouncing collusive action as monopolistic. This apparent contradiction will disappear when it is recognized that collective action is not in itself reprehensible, but only becomes so as a result of the end for which it is organized. Trade associations can perform many useful functions, but these should be clearly and publicly laid down, and any empire-building by trade association officials sternly discouraged. Justifiable fields of action for trade associations are the organization of change in face of a contracting market, or the building up of fresh capacity when the market is expanding. One particular form of instability, the so-called pig or cobweb cycle, is entirely due to the existence of a large number of small producers who in the face of price changes alternately over-produce and under-produce, so accentuating the fluctuation of price. A single large firm could organize its expansion more rationally and an association of firms could spread information of the likely additional production that is being planned.

Fourthly, economic institutions must operate *equitably*. They should not usurp the prerogative of constitutional bodies. Thus trade association tribunals should be abolished, however scrupulously conducted their proceedings may be. It is probable that they are suspect on other grounds as weapons designed to limit competition, but even if this were not so, or the limitation of competition were justifiable, it is manifestly against the public interest that a private body should have the power to punish an individual or to deprive him of his livelihood for actions which are not in themselves illegal.

In business, codes of behaviour will naturally be established, but there is a danger that these will be inflated to enforce uniform lines of conduct and will limit competition between business men. An ethical question is involved here. In certain circles it is not uncommon to describe the competition system as unethical, not only because it is held that it is generally wrong for individuals to compete rather than to co-operate, but because particular forms of competition are considered actually 'unfair'. It may be rather old-fashioned now to talk about 'jungle economics', but collusive action is often justified on the grounds that it is reasonable and right for business men to co-operate. The necessity of uniform practice in business is compared to the indispensable 'rule of the road', but even admitting that trade associations do have useful functions to perform (provided that these are clearly defined) it is essential that business men should realize that by indiscriminate defence of such associations they undermine the foundations of the private enterprise system itself.

More frequently it is urged that competition must be regulated because if it is unrestricted it will be 'unfair'. It might be asked to whom it is unfair, whether to the other competitors, to the consumers, to workers in the industry or to the shareholders. For the consumer, unfair competition is best defined as *uneconomic* competition which reduces the efficiency of the economic system. This has already been discussed. But, though traders often declare their solicitude for the buyers, and make a considerable show of what we have called 'consumer paternalism', by unfair competition they usually mean competition from their rivals which is 'unfair' to themselves.

Is there any criterion by which we can judge competition to be unfair in this sense? Certainly not the criterion of loss, for there can be no unfairness if a trader loses his profit or even his living, if he is driven out of business by the greater *efficiency* of a rival. Behind much of the feeling that competition is unfair lies the assumption that each individual is entitled to make his livelihood in the profession or occupation he chooses, and to reap the fruits of investments made and ideas originated. There is, however, no such right in modern economic society, especially in this country, where we have to make our living in the face of fierce foreign competition, though there is *social* obligation to soften the blow to those hardest hit by economic change. In nineteenth-century Britain the hand-loom weaver merited assistance in adjusting himself, but not a guaranteed livelihood at the expense of economic progress. The latter would be pure Luddism.

There are, then, a number of practices which without being illegal appear to outrage business ideals of decency and are generally considered 'not cricket'. These practices vary, of course, from one business community to another, but on the whole it is true to say that most business codes go too far in limiting legitimate competition and consumers' choice. State legislation goes even further: fair-trade laws are invariably widened to cover practices which do not appear anti-social, such as selling more cheaply, offering discounts on quantity and so on. Probably the remedy is best left to society, given the fullest publicity about these methods. If full publication of the facts were distasteful to the parties concerned it would become obvious that the practices *were* unfair.

Fifthly, the economic system should operate so that individuals have as much freedom as possible with a minimum of coercion and direction. It was one of the attractions of perfect competition that it fulfilled this condition and in particular reduced the interference of the State in economic matters to a minimum. But in an advanced society freedom can only be considered in terms of choice — choice of livelihood or profession, choice of employer and of employee, choice of how and when to spend one's income and so on. Interference with choice in the name of efficiency is dangerous, besides conflicting with our first principle whereby efficiency itself is assessed in terms of choice.

It is very common today to deny that consumers are in fact capable of making intelligent choice, and a doctrine of consumer paternalism has been evolved, largely to justify the restrictions placed on choice by manufacturers and retailers. Thus competition by price is deplored on the grounds that the firms charging lower prices do so by reducing quality; and retail price maintenance is justified by the alleged need to provide the public with after-sales service. In fact, when you buy a car you are forced to buy a large amount of after-sales service, even if you would prefer to service it yourself or use a garage which is not a distributor. To play down this doctrine is not to claim that the customer is always right, but that he has more intelligence than the average manufacturer is willing to ascribe to him and that experience may be worth buying. Consumer education is another answer, and so is independent assessment of the quality of goods offered for sale. Furthermore, it might be as well if manufacturers did in fact do more to improve the quality of after-sales service beyond offering over-generous retail margins.

Sixthly, economic power should be spread, undue concentration being undesirable in itself and only justifiable on grounds that it promotes progress and efficiency. Perfect competition, because it was a system operated by a large number of small units of control, apparently solved this problem. It was the market that was all-powerful, and no consumer or producer was able to run contrary to its dictates. In a sense the market situation was the exemplification of Rousseau's General Will, since it was a compound of every decision made by those operating in it. Moreover, the system in theory offered equality of opportunity to all. For it must be assumed that there is a possibility of change in the group of those exercising control and that a distinct social class which can be labelled as capitalist is not created. Alfred Marshall maintained that firms were like the trees of the forest which grew to a certain size and then tended to decay, their place being taken by saplings; or, in the words of the homely expression, it was a case of shirt-sleeves to shirt-sleeves in three generations. Thus there was no established economically privileged group, but those in better positions had always to maintain them in the face of competition.

The business situation, however, has not borne out Marshall's description. There is a natural tendency for existing firms to grow larger, quite apart from the powerful forces conveniently labelled the economies of scale which make for concentration. The State too has undoubtedly favoured the large firms through the special privileges it has granted to incorporated companies. On these grounds alone the problem of the small man is worthy of consideration, though it must be cleared of the emotional and political overtones usually associated with it. The small man may be justified under Principle 2 as being an instrument of change and diversity or under Principle 5 where the satisfaction and freedom gained from being one's own boss should appeal to Liberals. Without being pampered, he should not be allowed to be suffocated either by design or through penal personal taxation.

However, many of the present-day restrictions, particularly in the retail trade, are designed to prevent the larger firms from exercising their legitimate right to compete with smaller by price. It is a form of Poujadism, and always attributes sinister designs to the larger firm, such as the elimination of *all* competition by price cutting and the exploitation of the monopoly so created. There is something in this argument, but not enough to justify legal discrimination against all competition based on superior economic efficiency. It is true too that small firms, especially if they specialize, need not be inefficient, but it is still essential that the public should know the cost if they choose (for convenience or preference for a personal relationship) to deal with a small shopkeeper rather than a large store that can afford to charge smaller mark-ups on a larger turn-over. Again, if the small shopkeeper chooses self-employment because he personally prefers to be independent rather than to work for others, he cannot logically expect to be able to charge the smaller mark-ups and enjoy the larger takings of the big firm as well.

The social danger of bigness and undue concentration was admirably expressed in the minority report of the U.S.A. Supreme Court in the case *U.S.* v. *Colinson Steel Co.* (1946):

'We have the problem of bigness. In final analysis size in steel is the measure of the power of a handful of men over our economy. That power . . . may be benign or it can be dangerous. The philosophy of the Schuman Act is that it should not exist. For all power tends to develop into a governance in itself. Power that controls the economy should be in the hands of the elected representatives of the people, not in the hands of an industrial oligarchy. Industrial power should be decentralized; . . . it should be scattered into many hands so that the fortune of the people should not be dependent on the whim or caprice, the political prejudices, the emotional stability of a few self-appointed men. The fact that they are not vicious men but respectable and social-minded is irrelevant.'[1]

It is true to say that in this country we tend to dismiss the danger that undue economic power might lead to the exercise of undue political power. Socialists occasionally inveigh against sinister vested interests which in a private capitalist system distort the democratic process. But it is really up to those who dislike the prospect of centralization of power, economic or political, in the hands of a few, even if these few are theoretically servants of the public, to ensure that under a free enterprise system there is a reasonable dispersal of control.

The American economist, Professor J. K. Galbraith,[2] has evolved an ingenious explanation for the fact that bigness has not had the disastrous effect which might have been predicted from the classical analysis of the competitive process of large business units, which appear highly efficient and progressive and have developed despite statutory hostility. These apparently represent very large concentrations of economic power. Galbraith contends that this system is contained by the parallel growth in other power-units, such as trade unions and retail organizations. For the competition of other producers in the same line of business is substituted that of suppliers of labour, buyers of the product and the general supervision of the State. Countervailing power (C.V.P.), as Galbraith calls it, is substituted for competition as a limitation upon economic power. He in fact accepts the view that big units are in the

[1] Fritz Machlup, *The Political Economy of Monopoly* (Baltimore, 1952), p. 226.
[2] *American Capitalism* (Boston, 1952).

H

forefront of economic development. The theory does however beg several questions: whether this view is true as an historical analysis; how effective C.V.P. is; and whether C.V.P. is always exercised in the public interest. Galbraith draws certain interesting conclusions regarding C.V.P. in its applicability to anti-trust action by the Government: (i) that C.V.P. should be encouraged and not discouraged as in the past some of the big retail organizations have been; (ii) that discrimination is not necessarily contrary to the public interest, but may even be considered part of C.V.P. itself; and (iii) that oligopoly is essentially better than monopoly. The rôle of government, in fact, becomes that of tolerating and indeed encouraging C.V.P.

5. MARKET BEHAVIOUR

Even though it may be impossible to evolve a general theory of market behaviour, yet classification and categorization is not without advantage and may simplify the task of investigators.

One division has been price-makers and price-takers — that is, between those who can set prices independently and those who have to accept the price established in the market or by other producers. But a broader distinction would be between Monopolists, who can act independently of others in the market; Oligopolists, whose action will determine (and be determined by) the policies of rivals, and who will therefore adjust their activities in the light of possible reactions; Collusionists, who act in conjunction with other firms, implicitly or explicitly, in respect to some of their policies; and Market Competitors, who act independently of other firms and whose policy is determined by the market situation.

It is clear that in our definition of monopoly there is an element of it in the first three situations, and it is true to say that the policy of monopolists, oligopolists and collusionists all in their separate fashion must be considered under the broad definition of monopoly.

Monopoly and collusive situations have most in common, since a monopolist represents the fullest form of control, while a group of collusionists acting together are really a limited mono-poly. This is the distinction sometimes made between the Com-bine and the Cartel. However, the Trade Association may have grown so powerful that in reality the individual producers are as much and as permanently restricted in their freedom of action as if they had joined a combine. Moreover, a monopolist is rarely completely free from the fear of possible competition, and is per-haps the more keenly sensitive to public opinion simply because he is a monopolist. On economic grounds too a monopolist will be in a position to exploit the economies of scale, concen-trate production on the more efficient plants, plan ahead more con-sistently, avoid sudden and unnecessary shocks to the econ-omy, not be carried away by mob panic. Collusion may be for good social reasons — in fact to achieve by co-operation some of the advantages of the co-ordinated decisions listed above, while retaining independence and variety — but too often col-lusion represents the worst of both worlds, by stifling healthful competition and maintaining stubborn and uneconomic indepen-dence.

Collusive practices designed to limit competition among pro-ducers and sellers take many forms. Some are designed to limit competition between existing concerns, others to hold the ring against newcomers or against those who refuse to compete 'fairly' or 'in an orderly fashion'. Arrangements may take the form of organizing prices, production-methods or marketing. We can-not here discuss the manifold complications involved. Enough has been said to show that any scheme can be abused and must therefore be reviewed by an outside and independent body. But this is not to say that every such scheme is in fact abused. Actual operation, motivation and results on the market structure must all be carefully examined.

6. THE CONTROL OF MONOPOLY

The new Restrictive Trade Practices Act (1956) has not made the drafting of this chapter easier. But only time can show how effective the new mechanism will prove. The important thing is to realize that the Act has done nothing beyond creating a new mechanism and that the principles of its operation have scarcely been discussed. Nevertheless it is welcome, and the courage of the President of the Board of Trade must be applauded. Various objections can properly be made: the outright outlawing of certain restrictive practices might have been more effective; and it is certainly unfair to presume an individual or a firm guilty with the onus of proving innocence on the accused. Again, it might have been better if the Tribunal had consisted entirely of High Court Judges without a lay element. These are interesting problems — but basically they are administrative problems. The *principles* on which the Registrar and the Tribunal are to act still remain obscure. We have tried to consider the nature of these principles and to draw up a code of business behaviour which would operate in the public interest.

Such a code could develop more readily if four conditions were fulfilled:

1. Firms must co-operate openly. Secret agreements, concealed business practices and secrecy over methods of operation almost certainly work against the public interest. The solution is that agreements of a type specified by law should be registered, practices should be open to inspection and technical knowledge as widely diffused as is consistent with a reasonable reward for innovation and risk-taking. The onus of proof whether a certain type of agreement operates for or against the public interest should rest sometimes with the firm and sometimes with the public body set up for this task; the more obnoxious the practice *a priori*, the more certain it is that the onus of proof should lie with the firm. Collective retail price maintenance should be in this class, while for individual price maintenance the onus of proof should rest with the public body.

2. There must be a permanent commission whose duty it is to investigate and publicize business practices. It should probably be allowed to operate much more informally at first than does the present Monopolies Commission, more on the lines of the Can-

MONOPOLY   229

adian body.[1] There might well be a division between formal and
informal investigation. It is much to be deplored that the Commission is being weakened just when it was growing in confidence
and authority. It is to be hoped that the new Registrar will act
aggressively in uncovering malpractices.

3. It should be the business of the Commission to assess the
evidence and recommend whether action should be taken to mod-
ify the existing situation. One Minister (presumably the President
of the Board of Trade) should be responsible for implementing
this. Firms should have the right to refer the evidence and conclusions drawn from it to an independent tribunal. This sounds
cumbersome, but there has always been criticism of the fact that
the Monopolies Commission is investigator, prosecutor and to a
great extent judge in the same case. With the division between
formal and informal investigation and with the possibility of
taking the case to a separate tribunal these functions would become, to some extent, distinct.

4. The composition of the tribunal could be lay or judicial.
Business men have expressed a preference for the latter, which is
not surprising in view of the extremely helpful interpretation of
the common law 'restraint of trade' which has sprung from the
notorious decision in the Mogul case of 1894. Yet Judges are not
well fitted by training to interpret the public interest in complex
economic and social matters and most people (without really
assessing the evidence) are highly critical of the working of
judicial interpretation based on the Sherman Act.

But the problem of monopoly is not capable of solution solely
through mechanisms for investigating or evaluating evidence,
however ingenious these may be. We need general discussion and
acceptance of the economic and social principles upon which a
Liberal society should function. It is true that a referee must be
present, as in football, to penalize infringements of the code of
rules. But basically the game is only possible because the players

[1] The Combines Investigation Commission. See F. A. McGregor, 'Pre-
venting Monopoly: Canadian Techniques', in *Monopoly and Competition*, ed.
E. H. Chamberlin (1954).

accept the code, however much circumstances may tempt them to break it. Every game, moreover, has a code of behaviour which goes far beyond the written laws, and there are spectators who by their behaviour do much to ensure that the game is honestly played. The parallel holds good for restrictive practices on the part of labour as well as those in capital: remedial measures must go far beyond the Statute Book.

C. N. W.-P.

CHAPTER XI

AGRICULTURE

I. A STATEMENT OF PRINCIPLES

BRITISH agriculture is not an economically efficient industry. Protected in various and muddled ways, it does not help as much as it could either the economic recovery of Britain or the economic development of the poorer parts of the world. A standard argument is that British agriculture must be protected in order to reduce the scarcity of world food supplies. This it does not. Our refusal to buy in world markets is a direct cause of restrictions on agricultural output elsewhere. For example, because we protect sugar-beet Cuba finds it profitable to restrict her cane-sugar production. The way we shall really help the underdeveloped world is by exporting capital, which means a higher national income for Britain and so cheaper food.

At the same time, as we seek a new economic policy for agriculture we should recognize that eight conditions are necessary if it is to be socially worth while:

(1) The basic production-unit should be the 'family farm', relying predominantly for labour on that supplied by the farmer and his family. While cereal-producing farms would continue to use hired labour the number of self-employed and family workers would greatly exceed the number of wage-earners in agriculture as a whole. It must be frankly admitted, as is shown later, that by maintaining the family farm one route to greater efficiency is being largely abandoned — that of larger farms and their economies of scale. However, this is a minor route and can be sacrificed if others are followed with determination.

(2) Land ownership should be predominantly in private hands

and diffused. This means either that recent tendencies for an increase in owner-occupiership and the break-up of large estates under the pressure of death duties should be encouraged or that the public limited company must become a major instrument for running and managing land.

(3) There should be equality of opportunity in the obtaining of both farms and working capital. So far, with the exception of a few of the professions, agriculture is the one occupation where talents, both proven and equal, most frequently face disparate opportunities.

(4) In supplying means of production and in marketing farm produce neither farmers nor middlemen should have overwhelming bargaining power against each other, or individually or jointly against the consumer. Not only the exercise of monopoly power, but also the open or tacit collusion which competition among a few large organizations so often produces must be prevented.

(5) Unearned income must arise in agriculture (as a surplus return to the more fertile or better situated land — 'rent' in the strict economic sense) if the industry is to be efficiently organized without costly and complicated administrative arrangements. Yet it should not accrue to the few fortunate individuals who own or occupy land, but rather be taxed away and more justly distributed. Within agriculture there should be greater equality of earned income than at present, as long as this equalization is consistent with a higher level of efficiency. Where the elimination of this unearned income depresses the incomes of the poorest among farmers the problem is one for fiscal and social security programmes and should not be allowed to influence the making of agricultural policy or to complicate its administration.

(6) Physical controls should be abandoned in favour of planning through the price mechanism.

(7) The farmer should be offered what to him has the same significance as full employment to the factory worker, namely short-term guarantees that his income will not vary substantially in an unforeseen manner. In the same way as full employment should

not mean continued tenure of one job with no possibility of a fall in earnings, guaranteed prices are not a *permanent* insurance against substantial technical and productive adjustments.

(8) Finally, the proportion of the country's population at present engaged in agriculture should be maintained. There are strong social and political reasons for keeping a substantial agrarian population in this abnormally industrialized country. To keep a substantial minority of our people in close contact with organic processes and in day-to-day appreciation of the importance of the subtle relationships existing between living things is an essential safeguard of a humane society. Agriculture provides a continuing reminder, less subtle but as far-reaching as philosophy, that man is something more than matter.

The key issues are, therefore, whether the first five objectives are consistent with the last two and whether all of them are compatible with the measures necessary to remove the now serious economic inefficiency of British agriculture and with the revival of the free market as the predominant means of directing agricultural production. The eighth objective is certainly the most controversial. But the policy outlined below is not greatly modified if the free market is abandoned; then the case for giving direct income support to smaller farms, which we put later in this chapter, becomes less important.

2. THE CASE FOR FREE TRADE

In the farming year 1954/5 food was available in world markets at 76% of the prices being paid for comparable home-produced supplies and on the basis of this comparison it has been calculated that the average net output per head for British agriculture is some 40% of that in manufacturing industry. Importable supplies of animal products were available at 77% of home produce prices and of crops at 73%. Only for wool were the home and foreign prices equal and for only two other products, beef and mutton, were the import prices more than 81% of the home prices. The situation has not changed radically since then, except to underline

Britain's relative advantage in beef and mutton production.[1] The British factory worker is indeed entitled to ask whether it would not be cheaper for him to get more of his food by exporting to North America or the Caribbean than to East Anglia or Wiltshire.

Recently these essential facts have been completely lost in the welter of arguments concerning the effects of increased exports necessary to pay for increased food imports on the terms of trade of Great Britain; it is argued, generally with the flimsiest of statistical support and the most virulent of economic preconception, that any increase in exports would so force down their price and any increase in imports so force up their price that any re-development of our national resources from agriculture to export industries would prove worthless after the event.[2] In addition we are reminded that sooner or later the price of agricultural produce in all markets will rise in terms of the price of manufactured produce, so that Great Britain will ultimately need to devote more of her resources to agriculture and that it would be advisable to maintain the present prosperity of the industry in anticipation of this expected change in circumstances.

Whatever the intellectual fascination of these arguments they are irrelevant to the present situation. An increased demand for foodstuffs in world markets *could* obviously force up their prices, especially as many of the so-called world markets are extremely restricted, selling only the left-overs from national support programmes and international preferential trading systems. But the supply of imports is much more flexible in the short run than is usually recognized and it would be possible to seek a greater quantity of our needs there without significantly pushing prices

[1] Professor Nash, from whose earlier work the above statistics are taken, has brought them up to date in *Lloyd's Bank Review*, July 1956. For 1955–6 expected import prices to home prices are: wheat 74%, barley 82%, sugarbeet 66%, beef 100%, mutton and lamb 91%, pig meat 73%, milk 70% and eggs 81%.

[2] If the mid-nineteenth century economists had been as preoccupied as modern Cambridge with the terms of trade we would probably now have an economy as backward as that of France.

up. Both Canada and the United States have large grain surpluses; there is acreage restriction in the United States. In the farming year 1953/4 the wheat stocks of the main exporters were equivalent to over nine times the quantity of British imports in 1953; maize stocks were sixteen times the quantity of British imports. The situation today is much the same. Moreover, the long-term tendency, registered over the last fifty years and not simply in the 1930's, is for world wheat supplies to grow more rapidly than effective demand for them. A similar tendency exists for sugar and Cuba is already restricting her production by one-third. It is likely that we could buy greater quantities of sugar, wheat and feeding grains at lower prices than we now pay simply because such a policy would reduce existing cost-raising restrictions on foreign output. The flexible supply of grains also makes relatively easy the expansion of pig and egg production among the low-cost producers. Under these circumstances, even though an increase of exports will lower prices, a substantial re-direction of British demand for food towards world markets could take place before the prices of home-grown and imported produce were made equal. If the re-direction is effected gradually over a period of years we should be able to judge by experience, rather than by statistical sorcery, when the process had gone far enough.

The argument concerning long-term movements of the relative prices of agricultural and manufactured produce is irrelevant because in a fully employed world economy such changes, as far as any can be reasonably foreseen at all, will take place gradually. We are not likely again to experience any but minor vagaries of the international trade cycle. No policy of forcing British agriculture to withstand the competition of imported supplies is going to depress the industry so as to make it incapable of adjusting itself smoothly and quickly enough to such gradual long-term movements in the terms of trade.[1]

[1] As a cautionary tale one should remember that the dismal prognostications by Colin Clark and Arthur Lewis concerning the deterioration in the purchasing power of manufactured produce in terms of primary produce to be expected by 1960 are proving to be very wide of the mark.

There is a case for guaranteed prices, but it is not that of protection. Their purpose is to remove uncertainty about the future course of costs and prices, so inducing farmers to plan on a more long-term and cheaper basis, and to eliminate the cycles in production, of which the pig cycle is the best known, which plague agriculture in a free-market economy. It follows that guaranteed prices should be fixed at the prices which we expect to pay in the more immediate future in world markets. No further modification from the simple principle of comparative advantage is involved.

However, our last objective — to maintain the present size of the agrarian population — will be seriously jeopardized by a quick return to such a free-trade basis for British agricultural policy even though farmers at the moment are receiving higher incomes than they require as inducement to stay in the industry. This is shown by the great premiums commanded by farms sold with vacant possession — about 100% of the purchase price for farms without vacant possession. The extent of this 'unearned income' can be estimated as follows. Since 1937/8 the sale value per acre of farm with vacant possession has increased threefold. Is this change in sale value an adequate measure of how far rents for all farms would increase if there were a free market in land and if, by bidding for it, new farmers were able to indicate their willingness to do the job for less reward or with more efficiency than many existing farmers? It is true that the market in agricultural land is at present extremely restricted and that in consequence the values of those farms now being sold might be inflated much above true free market value. On the other hand many potential applicants for farms are excluded now since they have only sufficient capital for working purposes and cannot afford to invest in the fixed capital embodied in land. If once again there were competitive bidding for rented farms the total demand for farm land in relation to the available supply might well be greater than it is at present. An additional reason for thinking this is that since 1937/8, in contrast with the threefold increase in capital values and rents now postulated as likely under completely free-market conditions, the gross receipts from farming have risen fourfold and the net incomes of farmers fivefold.

Immediately before the war farmers paid £43 m. on rent and on interest on fixed capital (where farms were owner-occupied) and in 1954/5 £77 m., in contrast with a suggested free-market rental value of some £129 m., suggested in the previous paragraph. Accordingly it seems reasonable to assume that there would be enough farmers to occupy all agricultural land if they were required to pay £50 m. more than at present for its use and for the fixed capital associated with it. This is equivalent to a drop in the net incomes of farmers of about one-sixth and of prices received by them of 5%. Under existing world market conditions a free trade agricultural policy would almost certainly involve a fall in farm prices of much more than 5% on the average and the £50 m. of 'unearned income' would be more than eliminated. There would admittedly be many consequential changes of such a fall in prices, improving the efficiency and the income-earning position of British farms, but one of these would be a reduction in the total number of farmers accompanied by an amalgamation of some farms and an abandonment of others.

3. SIZE AND EFFICIENCY

The small average size of British farms is often advanced as a reason for their inefficiency which, it is claimed, is due to an under-utilization of costly capital equipment and, to some extent, of labour on the small farm.[1] The relationships between farm size and efficiency have not yet been examined in sufficient detail to clarify

[1] The exact average size of British farms is difficult to assess. The average size of farms run by farmers with no other employment (about three-quarters of all farmers) is probably around 100 acres, although since about 5% of them occupy more than one holding the individual operating unit (measured as a geographical entity) has a slightly smaller acreage. However, a large proportion, probably as many as 50% of farmers with no supplementary occupation, farm less than 50 acres each and over 20% less than 25 acres. The smaller farms will generally be livestock producers where acreage is much less of a limiting factor on the size of *enterprise* than in arable farming.

the situation. Some evidence is provided by the following statistics which, although the best available, are in many respects so imperfect that their interpretation must not be pressed closely:

Net Output per £100 Expenditure, Average 1951/2 and 1952/3,
England and Wales

Type of farming	50 acres and under	50–100 acres	100–150 acres	150–300 acres	300–500 acres	over 500 acres
Dairying	106	111	115	119	119	—
Livestock	97	115	122	126	132	140
Mixed	106	111	116	117	126	134
Arable	112	118	126	134	133	133

Note: 'Net Output' is the value of gross farm output less the value of purchased seeds and feeding-stuffs. 'Expenditure' is similarly adjusted.

The statistics are calculated from a sample of 2,262 farms, unavoidably *not* randomly selected. Individual farms are not classified according to their own type of farming but according to the predominant type of farming in their districts.

Source: Farm Incomes in England and Wales, 1952–53 (Ministry of Agriculture and Fisheries, 1955).

No matter how cautiously one interprets these statistics farms of all types with less than 50 acres each make a poor showing. In comparing the other size groups those farms with more than 300 acres each should be excluded as being controlled by farmers with exceptional skill, at least in the management of men. Allowing for this fact, the performances of farms of sizes between 50 acres and 100 acres in dairy and mixed farming are reasonably satisfactory; in the more extensive livestock and arable groups there are more signs of increasing efficiency associated with increasing size. But few of these reductions in costs result from the more intensive use of costly equipment possible on larger farms. They are due to improvements in techniques and in management which happen to be associated with increasing size of farm. The farmer who has the ability to manage a larger farm has also the talents to ensure better technical management of stock.

Although the inequality of opportunity already discussed denies to many farmers the opportunity of managing larger farms more

appropriate to their capabilities, these skills are scarce and a wholesale creation of more large farms by amalgamating the smaller ones
would not be accompanied by a maintenance of the average standards displayed on the larger farms in the Table above. The Table
reflects the present situation; it does not tell us that more use of
large-scale farming is the way to economic salvation.

Particularly in the case of the 25% or so of farmers with no
supplementary occupation on the smallest farms, there is a clash
between the need to maintain our farming communities and the
needs of economic efficiency. This difficulty will be discussed later.
In general British farming should not suffer any significant con-
straint upon its competitiveness because of the size of its farms.
The average size of farm in Denmark is less than one-half of that
in Britain and the Danes do not secure substantial off-setting advantages through cheaper imported feeding-stuffs (even though
there are no tariffs on these in Denmark), while Danish hired
farm labour is no cheaper than that in Britain. The Swedes have
given great thought, as a basis of their energetically pursued policy
of eliminating small farms, to the minimum size of a farm under
present conditions to be economically viable and have decided
that it should fall within a range of 50–75 acres. It would not be
pretended, of course, that such a size exhausts all 'the economies
of scale'. While size of farm undoubtedly confers some economic
advantages there are many more effective ways of reducing costs;
most agricultural economists would probably regard size of farm
as one of the least important factors influencing agricultural efficiency.

In any case much of the need for larger farms can be avoided by
a greater emphasis upon livestock production and many of its advantages secured by greater specialization within individual farms.
Greater emphasis on beef and mutton production is essential
since their prices are likely to rise the most in world markets in the
next few decades. The average size of pig herds in Denmark, notwithstanding the smaller farms there, is substantially greater than
in Britain, where in 1948 pigs were produced on over 60% of all
holdings, on 40% of them in herds with fewer than five pigs each. In

the United Sates the average price of eggs was less than half of that in Britain in 1953,[1] the ratio probably having risen slightly since then. This greater saving results predominately from the larger average size of American poultry flocks. Yet even the importance of size of enterprises must not be exaggerated. For example, the available evidence suggests most strongly that economies in milk production are much less influenced by size of herd than they are by the average yield per cow in the herd. The competitors whose agricultures we should most imitate, the New Zealanders and the Danes, base their efficiency predominantly upon a much higher level of technical achievement and not upon flocks or herds of optimum sizes. The overwhelming reason for the cheapness of Danish bacon is the efficiency of the Danish sow as a mother and of her progeny as a converter of food, advantages secured by extremely skilled stock management aided by some seventy years of careful selected breeding. Thus in one year a Danish sow produces 25% more pigs which are reared to the point of slaughter than does her British counterpart. The basic problem of British agricultural policy, therefore, is to speed up the rate of technical progress and to ensure that those who become farmers are the most capable of applying it.

4. OPPORTUNITY AND ADVANCE

The conditions are now much more favourable than before the war for technical advance: guaranteed prices enable the farmer to give more of his attention to the technical and less to the financial aspects of his business; and the higher prestige enjoyed by agriculture is attracting more people of real ability to the industry as a permanent career. Even so the industry has less power of attracting or using talent than its present or potential prosperity warrants. The effects of excessive security of tenure enjoyed by established farmers, the absence of a free market in land and the lack of capital among many would-be entrants are clearly the most

[1] Converting dollars according to the purchasing powers of the currencies, not at the official exchange rate.

serious barriers. The last is becoming more and more severe as a result of the breaking-up of large agricultural estates under pressure of death duties, the failure to create other institutions to fulfil their function and the consequential decline in farms available for renting. There are extremely limited opportunities through small-holdings (and obviously poor ones at that in view of their usually small sizes) for those with little capital and virtually none for those without capital to secure promotion. Equality of opportunity is the social and economic crux of a Liberal agricultural policy and the farming oligarchy, now rapidly being created, is the most serious restraint upon technical progress.

The political organization of farmers' interests has led to many wasted opportunities of fostering technical improvement. Emphasis on the affairs of the National Farmers' Unions and on the promotion of national Marketing Boards have brought politician farmers forward as leaders in the industry. Those capable of serving the country more usefully by providing technical and commercial leadership, even at the parochial level, have had fewer incentives or channels through which to exercise their talents. The absence of a thriving farmers' co-operative movement has been a severe handicap in contrast with the situation in Denmark, New Zealand and Holland.

Four measures are essential to provide full opportunities for talent:

(a) Landlords should be allowed much greater powers to dispossess tenants if there are alternative claimants whose technical and other standards seem higher; security of tenure for periods of three or four years and recognized compensation for improvements and disturbance to ejected farmers would ensure the best of both worlds.

(b) A land tax may be required to ensure that economic prices are charged on all lands whether tenanted or owned by the farmer and that thereby landlords receive as little 'unearned' income as possible in consequence of freeing the land market. This tax would not be difficult to administer nor land values hard to assess, notwithstanding much opinion to the contrary. Land could be classified into twenty or so categories according to its fertility or location. For each category a tax on an acreage basis would then be levied to produce land prices just sufficient to balance the demand and supply of it, while allowing capital a return adequate to induce its replacement or, if necessary, augmentation. If the tax on any farm made these two objectives unattainable this would simply show that it should be re-classified and the direction in which the re-classification should be made, the tax being changed accordingly.[1] Several countries already have land taxes intrinsically more complicated than this, such as New Zealand and Denmark.

It is obvious that some land would be unlikely to earn a return above that necessary to maintain its proper management and the capital invested in it, and so pay no tax. The purpose of the tax is not only to net the surplus on the more fertile or favourably located land but to recoup the subsidies proposed later when they are unavoidably paid to farmers who do not require them as an incentive to remain in production.

(c) Equity financing in agriculture must be extended from an almost non-existent base so that integrity, perseverance and ability can become adequate collaterals in securing fixed or working capital. This is a large part of the case for a specialized agricultural credit agency. Share farming, whether of product or of profits, is another most effective way of providing a needed rung in the farming ladder;[2] it is now virtually non-existent in Britain yet it is one of the main reasons for the high efficiency of New Zealand dairy farming. Share farming (or, as it is more often called, share cropping) has a bad name yet it is only a source of social abuse in over-populated countries and of economic stagnation where land-lords have no interest in agricultural progress. Another possibility is the public company as the successor to the large-scale land-

[1] For a fuller indication of the possibilities of a land tax see Professor A. C. Pigou's classic, *A Study in Public Finance* (1928, revised 1947), Ch. XIV. The caution towards the end of his chapter is due to Professor Pigou's value judgments and not to the technical and administrative difficulties of a land tax.

[2] See A. H. Maunder, 'Some Alternatives to Cash Tenancy', *Westminster Bank Review*, May 1956.

owners now being displaced by death duties. But the scope for such a development is probably limited. Subject to the important proviso discussed two paragraphs below, personal ownership and management of land is likely to be cheaper, which is probably the reason why the public company has not yet literally entered the field.

(*d*) The State will need to take a more direct interest in the promotion of technical efficiency than is necessary in (say) Denmark or the United States, at least for some very considerable time, until the National Farmers' Unions are weaned from their concentration on political and commercial action to the exclusion of fostering technical progress; but this is not an intervention inconsistent with our eight objectives, nor need it be self-perpetuating. One can hardly regard the subsidizing or administration of progeny-testing schemes to raise the standard of British livestock as a threat to individual human liberty. Nor can any substantial objection be raised against subsidies designed to encourage new techniques. They would not support inefficient or lethargic producers and they would be extremely cheap. For example, recently introduced progeny-testing schemes involve a subsidy of less than £1 m. They are distinct from most existing subsidies which favour the efficient and the inefficient alike, the lethargic as well as the enterprising, and which only boost production within a known and generally accepted framework of techniques. Given these modest interventions and the proposals for easing entry to the industry, State action to control the techniques of production or the quality of production can be ended. Not only is the right to dispossess farmers not conforming to given technical standards hardly ever used; it is in itself a false yardstick (technical and not economic efficiency) which should be replaced by charging an economic price for land.

The proposal for increased diffusion of land ownership, when some 40% of farms are already owner-occupied, poses the important question who is to fulfil the functions of estate managers once undertaken by the large landowners. The economic utilization of land requires in most situations the co-ordination of

THE UNSERVILE STATE

activities, both complementary and competitive, over extremely large tracts of land, often tens of thousands of acres. If there is to be pure *laissez-faire* in land management the individual owner will carry out investments only to the point where the cost is equal to his own private return, and as a result worth-while investments from the view-point of his neighbours and of society as a whole will not be carried out. For example, hillsides may need afforesting in order to prevent flooding in the valley below. This situation has been shown in its most dramatic form in a recent report on the Monmouthshire Moors by the Welsh Agricultural Land Sub-Commission, an area of 26,800 acres stretching roughly from Chepstow to Cardiff and bounded on one side by the main railway line through the Severn tunnel and on the other by the sea. The land is owned by 489 persons and its control complicated by the existence of many tenants who rent from more than one owner. The land is flat and scarcely above sea-level and needs a co-ordinated system of drainage. It receives abundant water from the surrounding hills through most of the year but dries up rapidly in summer. Consequently, in default of an adequate drainage and irrigation scheme, farmers often deliberately keep land poorly drained, allowing many of the channels to become partially blocked so as to ensure sufficient water during summer. Many of the access roads are of grass and become mud-bound in wet months. The Commission's report considered that an irrigation scheme for the whole area, involving the construction of pumping stations, and the building of hard-surface, hard-access roads would be financially sound. The inability to co-ordinate the activities of a multitude of owners has created a situation where the return on investment to the whole community is greater than that expected by individual owners, so that the area has not been fully developed. There are many other areas of similar underdevelopment through failure to treat the districts as unities, such as the Bridgewater plain in Somerset and the valley of the Hampshire Avon. In addition there is a need, the extent of which cannot be clearly indicated, for reorganizing the boundaries of farms, in a few cases such as Yetminster in Dorset where there is extreme fragmentation of individual holdings (akin to the continental agricultural land-scape) but more generally where exchanges between farmers of fields of reasonable size would make farms geographically more compact.

On such arguments is usually rested the case for land national-ization. The economic objection to it is that private landowners are certainly cheaper managers of land than would be a central salaried staff and that, therefore, the functions which they can adequately carry out as individuals need not come under the sur-vey of any central authority. What is needed are regional planning bodies able to impose regional investment programmes where these are economic, even against the opposition of individual landowners in the districts concerned. Since only economically sound investments would be carried out they would be completely financed by the land tax which could be recouped on 'betterment' to the properties concerned. In fact, to ensure that no individual landowner suffered financially it should be required that recoup-ment would be collected only to the extent of any 'betterment' actually reflected in subsequent changes in land values.[1] Many of these improvements would virtually be of a once-for-all nature and many others would require only routine maintenance work, so that the State would not have to exert a large and continuing direct interest in estate management. Where land has to be taken over as part of any regional improvement scheme, such as for afforestation or to provide shelter belts, it should be rented from its owner at current market rates unless he wishes to sell at exist-ing market values. These proposals involve no significant en-croachment upon the principle of diffused ownership and the compulsory regrouping of fields and consolidation of individual farms involves only temporary and self-destructive restriction upon individual freedom.

In principle there are four objectives for monopolistic agri-cultural marketing boards: to raise farmers' incomes by restricting total supply (as done by the Hops Marketing Board and as could

[1] This is more or less the system in New Zealand's 'unimproved value' land tax.

be done by the Tomato and Cucumber Marketing Board) or by
discriminating in the prices charged to different purchasers (as
done by the Milk Marketing Board); to secure reductions in the
costs of distribution; to improve the quality of marketed produce;
and finally to give greater short-term stability to production and
income. The first objective is one which more properly belongs to
the realm of general fiscal and social security policy and should not
influence the type of marketing system used or justify agricultural restrictive practices.

The second argument has very little substance, since it implies
that there are such economies of large-scale production that
monopoly is in any case inevitable, or that such a few firms would
remain in competition in collusion with each other, or that there
is such inertia and ignorance of opportunities amongst a large
number of otherwise competitive marketing enterprises that only
by administrative action can both be removed. Detailed consideration of these possibilities elsewhere has shown that none of
these arguments has much weight. There are, indeed, many imperfections in the marketing of farm produce but these are not
going to be eliminated by organizations which are superimposed
upon the existing industry and which essentially would carry out
the same functions. There are, for example, good grounds for believing that about one-quarter of home-grown horticultural produce is unnecessarily consigned through the main London fruit
and vegetable markets, instead of going directly to provincial
markets, and that growers and their agents do not have complete
success in directing supplies to the markets where they are most
needed. Similarly, with a highly perishable product like milk there
is a real need for some central organization which will act as a
clearing-house in order to get supplies moved where they are
most needed.[1] While Government action is required to establish
improved arbitrage facilities and to ensure an efficient location of
markets no limitations should be placed upon established or new
marketing organizations to use all available facilities as they think
most appropriate. The development of grading, if it is to be in

    [1] The Milk Marketing Board certainly gains high marks on this one score.

response to genuine consumer wants and not simply a disguised restriction scheme, can equally be developed most effectively within a competitive framework.[1] In fact, since all-embracing marketing schemes have to set standards achievable by the least efficient of their members they retard the development of economically justified grading.

The most effective way of removing any inertia in the marketing industries is to develop a vigorous farmers' co-operative organization, in the reasonable expectation that greater diversity of social background and economic interest among marketing enterprises would make for more effective competition. Not even the most Utopian enthusiast for co-operatives could argue that the British farmers' co-operative movement has been outstandingly successful, except perhaps in the marketing of eggs. This fact gives no ground for pessimism concerning the possibilities. A farmers' co-operative movement is somewhat akin to an 'infant industry' and often needs temporary support or shock treatment to ensure its overcoming initial growing pains, especially where private enterprise is reasonably competitive and not obviously exploitative. For example, the highly successful Dutch horticultural co-operatives owe their development above all to a period in the first World War when all produce was compulsorily marketed through the auctions. If British farmers were told that marketing boards were no longer politically acceptable there would certainly be a vigorous development of co-operative enterprises, as was shown in 1954 by the speedy and effective formation of the Fatstock Marketing Corporation when it became clear that the Government was not prepared to set up a marketing board in sufficient time to control the trade when meat was de-rationed. Yet in co-operatives there is a danger, as has already materialized in Sweden, that group loyalties would enable the farmers' co-operatives, in federation, effectively to dominate the marketing industries in which they operate. Not only must the Government be prepared to encourage the development of many more co-

[1] As the contrasted failure of the National Mark Scheme and success of various private grading schemes before the war show.

operatives than there are today, but at the same time it must set limits to the growth of these or private trading organizations to prevent domination of or collusion (open or tacit) between rivals, as is already the case in bacon marketing and grain milling.

A limited but fairly strong case can be made for certain marketing boards where there are cycles in production which cause serious year-to-year price fluctuations and avoidable physical waste. This is but one special aspect of the general case for short-term guaranteed prices which the farmer can claim on grounds of equity but which are also probably in the interests of consumers. The wastes of the pig cycle are fairly well-known yet similar cycles are found with other livestock and, in less clear cut form, in the production of vegetables. Moreover it seems reasonable to expect that in an industry of predominantly small-scale *entrepreneurs* with generally limited capital resources the prospects of a fluctuating price level will induce farmers to play safe in their production and investment programmes. If future prices are uncertain, given the slow turnover of capital in agriculture, 'the bird in the hand' and 'not every egg in one basket' psychology is likely to be a strong deterrent to desirable intensification and specialization of production. In recent United States and British experience there is evidence that guaranteed prices accelerate substantially the rate of technical progress in agriculture and of increase in output. Looked at from this point of view the 'fiddling the riddle'[1] of the Potato Marketing Board is not the economically obnoxious device which its critics would have us believe: it is the only effective administrative means of removing serious year-to-year price variations which for the grower become even wider percentage variations in income. The same type of control might, to the consumer's long-run advantage, be applied to carrots. These, however, are the only two important crops for which an element of monopolistic marketing is required in order to stabilize prices in the short-run and no defence is intended for actions which

[1] The output of potatoes is stabilized from year to year by varying the size of the grids on the riddles through which potatoes must pass if they are to be sold for human consumption.

restrict supply in years of very poor crops or keep out new lower-cost producers. The buffer stock technique is satisfactory for storable products. For the remainder subsidies should be paid, as at present, when ever prices fall below the guaranteed prices. In theory one can object that there is no immediate recoupment if prices rise above the support levels. In practice this is not a serious objection, because such gains are unlikely to be great if a real attempt is made to fix support prices at expected world prices in the near future, and in any case any such 'unearned income' will tend to be used in bidding up the price of land and so be regained through the proposed land tax.

Our analysis shows that the first seven objectives are mutually consistent and that, when economic efficiency is considered from a long-term and non-static point of view, their fulfilment will greatly accelerate economic progress in the industry. In no way do they create a substantial barrier to this progress. How we may obtain them has been set out already, except the achieving of greater equalization of earned income in agriculture. This would result from the proposal to place much greater emphasis upon livestock production, from the policy of paying ultimately prices equivalent to those ruling in world markets and from the imposition of a land tax. Notwithstanding various subsidies designed to aid the small farms and geographically less favoured regions, it is the arable interest (for example, on the large farms of East Anglia) that derives the truly unearned income generated by the present price supports and by a production programme which lays unnecessary emphasis on cereals and sugar-beet.

The difficulty is to reconcile a competitive market for British agriculture with the aim of maintaining the proportion of the country's population engaged in the industry. Even given the improvements envisaged earlier it seems likely that many small farms would not be financially viable if required to compete freely with foreign producers. On farms of less than 50–100 acres, depending on the region, unless the land is used for specialized horticultural or fruit farming or as nothing more than a parking place for intensive pig or poultry production, the diseconomies of small-scale production are clearly important and in such circumstances an advanced level of techniques would be inadequate to offset the low labour costs of many foreign producers. On farms with less than 25–50 acres, according to region, these diseconomies will be substantial and any protective price or income support designed to keep them in production would contribute so heavily to farmers' revenues as to make them virtually pensioners of the State. It is not on such terms that one wishes to maintain an agrarian population whose value should rest partly on its economic and political independence.

Farms of size between 25 and 50 acres on the most favoured land and those of between 50 and 100 acres on the least favoured would probably need only small support to ensure their viability as long as they adopted advanced techniques. Therefore it is proposed that a grant be made to all farmers on the smaller farms, excluding the specialist fruit and vegetable farms, with the aim of maintaining the existing number of farms between 25 and 50 acres in the most favoured regions, the size limits being raised according to the declining geographical advantages of districts to a maximum of between 50 and 100 acres. This last size range would cover the marginal farm regions, namely the upland and hill regions of Exmoor, Wales, Northern England and Scotland, where natural conditions require a much more extensive system of cultivation than elsewhere in Britain.[1] It must be stressed: the payment should not constitute a featherbed but be just sufficient to make small farms economically viable as long as producers adopt improved techniques.

Since a few farms larger than the upper size limits specified might need the income support, the payment should be made in amounts decreasing with the size of farm, so that no farmer with more than 75–150 acres, depending on the region, would receive aid. The payment to the farms below the lower size limits would simply be intended to assist the transition of many of the farmers

[1] The problems of many marginal farming areas are not essentially agricultural but arise from the underdeveloped nature of their regional economies. See George Allen in *Town and Country Planning*, May 1956.

concerned out of the industry and of the amalgamation of these intolerably small units. Payment would be integrated with the administration of the proposed land tax, the existence of which would ensure that any payment made to particular farmers not requiring it as an incentive to remain in the industry was recouped by the Exchequer since in such a case the payment would be capitalized back into land values. A *sine qua non* of this proposal would be that small farms would be the first to receive the attention of the proposed regional land planning boards for the regrouping of fragmented holdings and, where appropriate, regional development schemes designed to promote more intensive production.

Given direct income support to farmers with limited acreage our eight objectives are adequately attained except for a minor sacrifice in respect to the last. The final problem is whether there would need to be any interim asistance, given income support to small-scale farmers, while British agriculture was adjusting itself to meeting the free competition of foreign producers. A rapid switch from cereal and milk production to the raising of fat cattle and sheep would be essential and would undoubtedly be speeded up if the proposed Agricultural Credit Bank were required to make interim payments on fatstock production.[1] The payment of income support would cover most of the present marginal producers. If it were found to be insufficient during the period of adjustment to prevent larger farms going out of production interim support would best be given as subsidies to methods and means of production which are likely to secure more intensive use of the fixed factors of production and a switch to greater livestock raising. Probably the subsidy paid for ploughing up land in order to produce temporary grass, at present costing about £10 m., would be the most important. Assuming that British prices would be scaled down gradually to world levels nothing more would seem necessary.

In all, many substantial changes are required in the agricultural

[1] In much the same way as interim payments are made to builders before their work is completed.

legislation of the last ten years, especially that deriving from the Agriculture Acts of 1947–9. The present system of *support* prices must become a system of *guaranteed* prices, the guarantee being against short-term, unforeseen price changes, but not longer-term support of prices above those in world markets. The right of compulsory dispossession should be abandoned but replaced by powers to impose improvements and to charge for them at their economic price. Security of tenure needs to become much less rigid, a return to the legislation operating immediately before the last War being in general sufficient. The various indirect subsidies to low-income producers, those which help all farmers in the less favoured regions irrespective of the individual needs of these farmers or those which cheapen means of production without encouraging a new or more desirable set of production habits, should be abandoned; these include subsidies on lime and fertilizers, differential payments for milk in favour of small-scale producers and the costly subventions for capital investments paid to farmers in the marginal areas. In the place of all this we offer a set of proposals based explicitly on a defined set of social objectives and capable of ensuring that agricultural policy serves the nation's economic interests as at present it manifestly does not.

G. A.

BOOK FOUR

THE INTERNATIONAL SETTING

CHAPTER XII

BRITAIN IN THE WORLD

I. THE PRE-EMINENCE OF FOREIGN POLICY

IT is too often forgotten that the first need of a politician in power is a foreign policy and the means for conducting it. We live in a century which the historian of the future is likely to think of as an age of great wars, characterized by the downfall of states and régimes. Yet the conduct of foreign affairs is ordinarily ignored or at best set aside with the most perfunctory notice in contemporary political discussions. It is not difficult to see why this should be so. But it is important to take account of the fact and it may be profitable to give some attention to the reasons for it. They are of the essence of the political facts of life, at any rate in our own times.

Political action is necessarily directed towards achieving one condition which is the first objective of all politicians and their supporters — namely the attainment of political power. In states where political democracy as we know it is practised, their best tactic is to persuade the majority of the electorate that its own recognizable and immediate interests will best be served by their coming to power. It is in the nature of things that the greater part of the proposals which political contenders set before electorates are concerned with domestic affairs. This being so it is not even very surprising that, with rare exceptions such as are unlikely to occur except in moments of unusual and unusually obvious common peril — as in 1940 — changes of Government are usually brought about as the result of election campaigns or of political crises during which the bulk of the discussion has been of domestic and personal issues.[1] Dr Johnson once epigrammatized the inability of

[1] Cf. D. E. Butler, *The British General Election of 1955* (1955), pp. 74-5.

the ordinary member of society to give more than the least part of his attention to the grave concerns of foreign policy and war by asserting that no news of a military disaster on foreign soil had ever diminished anyone's appetite for a single meal. In these days, when the more conspicuous consequences of an unsuccessful foreign policy are apt to make themselves apparent by way of an explosion in the voter's back garden, it might be supposed that the importance of such matters would be more widely accepted. Yet a glance at the issues which have had most of the attention of voters and candidates in recent General Elections, analyses of candidates' speeches and election manifestoes seem to show that what Johnson believed to be true of the average Englishman of the eighteenth century is still more or less true — at any rate most candidates appear to think so.

Perhaps because self-sufficiency and independence have always been a primary object of the modern Nation-State, its own internal and domestic affairs seem to have an importance which overrides all other considerations to an extent which is certainly very far from being justified by the harsh facts of any imaginable international situation. As a matter of history, whenever it has been safe for a people to pursue their own internal development with little regard for their external circumstances this has been due to fortuitous and temporary factors, largely beyond their control. Thus the Swiss, during the last century and more, have owed their immunity from external dangers to the chance that powers stronger than they would be certain to regard their subjugation as a direct menace to their own security, and to the consequent calculation of potential aggressors that the cost of conquering Switzerland would more than outweigh its advantages. Similarly the people of the United States, for so many of whom during the nineteenth century politics was a matter which 'ended at the sea', found themselves in the fortunate situation of being able to concentrate the whole of their attention and energies upon the development of their own continent. This was because the seas, across which a serious threat to their independence must come, were denied to any possible enemy by the fleets of the United Kingdom in pursuit of a policy which was adopted for British interests alone and of which the immunity of the United States was a by-product. Such an immunity from the preoccupations of foreign affairs and from the heavy burdens, military and other, which an active and effective foreign policy involves has occurred only very rarely in the history of modern states.

It follows that a Liberal administration would, like all of its predecessors recent or remote, find itself obliged to accept as the first charge on its attention the care of British interests in the world at large and the conduct of a foreign policy directed towards this end. It is no doubt one of the ironies of the contemporary situation that the politician, once he has achieved what is always of necessity the first and is not seldom the principal object of his ambition (in the shape of power) is by that very achievement obliged to give his mind to a branch of political activity of which he is likely to have had but an indirect experience and to which he has directed a small part of his attention.

The 'practical politician' of today is thus a man who occupies himself first with the task of persuading his fellow-citizens to vote him into power and who, when he has succeeded in doing so, finds himself confronted with the necessity of conducting the affairs of his country in the vital field of international politics. It is the purpose of this book to concern itself with practical politics in a rather different sense. For us practical politics means those policies which seem likely to stimulate and accelerate the country's development as a liberal society and in the framing of which all likely obstacles and difficulties have been considered but one — that obstacle to which most practical politicians are obliged to give a great deal of weight — the likelihood that they may not immediately commend themselves to the majority of the electorate. We attach an overriding importance to the proper conduct of international policy and to the necessity for educating the public in the importance and realities of foreign policy. We believe too that the pursuit of a foreign policy adequate to the needs and resources of the country will involve the acceptance or the continued acceptance of very heavy burdens and — more original

I

and no less difficult to achieve — the shedding of many long-
cherished and no doubt still exceedingly comforting illusions. In
the light of these things we may be thought fortunate in our
temporary freedom from the obligation to consider more closely
the wishes of the electorate.

2. SOME LIBERAL ILLUSIONS

Surprising though it may be, it is important not to lose sight of
the fact that Liberal thought is deeply historical, more so perhaps
than the thought of either of the other British political Parties.
This is essentially true of thought about foreign policy. In this
respect much 'liberal thinking' is still embedded in ideas and
beliefs which date from the time of the great flowering and pre-
dominance of Liberal thought in the middle of the nineteenth
century. It has for long been all too apparent that the calculation
of the Liberals of a hundred years ago, in these matters, was seriously and often dangerously wrong. Like the Marxists, the early
Liberals were more than merely the proponents of an ideological
view of the nature and prospects of international relations. There
was a powerful prophetic element in their calculations. They believed in an inevitability. They expected that freedom in the sense
of self-determination and free institutions would soon come to
each unit of international society or 'nation' and they believed
that when it did so international peace and co-operation would be
assured. The advantages of altruism would, they thought, be as
readily apparent to the members of the international society as they
were to those of a Quaker conventicle. This attitude was strongly
reinforced by the current economic doctrine, to which there was
scarcely any effective intellectual opposition at the time. The
triumph of the doctrine of economic freedom had coincided with
the peak of British economic ascendancy. This happy state was
thought, among Liberals, to be the result of no especial virtue or
good fortune on the part of the British people other than the
recognition and acceptance of the superior merits, not to say the
ultimate wisdom, of the practice of political and economic freedom.

The Liberal expectation was soon shown to have been wrong. The Cobdenite Liberals, who postulated the existence of the 'economic man' and brought him into their discussions of economic affairs equally, implicitly postulated a 'political man'. There was nothing essentially new in this, and a very large part of what it implied in their belief still has the widest currency among the peoples of the more conspicuously benevolent and satisfied, the less consciously aggrieved and resentful societies — notably of course the British and American but equally the Belgian, Dutch, Scandinavian and Swiss, in fact among the more liberally-minded. The essential constituent of this 'political man', like that of his economic counterpart, was held to be his need for freedom. It was thought certain that if he were given his freedom he would develop his talents and pursue his own happiness in a manner which could only serve to increase the happiness of his fellows — free from the embarrassment of all mutual rivalry and competition except, of course, the indispensable competition of the free economy, upon which his prosperity was supposed to depend.

Moreover, for the Liberal thinkers of the nineteenth century, and for the great majority of those people who create the public opinion with which the Foreign Secretary of today has to reckon, international society is composed of a number of corporate 'political men' — the Nation-States — and of a further, progressively decreasing, group composed of the still dependent States which are not yet regarded — whatever they themselves might think about it — as having reached a sufficient degree of maturity for them to be accorded the independent status which goes with political manhood. Behaviour as a member of such society — foreign policy — is necessarily conditioned by a belief, conscious or not, about the nature of the society and of the units of which it is composed. Whether they know or not, those members of the electorate who have the least awareness of the existence of a problem of international relations have a doctrine of man which they apply to the units of international society. It has been the great weakness of the foreign policies of the democracies in time of peace that their international doctrine has been based on the in-

dividual's experience of men in a law-abiding and law-enforcing
society to which the international society does not correspond.

3. THE NEED FOR ADAPTABILITY

Given the essential facts of the international situation we must
consider what should be the foreign policy of a British Government.

The basic miscalculation of the classical nineteenth-century
Liberal was his assumption that the international society resembled
in all essentials the law-abiding domestic society which was the
background of his individual experience. A Liberal Foreign Secretary must base his policy on the recognition that this is false.
Nations advance their purposes by the acquisition and exercise of
power and influence, and one principal duty of a Foreign Secretary
must be the maintenance and extension of British power and influence. But, for Liberals at least, these things are not ends in
themselves. Rather they are essential practical means to an ideal
ethical end — namely to bring about in the international society
such changes as will cause it to resemble more closely the law-
abiding societies of those states upon analogy with which the
early Liberals based their misconception. Situations change and
with them the dangers and needs of the moment. The 'pattern of
alliances' is itself a changing thing. There is at present no prospect
of survival for the purely pacific State, certainly not for a rich
State and one worth plundering such as Britain is. Indeed there
would be in all probability no pacifists at all if it were not for the
existence of some societies so much wedded to the principle of
individual freedom that the majority of their citizens have been
prepared, if necessary, to fight in order to preserve a state of affairs
in which the individual pacifist might practise and propagate his
beliefs.

Twenty years ago the most serious danger to this Liberal way
of life — and to Britain — came from Nazi Germany. By this
reasoning the interests of both British independence and Liberal
principles were best served by taking advantage of the fact that the

very different and illiberal interests and principles of the rulers of the Soviet Union were equally in jeopardy from Germany — and so our alliance with the U.S.S.R. Today the overriding fear is of the U.S.S.R. and of the system or conspiracy of which it is the moving force. It is a fear which seems to be justified by all the indications, but the circumstances of international politics are rarely so permanent as they seem. Thus it appears likely to be merely a matter of time before China outweighs her Soviet partner in the resources which make for power. On the other hand it should not be taken for granted that the full recognition of this, when it comes about, will be followed merely by the substitution of Chinese for Soviet leadership in the Communist half of the world. A split between the U.S.S.R. and China and a complete transformation of the world power situation would be by no means out of the question. Further, the world ideological situation may also be transformed. Suppose that the Central Committee of the Soviet Communist Party, as well they may, move towards ever greater moderation, while the Chinese remain — what they actually are as we go to press — rigidly Stalinist, and allied with a reactionary, nationalist Japan? Then our whole moral view of the world would be altered too. But for the present and for the more immediate future at least, the situation is dominated by the existence of the two gigantic blocs of which the U.S.S.R. and the United States are the leaders.

4. BRITISH NEUTRALISM?

For Britain, in these circumstances, a policy of neutralism would not be practicable or safe even if, which especially for Liberals is very much more than doubtful, it could be justified on any ground of principle. The strategic and industrial importance of her metropolitan and some of her overseas territories would soon involve their absorption by one or the other of the contending parties in a global war. Nor, since the conflict between East and West is still substantially an ideological and even a moral one, can the British people be said to be intellectually and emotionally

capable of 'non-involvement'. But alignment with the United
States does not necessarily mean subordination to the policies and
requirements of Washington. There have always been grades of
powers possessed of more or less freedom of action and choice
within the circumstances of their situation and resources. The
fact that two powers now so far overshadow all the others and
have gathered most of the others around them into separate camps
does not necessarily involve their allies in the dependent rôle of
satellites. There is plenty of evidence to show that even in the
Communist camp the separate states continue to represent genuine and separate political entities. West or East of the 'Iron Curtain'
national feeling is a powerful political sentiment and the demand
common to all who share it is for an independent administration.

Britain's policy in this situation must be to recognize the
strength of this sentiment and to pursue a policy based upon this
recognition. Her alliance with the United States is fundamental. It
is an association in which the dictates of necessity coincide — as
they did not, for example, in the war-time alliance with the
U.S.S.R. — with the broad community of ideals and political
principles so obvious that the necessities themselves are often
overlooked. They arise not so much because of the division of the
world — however temporarily — into two camps makes it likely
that even comparative safety can only be achieved by adherence
to one of them. It is not certain that for all nations this is so. But
the United Kingdom owes its present influence and its ability to
support a population of fifty millions to the fact that it once enjoyed the command of the seas — and since it no longer does so it
is dependent in the last analysis upon those who do. It may be no
more than chance that political liberty and naval power have continued to go together — but it is a fortunate chance for liberally-
minded Englishmen.

To abdicate what remains of British 'Great Power' status in the
hope of enjoying what appear to some publicists as the quiet and
comfort of the rôle of an outsize Switzerland might or might not
entail economic suicide for the swollen population of the British
Isles. It would certainly mean the surrender of responsibilities and

the rejection of our principal means of influencing the future course of international political development — namely the conservation and the principled use of the power Britain has. Alliance even between powers of disproportionate strength need not involve the entire dependence of one of them. And since it is an axiom of political freedom that dependence is not an ideal state for either of the parties concerned it follows that it is the duty of any British Government to acquire and exercise as much power as it is able. It follows too that the Conservative Government was right in deciding to develop the thermo-nuclear weapon just as its Labour predecessor was right to make the atomic bomb.

5. THE IMPERIALIST HANGOVER

The translation of Liberal principles into action in the field of international relation has suffered, as we have seen, from a refusal to face the facts of international society in an age of sovereign states and from the aversion which most reasonable people feel to the use of force and even to the existence of the instruments and habit of mind which make its use possible. Foreign policy in the democracies has also suffered much from the refusal even of those whose doctrine has been one of trusting the people to present the people with the plain, and often disagreeable, facts and to trust them. It has too often oscillated between the two poles of electoral attraction: pacifism and jingo-like bellicosity; finding a not very glorious and sometimes nearly disastrous expression in a desire to appease the strong — as Nazi Germany — and to get tough with the weak. If it is important to persuade the electorate to accept the realities and necessities of the power situation it is scarcely less so to make sure that they are not deceived by the superficial reassurance to be derived from a policy of merely 'getting tough'.

The decisions to make the atomic and hydrogen bombs were in fact decisions not to surrender the status and opportunities which go with being a major power. The advantages to be expected of them are, first, the power in time of war of striking at targets from which might be apprehended a danger mortal to Britain but not to

her ally; and second — and scarcely less important, indeed not less
important at all if the hope that the accumulation of thermo-
nuclear weapons might prove an effective deterrent to major war
should prove to be a just one — it will enable her to participate in
an altogether different way from that enjoyed by her other
European allies in the framing of the collective policies of the
alliance.

But the rôle of a great power is far from being the same as it has
been and as many people still expect it to be. Almost the last thing
that can safely be said about British foreign policy is that it should
follow a line of no change. In particular we must expose the fallacies of the alleged dilemma between near-pacifism and imperialism which is the form in which the choice of possible foreign
policies has too often been presented to the electorate. Quite apart
from matters of principle which, especially in the case of a Liberal
administration, must be seriously considered, an empire or aggregation of different nationalities can have no secure place, other
than as a voluntary association, in a policy founded upon the recognition of the force of national feeling. It follows that to conduct
a satisfactory British foreign policy our rulers must disabuse themselves of the more pervasive and persistent elements of the imperial
illusion which has played so large a part in soothing the con-
sciences of the British upper classes and in persuading the electorate to accept the burden inseparable from the pursuit of a strong
foreign policy. This is not to say that the achievements of British
imperialism have not been real and often beneficial ones. But it can
hardly be denied that the British recollection of these achievements and of these entirely praiseworthy purposes is a positive
handicap to the successful pursuit of a contemporary foreign
policy. Chiefly perhaps because Liberalism has taught the British
people to look for moral principle as well as the care of purely
national interests in their policies, there is still a good deal of hum-
bug in the conduct of British relations with lesser and weaker
states. Thus, while it is no doubt true that the British during the
second World War preserved Egypt from the disadvantages of a
German occupation, it is quite untrue — and quite plainly untrue

— to represent this as having been anything but a minor purpose of the campaign. Britain defended Egypt because to do so in the circumstances of the time was held to be an important contribution to the achievement of the overriding British interest of the the time, namely the military defeat of Germany. Similarly, the original occupation of Egypt in 1882 was undertaken — much against its own inclination, by a Liberal Government — because from a purely British point of view there was no other sensible course. The benefits which Egypt derived from the period of effective British rule that followed were real, but they were the by-product and not the purpose of the British position in the country. It is a psychological necessity for successful dealing with the Egypt of today that this plain fact should be plainly stated.

The same reality of British interests and the same cloud of self-deception and misrepresentation exist today in respect of Britain's vital interests in the strategically important and oil-bearing lands of the Middle East. Most of the countries of which it is composed are now independent states with interests and ambitions of their own. It is well to remind ourselves that the first political duty of a foreign statesman, even of one who rules over what was once in effect a British possession, is to his own people, and moreover that it is a condition of his continuing to rule that he succeeds in convincing his people that he is successfully fulfilling his duty. The approach of British policy to the governments of lands, such as those in the Middle East, in which Britain has important interests might with advantage be made more like that of the individual politician in his relationship with his constituents.

It is in this connection that an adaptation suitable to contemporary circumstances of the concept of the 'political man' as applied to the units of international society might prove fruitful. In the past century and a half most rulers have learned to maintain their position and to seek their ends by securing the consent, or at least by avoiding too great a measure of the active opposition, of their fellow-countrymen. They do this largely by seeking to establish the belief that they are pursuing the interest of their fellow-countrymen. It would be well if those charged with the

12

conduct of British foreign policy could persuade themselves to regard the nations and colonies with which they have to deal in something of the same way as a politician regards the electorate as a whole. In so doing they would need to remember that the two most powerful forces at work in the contemporary world outside Europe are the sentiment of nationalism, always strong and all too easily strengthened by seeming opposition or disparagement, and the desire for material betterment which now amounts among the non-white peoples, as it has long done among the British electorate, to an expectation and a right. A conflict with national feeling is sometimes inevitable. But it should be avoided with no less care than politicians have learned to take in domestic affairs to avoid conflict with a church or with a trade union. The expectation of a rising standard of living and of the progressive elimination of conspicuous disparity of personal fortunes is a characteristic of modern European and American men which is rapidly becoming characteristic too of the rest of mankind. It is an expectation to which domestic politicians have long learned to pay conspicuous attention. It would be as well to pay comparable attention to the conspicuous difference between the living standard of even the least fortunate Englishman and the great majority of the world's peoples.

6. THE SACRIFICE OF SOVEREIGNTY

A realistic view of foreigners and foreign affairs, and a preparedness to make H-bombs and wage cold wars, do not in the least exclude idealism or imply selfish and aggressive nationalism. In modern diplomatic conditions idealism *is* realism. It was often so in the past, too: consider how much in Britain's selfish interests, well considered, it was to support the League of Nations.

'How many divisions has the Pope?' asked Stalin. The answer was, of course, an uncertain but very large number. In the same sense the movements for world government and above all European unity have 'many divisions'. If a sufficient number, even of woolly idealists, are discontented with the notion of national

sovereignty, national sovereignty is *eo ipso* less desirable. Fewer
soldiers will fight for it and more allies will be won by supporting
supra-national bodies.

It is the object of the Liberal State in foreign policy to protect
Liberalism, not the State. The existence of states is or ought to be
a mere device to that end. If, owing to a widespread change in
human ideals, a supra-national body looks as if it could better discharge the function of protecting Liberalism than any State, then
it is the duty of the Liberal State to liquidate itself. But realism is
necessary in examining the claims of the supra-national body to
permanence, efficiency and reliable Liberalism; always remembering of course that the adherence of any State would vastly
strengthen it.

In fact considerable scepticism is called for in examining the
existing or proposed supra-national bodies that are candidates for
the great privilege of absorbing our sovereignty. Engagements between states have a disconcerting tendency to be entered into *ad
hoc* (or even occasionally *ad hominem*) rather than in the light of
such larger-term and more ideal considerations as Liberals would
rightly prefer. Of such necessities were born the militarily reasonable yet ideologically incongruous Anglo-Russian Agreement of
1907 and the Anglo-Soviet treaty of 1941. Necessity makes for
uncongenial bedfellows and the liaisons of international affairs are
notoriously temporary. However since the end of the second
World War diplomatic regroupings have assumed a more logically satisfying because a more ideologically coherent shape.
Common fear of the frankly illiberal Communist states has drawn
most of the liberal states of Europe, along with the United States
of America, into an unprecedentedly close association with one
another.

Take first the North Atlantic Treaty Organization. This is
clearly composed for the most part of nations so like-minded that
it would be the plain duty of a Liberal Government to encourage it
to develop into an association with more long-term aims and
likely as such to survive the overriding fear of Soviet Russia. But
it is unlikely to develop very far, so long as U.S. public opinion

remains isolationist in many minor matters and strongly opposed
to sacrifices of sovereignty. Further, we may doubt whether it is
wise, if our object is to preserve a liberal Britain, to place our internal affairs at the mercy of such powerful and unstable bodies as
the American electorate and Congress. France, Italy and possibly
also Germany are unstable, but they are quite unlikely to veer in
the same direction at the same time. In a united Europe they would
be checks on each other and we their highly respected and powerful colleague. An access of isolationism, deflationism or McCarthy-
ism in U.S.A. would be less manageable than the large Communist minorities of France and Italy or the understandable irredent-
ism of Germany.

More immediately susceptible to positive action than NATO,
perhaps, are the liberal-democratic states which form the greater
part of Western Europe. The advocates of European Union are
today propounding a doctrine for which there appears to be the
unusual combination of good short-term and long-term arguments. The argument of the relatively short run is similar to that
for NATO. But there seems, too, to be some prospect that practical political and economic expression might be given to the
many ideas and aspirations which the European democracies continue to have in common — and of which perhaps their peoples
are more keenly aware than ever before, in spite of the effect of
some 400 years during which the most conspicuous characteristic
of European society has been its political fragmentation. Most of
the qualities they have in common are thoroughly congenial to
Liberals — Parliamentary government, respect for the individual,
freedom of speech, the rule of law and the rest — and no Liberal
Government could fail to use the present opportunity to give this
high degree of common belief and practice more and more expression in common institutions.

The opportunity is great and must be accepted, but the task is
not an easy one nor is the precise means to its accomplishment at
all clear. The melancholy fact is that neither Conservative nor
Labour opinion in this country is at all favourable. Europe was
ever a purely Liberal cause. Conservatives and Socialists who look

abroad at all look to the English-speaking world. They urge that closer ties with Europe are incompatible even with our present relations with the Commonwealth; but in fact it is not true that any other Commonwealth Government wants us to keep clear of Europe, nor is there, when we come to a hard-headed examination of practical details, any contradiction or even difficulty in our simultaneous membership of both clubs. In particular Imperial Preference — not much liked by our sister States but emotionally important in this country — can be combined with European free trade. True, if we were to let West European goods in free we could not give Commonwealth exports preference over them — the latter could not have lower than zero tariffs. But Commonwealth preference over all other imports would still be possible. As for our exports to the Commonwealth a *certificate of origin* could be appended to each export: if it were a genuine British good it would pay the preferential tariff, whereas if it originated on the Continent and were trying to creep in *via* Britain it would have to pay the full tariff.

Nevertheless public opinion would need a great deal of persuasion before a British Government could enter any sort of European political union with enough popular support to make its action anything but an empty gesture. In particular, many British business men and trade unionists would have to be coaxed out of their fears that the peoples of Europe are too much addicted to the practices—admirable rather than endearing—of uninhibited competition and unrestricted labour. A Liberal policy with regard to *internal* restrictions and monopolies (cf. Chapter X above), would have just this effect on the climate of British economic thought and make European free trade far more acceptable.

Yet, if the difficulties are great, so is the prize; and a Liberal Government would be bound to undertake the double task of educating opinion at home and exploiting such opportunities abroad. Almost any step in this direction would, of course, involve some surrender of sovereignty. But so does the signature of any international treaty and adherence to, for example, NATO and UNO. A most obvious field for practical co-operation is in our relations with dependent or recently dependent territories. A concerted policy towards their colonies and towards once-dependent states such as those of the Middle East would — if it were conceived in a liberal spirit — enable the European states to bring greater resources to bear upon their development and to exercise a greater understanding and tolerance — born of a sense of strength — in their dealings with them. It would be an immense advantage to Britain as well as the colonial powers of continental Europe to be freed, by virtue of a real strength and unity, and of a common and genuinely liberal policy, from the frustrating and undignified concern for prestige. Not least would we benefit by being able each in turn to restrain the other from emotional excesses when, as will necessarily happen, the historical pride of one particular power is flouted. It has been comical recently to observe how in turn Britain and France restrain U.S.A. over Formosa, U.S.A. and France restrain Britain over Cyprus, U.S.A. both the others over Suez, all three restrain Holland over Indonesia, etc. These controls need systematizing.

Of course our Commonwealth connexions are quite as valuable as the new European connexions we should form. Since they are, to repeat, in no way incompatible, and since the Commonwealth is dealt with in the next chapter, we say no more about it here. Its importance is not at all to be judged by the small space it takes up in this chapter.

A Liberal Government would regard UNO with the respect due to the only institution apparently capable of being developed into an instrument of a world-wide rule of law. In principle it would be prepared to surrender some elements of national sovereignty whenever it appeared that it could thereby bring such a rule of law nearer and so promote the most vital interest of Britain herself. The very comprehensiveness of UNO, which is the reason for its relative lack of homogeneity, is its principal merit. It differs from other and lesser international organizations in that it is essentially a meeting-place for diverse and opposed interests and as such it must be purged of all exclusiveness — notably in the matter of Chinese membership. But obviously a body full of the representatives of Communist and other dictatorial governments is not one to which we could yet sacrifice any vital elements of sovereignty. UNO — or rather some of the régimes represented in it — must undergo radical change before we could do so.

7. PAX URANICA

It cannot be very long before the powers which today possess atomic weapons will be faced with the urgent necessity for a major decision of policy. In the nature of things their monopoly of these weapons will not remain unbroken unless they are prepared, *jointly*, to take steps to see that it does so. The source of the relaxation in international tension early in 1956 was the knowledge that the major powers are at or near the point of mutual destruction (and perhaps incidentally of world-wide destruction) in such weapons, and the belief that their governments are sufficiently hard-headed to be restrained by this thought. But a growing number of states possessing these weapons will increase the danger of — and perhaps make likely — the emergence of a ruler with less cool nerves and less to lose, one who would be willing to endanger the existence of his own people and perhaps that of humanity on some such principle as that of *Weltmacht* (or the Oder-Neisse line, or the Gaza Strip or British Honduras) *oder Niedergang*. It should be British policy to encourage the H-bomb powers to prevent by whatever means they may have the more widespread possession of these weapons. Even if they were to agree to the Soviet proposal for the abolition of such weapons it would be necessary to make sure that other states did not acquire them. In any such transactions the UNO would be the proper point of contact between the thermo-nuclear 'haves' and 'have-nots'.

We have implicitly made a bold prophecy: across the enmity and tension that is bound to subsist between liberal and Communist nations — it would be immoral were we to relax it — there will be more and more practical and intimate co-operation between the U.S.S.R., U.S.A. and Great Britain. Their common interests as atomic powers and capital exporters will force them to work together. We are constantly told that there is economic competition between the two blocs; competition leads to gentlemen's agreements. Where the sacrifice of sovereignty to even a quasi-Communist power would be betrayal, there is nothing immoral about such agreements as these. Quite the contrary, they all help to hasten the disintegration of the Communist bloc which is the only ultimate hope for world peace. Even an Anglo-Soviet consortium for some large project in (say) India is possible; it should even be an aim of our policy to bring it about.

8. FOREIGN INVESTMENT

All this emphasizes that the ends of foreign policy are not always best achieved by the possession of military force. Hitherto the exercise of influence in international affairs has depended upon the possession of armed strength, of sovereignty — to be bartered for allies by way of treaties — and the less definable but real and perhaps growing factor of ideology and sentiment. To these must now be added the power to aid both financially and technologically the 'underdeveloped' peoples. Such peoples are increasingly aware and resentful of their relative poverty and are convinced, for the first time in history, that their lot could, and therefore should, be progressively improved. The resentment which they show towards their own governments when they are dissatisfied can be all too readily redirected against the Western powers in the form of nationalism or 'anti-colonialism', however unjustly. Popular hostility has already led to the abandonment of some strategically important bases and has undoubtedly reduced the potential usefulness of others. Where such feeling can be attributed to the consciousness of a low standard of living it should be our policy to improve that standard rather than to strengthen the police force.

Nor should we look for gratitude if, at considerable expense to ourselves, we succeed in contributing to a rising standard of life in the Orient and elsewhere. The motive of such expenditure will be not only benevolence but also self-interest which is none the less so for being enlightened; and it is as self-interested alone, let us always remember, that our actions will be regarded. The rendering of aid may actually create ingratitude in particular circumstances and render the recipient more hostile than before. We have not recommended that Britain render aid, but that she put herself in a position to do so. If foreigners know we have capital to spare we shall have influence even if they do not actually borrow it. In just the same way no country needs to use its H-bombs; it needs to have them. Expenditure of this kind should properly be regarded in the same light as expenditure upon armaments. If a Conservative Government was right to order the development of the thermo-nuclear weapon, the Labour Leader of the Opposition was equally right in principle to suggest the setting aside of 1% of the national income for use in underdeveloped territories. Though aid to the poor ought primarily to be a matter of Christian charity it would be hypocrisy to deny its secondary effect; a well-conceived expenditure on 'aid' might often make unnecessary a greater expenditure on arms.

Considerations of this kind bring us to the final question: what place has an analysis of foreign affairs in a study of the Liberal Welfare State? The basic answer is simple: to have no foreign policy, with all that this implies, would leave us very little Welfare and perhaps no State at all. To survive in the short term the British Welfare State, whose citizens are, in world terms, highly privileged both politically and economically, must be able to defend itself. In the long term it must ensure that its privileges are progressively less exclusive. It must deliberately seek an improving standard of living, as well as the rule of law, throughout the world. For this we need not only the right policy but a good deal of money to spend in its pursuit. It is a commonplace that productivity is the key to domestic prosperity. It is no less true that it affords the instruments of a successful foreign policy. Plentiful fruits of industry are no less essential to British security today than were our armaments in the second World War. If the 'world is to be made safe for democracy' Britain must have an export surplus. Some of it, admittedly, can come from a reduction in arms expenditure — for we have seen that leaving all generosity aside 'aid' can be a substitute for arms. But much, surely, must come from our voluntary savings or from taxes. We cannot avoid having a foreign policy and we must pay for it.

H. S. D.

CHAPTER XIII

COLONIES TO
COMMONWEALTH

IT is sometimes proudly claimed that British colonial policy is bi-partisan, implying that the tide of its principles rolls on irrespective of whether the Government in power is Conservative or Labour. It might rather be said, not wholly cynically, that British colonial policy is such an agglomeration of platitudes that it does not matter which Party is in power: they will both recite the regulation incantations as they lurch from crisis to expedient, taking nourishment occasionally by eating their words.

Both these views contain elements of truth. The basis of bi-partisan policy is proven principle, but on the one hand principle is not consistently regarded and, on the other, some of it has become little better than a shelter in which the well-meaning take refuge from the storms of a bewildering world. The result, as Miss Margery Perham has described it, is that 'we are ... finding ourselves obliged to make concessions we never meant to make so soon. We yield to pressures without fully understanding what they are or where they come from. We claim — but it is only a half-truth — that what is happening is merely the fulfilment of our own policy and promises. We preside with a fair measure of dignity and good-will over these uncomfortable processes of decolonization.' Hoist only too often by the petard of our own virtues, when the very civil liberties we bestowed are directed against us we jettison our 'careful, leisurely programmes', and face our dilemmas with divided minds, conscious simultaneously of our undeniably good intentions and of our failure 'to match the dynamic urge of the times'. That in the event we do no worse than we do 'is to the credit of our adaptability and also to the high quality of our agents in the Colonies'.[1]

The object of this chapter is to discover whether Liberal policy can offer a better prospect than presidency over the lingering dissolution of a great legal, political and humanitarian system — lingering because, like Byzantium in the era of its dissolution, we command the finest administrative service the world has ever seen.

I. THE LIBERAL ATTITUDE

Liberal policy is not absolved from dealing in platitudes — or principles, according to one's viewpoint. The following is a digest of post-war resolutions at Liberal Assemblies.

Those elements which may be called bi-partisan or, in this context, tri-partisan, are:

(i) That the overriding aim of British policy is to train dependent peoples for full responsible self-government, subject to satisfaction of the requirement that the future and interests of all elements of the populations concerned shall be safeguarded;

(ii) That racial and religious discrimination is totally rejected by Her Majesty's Government;

(iii) That modern scientific and technical knowledge be put to the service of colonial territories, to develop their natural resources, agriculture and industry and to raise the standard of living of the inhabitants; and

(iv) That our civil liberties (equality before the law, right of free speech, free press, association and so forth) shall be bestowed upon the indigenous inhabitants of dependent territories.

Many of the methods advocated are also generally accepted by all Parties: development of local government institutions as an apprenticeship for self-government; development of the social

[1] 'Britain's Response to the End of Colonialism', *Listener*, 30 December 1954.

services, especially education and health; recognition of the dangers of the impact of 'modern' techniques, etc., on backward societies. One comes upon a few loose phrases about native aspirations and progressive devolution of power and authority to colonial Governments — dangerous because they have a comfortingly generous sound which tends to divert attention from close examination of specific and possibly sectional aspirations and the composition of the Governments on which authority is to be devolved.

In general terms, however, these statements add up to a classical doctrine of trusteeship with, perhaps, not much reference so far to the duality of the mandate; and as principles they are unexceptionable. There might be a certain amount of acid entertainment to be had by 'debunking' them with the help of modern (and, for that matter, historical) instances; but, as Professor Sir Charles Webster has cogently remarked, the cumulative effect of debunking is to render its practitioners incapable of constructive thought. It is more important to ask: where do we go from here? The Liberals have gone further, and do not in fact neglect the duality of the mandate of trusteeship. It is at this point that they part company decisively with the other two Parties, as the following extracts show:

'The Liberal Party, holding that Colonial dependencies are held in trust in the interests, firstly, of the indigenous inhabitants, and secondly, of the rest of the civilized world....

RECOMMENDS ... the encouragement of such industries as can in the circumstances of each territory be calculated to maintain themselves without fiscal protection....

REAFFIRMS the Party's traditional adherence to the policy of the Open Door, and condemns the imposition on any Colony of a fiscal system not designed in its interests' (1947).

In short, it aligns itself with Lord Lugard's forthright declaration of 'the principle that a trustee Power is not justified in arbitrarily restricting the markets of its ward'.[1]

These declarations, especially in conjunction with Liberal statements about civil liberties and racial and legal equality, imply a

[1] The Dual Mandate in British Tropical Africa (1922), p. 268.

recognition of something which, for a generation, few have dared
to assert aloud: namely, the paramountcy of the interests of the
indigenous inhabitants. In a situation bedevilled by the problems
of plural societies, an overt declaration on paramountcy only appears straightforward and is, in fact, ambiguous. But Liberal
declarations are mercifully free of another ambiguity: that blessed
word *partnership*. Instead, they stand firmly upon the principle of
consent — of the governed, of whom the great majority are indigenous.

2. MODERN INSTANCES

Resolutions prepared for Liberal Assemblies, however, afford
little more than an outline of policy. The test lies in filling in the
details. Will they conform to, or violate, the outline — or even
show the outline itself to be invalid? How much farther do such
more detailed proposals as may be contained in Liberal resolutions carry the development of policy? To afford some answer to
these questions it is necessary to set out and examine those pressures to which, as Miss Perham has said, we yield without fully
understanding their nature or origin.

Certain observations on the origin of these pressures are hardly
open to dispute, but perhaps should be made as a preliminary to
further analysis. The White Man's world has let loose on societies
which may be either primitive and tribal (as in most of Africa and
the Pacific) or rigid and hierarchical (as in parts of Asia) the impact of Western money economy, technology and science. In
addition, the British in particular have been missionaries not only
of a strongly protestant religion but, with equal conviction, of a
form of parliamentary democracy which has carried with it a
peculiar and largely uncodified legal system; and of their own code
of commercial morality and enterprise. The British mission was
not so much fervent as inevitable. It was fortified by domestic
experience and by the visible success of the political system in
Canada, Australia and New Zealand and, latterly, to a notable
degree, in Ceylon, Pakistan and India; by the fertility, adaptability

and pervasiveness of the Common Law; and by the results of commercial expansion in terms of the standard of living. The point is, however, that the economic and political-legal impact was not, for the colonial territories, softened by generations of apprenticeship to the methods involved. The capacity for adaptation and compromise, slowly built up in the West, had no time to grow. The social order of centuries, despite the protection of devices such as indirect rule, began to crumble.

The above, though brief and telescoped, is fact. In interpreting it, we do not hesitate to challenge the carping of critics. Not *all* the consequences of the impact were evil. On the contrary, the bulk of them were beneficial. Slavery and the slave trade were abolished. 'Peace, prosperity and justice without parallel were secured to the inhabitants'.[1] 'A criminal law common to all persons without distinction; a personal and civil law in accordance with everyone's particular traditions; a judicial machinery organized regardless of cost so as to make legal remedy available to practically every person in the land; relief and amelioration measures on a gigantic scale to grapple with famines to which India is so frequently liable; curative and preventive medical work to reach the ordinary ills as well as the emergency needs of a population as large as that of Europe (barring Russia); an ever-increasing supply of schools and teachers to overtake illiteracy . . . ; it is no exaggeration to say that each one of these lines of "official service" really implies an expenditure of human worth and personality the recounting of which would be more fascinating than a romance. . . . The Sircar is here, there, and everywhere. Its long arm can be touched wherever you are.'[2] If the old order crumbled, it was high time in many cases, as may be judged from the accounts of pioneer explorers.[3]

[1] Quoted from the protest sent to the Colonial Office in 1930 by the inhabitants of the 300 villages of Wei-hai-Wei when they learned that the British were to cede the settlement back to China.

[2] K. T. Paul, *The British Connection with India* (1927), p. 29. The author was an Indian nationalist.

[3] See, e.g., M. Perham and J. Simmons, *African Discovery: an Anthology of Exploration* (1942).

The 'my country always wrong' school is in its way as fatuous as
the Blimps and even drearier.

Nevertheless our failures in recent years 'to match the dynamic
urge of the times' stick out of the record of achievement like sore
thumbs. But are they so numerous in fact as the sound and fury of
the tale of British sins would make them seem? It is true that there
are embryo Harlems in Brixton and Birmingham because poverty
and unemployment are endemic to the economies of West Indian
islands. We have had crises of personalities in Bechuanaland and
Uganda because of ham-handed fumbling. We have a nationalistic
crisis in Cyprus because of early neglect and later lack of constructive imagination — and because of an intransigeant political pre-
late. We have launched an experiment in Central Africa of vast
potentialities, in which the evil may break through the tenuous
safeguards of the good because we denied the principle of the consent of the governed. We have suspended the constitution of
British Guiana — because we tried to remedy past indifference by
an act of faith? And we have an 'emergency' in Malaya — because
we failed to create a visible identity of interest between government and governed or because Pearl Harbour prepared the way
for Mao-tse-Tung's rule in China.

Some of these cases are special because they concern 'plural
societies', whose problems are peculiarly intractable even to the
most enlightened and liberal policy.[1] In a number of these difficult
cases the genesis of plural societies preceded the British. There
were probably Chinese in Malaya and the East Indian archipelago
in the twelfth century; Indian Tamils in Ceylon and Arabs on the
East African coast pre-dated the British. But responsibility for the
ubiquitous presence of Indian settlers from Entebbe to Fiji lies
mainly on the old system of importation of indentured labour,

[1] Sir Keith Hancock prefers to call the condition of intractability 'com-
munalism', but possibly 'plural society' is less prone to confusion with
'Communism'. A 'plural society' is an aggregation of communities of different race, religion, language and culture, living side by side in the same territory but never mingling or fusing. Moreover, no 'plural society' is exactly
like another, and all have their differing problems.

and partly on the freedom of movement accorded to British subjects ('old style') within British possessions. The creation of settlements of White Britons is, by definition, our work.

Of all the problems in the Commonwealth, that of progress towards self-government in plural societies is the hardest to solve, because where there is no community of purpose, outlook and will it cannot be imposed. A long-term effort to create a civic sense and social cohesion has to be combined with short-term safeguards for the rights of the different sections, and the latter may delay, or even conflict with, the former.

3. THE PSYCHOLOGICAL CHALLENGE

We submit that, despite undoubted historical and economic causes, the nature of our present failures is largely psychological, and psychological in two aspects.

On the one hand, communities recently 'liberated from the colonial yoke' (as they would express it), or on the verge of independence, are intoxicated and obsessed with this concept of 'liberation'. The intoxication vents itself in acute and inflammatory nationalism, at a time when the more mature nations tend to reject nationalism as a sin against international society. People in a condition of intoxication do not form cool judgments or see far ahead. They are profoundly impatient of Britain's 'careful, leisurely programmes' and blind to their merits. They are indifferent to what the West calls 'the Communist threat' because it threatens nothing they think they want. They ignore the economic penalties inherent in the fulfilment of their desires — no new phenomenon this, for cutting off one's economic nose in the pursuit of political face-lifting is a commonplace of history. Their attitude is Lord Hailey's in reverse: we offer them bread but they ask for a vote.[1]

[1] Lord Hailey, *The Position of Colonies in a Commonwealth of Nations* (1941), p. 41: 'In building up a political future, the stunted body is no less an obstacle than the dwarfed mind, and ... we should not give our native populations cause to complain that when they had asked for bread, we offered them a vote.'

The vocal nationalists are usually a small number, compared to the population of any territory. Doubtless there are among them the Nehrus and Tshekedis of the future, as well as the Bustamantes and the Jagans. We forget too easily that the men and the situations have had their parallels in our own history. For the time being they are apt to appear to the harassed colonial Power and its servants as blatantly irresponsible persons commanding the demagogic arts of invective, emotionalism and ridicule, too ignorant to appreciate that they may encompass nothing but destruction of the work of 'Government', but clever enough to twist half-truths and whole lies into a scourge for authority. Those who would cooperate with government receive their special flagellation as 'imperialist stooges'; and the concessions of authority are held in contempt as symptoms of weakness. In plural societies, the situation is further complicated by the manoeuvrings of rival communities trying to ensure that the heritage of power falls to themselves.

The second aspect of psychological failure concerns the British themselves. In 1875, Alexander Mackay of Uganda wrote: 'My heart burns to rescue Africa from the Slave Trade.' What young man would dare to write that now? One does not doubt that hearts still burn — to rescue Africa from soil erosion, hook-worm and *apartheid*. But the simplicity and readily comprehensible appeal of a crusade against a visible enemy is no longer with us. The British public, bewildered by the bitter rejection of their honest endeavours, does not support today's crusaders as it supported Livingstone. 'The British have allowed themselves to be fooled by the propaganda against propaganda. They have not dared to speak up for themselves for fear they might be accused of sordid and sinister aggression upon free public opinion. They have kept silent while their enemies damaged the prestige of their national life and their imperial record. Honest men have unwittingly aided this dishonest campaign.'[1] So have dishonest men. The concept of the 'civilizing mission' was condemned in ridicule along with Mussolini, so that one scarcely dares to write the words, still less defend the validity of the idea.

[1] W. K. Hancock, *Argument of Empire* (Penguin Special, 1943), p. 22.

There are more serious sides to this psychological retreat than lack of self-confidence. From a domestic scene curiously compounded of full employment and material emulation intermittently overshadowed by crisis, few are prepared to set forth on a life of uncertain rewards and almost certain ingratitude.[1] The numbers and quality of the Oversea Service may well be in danger. Lack of confidence has also affected the British sense of mission, and produced a negative attitude and policy, notably since the 1920's. This negativism is probably a major cause of the emergence of the so-called bi-partisan colonial policy, which at its best is deficient in dynamism and at its worst almost amounts to abdication.

But far worse is the plain fear that too obviously governs many European minds, especially in Africa. It gives rise to what has been aptly called 'a psychology of siege'[2] and is the tap-root of *apartheid*, as it was of the 'civilized labour' policy of the Union of South Africa in the 1920's. The white man, victim of this fear, visualizes himself as the defender of his 'way of life' — which he identifies with 'Western civilization' — against the double threat inherent in the political enfranchizement and economic advancement of the native. It is the threat of being engulfed by what was once called 'the rising tide of colour' and, in many Europeans' eyes, a sheer question of survival on which no compromise is possible as you cannot compromise with death. The nearer the European may be to the African or Indian level (that is, the 'poor white'), the nearer is he to that death, and for the sake of white solidarity he has to be supported by measures with which the more successful white man could dispense and which create a caste system based on skin colour. The European victims of fear bring to their aid every kind of economic as well as political stratagem, from distortions of loyalty and 'the civilizing mission' to differential prices and reserved markets, and appeal to such apparently sound principles as 'the rate for the job'. Many (not all) acts of social discrimination of a petty and some-

[1] A leader and correspondence in the *Times* on the calibre of potential future colonial Governors (September 1955) illustrates the situation.
[2] R. E. Robinson, *Listener*, 16 December 1954.

times insulting nature are manifestations of this psychology of siege.

If one lives in Bexhill or Berwick it is easy to assert the evident truth that a White civilization which cannot, despite an enormous flying start, hold its own in open competition with the native deserves only to go the way of other civilizations that have crumbled. It is far harder in Buluwayo or Blantyre, where the truth that all economic advance in the territory is due to the European is far more evident.[1] No blinking the facts is going to help, but the facts must be seen in relation and in perspective. Finally, it is useless to wish undone what has been done. The problems of plural societies, aggressive nationalism, White Highlands, 'poor whites' and so on, are real and must be faced.

4. NATIONALISM AND THE TIME-FACTOR

It has been well said of the British administration of India that, magnificent at its best, it was at its best at village level. The District Officer, as described by Lord Lugard,[2] was the heart of that magnificent administration, and he put his heart into it. He represented the long arm of the Sircar which could be touched wherever you were, the 'protector of the poor' from Africa to the Gilbert Islands as much as in India.

For the British the crux of the problem of the transfer of power to an elected local administration lies at 'village level' and not in any nostalgia for faded Imperial glory or sinister purpose of economic exploitation. It is a genuine ethical problem. Are we, in order to satisfy the vocal few, justified in handing over to inexperienced politicians and an untried electorate the responsibility for millions

[1] See Summary in East Africa Royal Commission Report (Cmd. 9475, 1955), Ch. 2, § 72 (p. 29).

[2] *Op. cit.*, pp. 131–3. By putting the District Officer in the past tense, we do not intend to imply that he is less essential or less valuable than he was. But there is the question whether the present can throw up great D.O.s any more than great Ambassadors, now that they are drowned in paper-work and readily accessible to 'higher authority' through the doubtful blessing of modern communications.

unfitted to protect themselves? *Relative* inefficiency will certainly ensue, the peasants' pathetic pence paid in taxation may be wasted, there will be some corruption and there may be native demagogy or an entrenchment of powers in the hands of a minority.[1] Are we deluding ourselves with talk of political progress when in fact we are committing moral abdication? Is it our bounden duty to face opprobrium (or worse) and put on the brake?

The answer may be sought in two directions: in history and in the relation of Liberal principle to history. The historical part of the answer is blunt: you cannot put the brake on. The pace may be fairly decorous, as it was in Canada, where the population was almost wholly European in origin and, as to a large part, trainees of the Mother of Parliaments. The Canadian *tempo* was even, but it was the *tempo* of a Canadian tune. In New Zealand, 'Great Britain had to pay the piper while the colonists called the tune,'[2] from 1855 to 1870, the period of the Maori Wars. This period of New Zealand history, like that of Southern Rhodesia under the 1923 constitution, illustrates the historical truth explicitly recognized by men as different as Lord Lugard and Professor A. Berriedale Keith: that it is not possible either to recall self-government or to hedge it about with limitations and restrictions, for these will not endure — more especially when those who have the *de facto* power without the ultimate responsibility are white settlers. In India, the *tempo* was jerky, and the tune disputed between two orchestras with different scores; but the final pace was precipitate. *Personalismo* in politics is an inevitable accompaniment to a nationalistic liberation movement (in South America, where the Imperial Power had no tradition of parliamentary democracy to impart, personalist politics still flourish), and the tragedy of attempts to put on the brake is that the 'extremists' of an earlier day

[1] Dr Danquah has described the alternatives as 'white imperialism or black dictatorship'.

[2] See W. K. Hancock, *Survey of British Commonwealth Affairs*, Vol. II, Part 1, pp. 53–70 (Oxford, 1940) for an analysis of the conflict between trusteeship and colonial self-government as demonstrated by the history of New Zealand up to 1870. This analysis contains much that is relevant to Kenya and Central Africa today.

are overtaken by others so much more extreme as to render their predecessors 'moderate' by comparison. Tilak succeeded Gokhale, De Valera succeeded Redmond, intransigence and even bloodshed succeed compromise and constitutionalism. The main sufferers are two: the 'village level', the peasants and the poor whom the British try to protect by going slowly; and the leaders called 'loyal' because their minds were broad enough to see British merits as well as nationalist needs.

What we must seek to do is to make an ally of nationalism, and enlist its dynamism for the progress and development of colonial territories. This means that we must try to adopt a policy that will anticipate events. Here we submit that two Liberal principles are essential. One is consent, the other that responsibility and power are inseparables in politics. Nothing will damp down the heedless quicker than the cold douche of responsibility. Whether we like them or not, the nationalist newcomers are the leaders thrown up by the people of their country and in that sense represent the consent of the people, and we must work with them, for we cannot hope to work against them. 'If the nationalists are left in opposition when they have mass support, they develop the opposition mentality. They grow irresponsible, and when at last they do win power they do not know how to use it constructively. But if they are made to govern and to cope with the real problems of their countries, they will be sobered by the challenge. And if they are not, it will not be long before their people discover their hollow incompetence.'[1] Signs are not wanting that this last is true.

A policy of anticipating events is even harder than a policy of 'go-slow', and will have to be both tough and imaginative. Consider, for example, the case of faithful chiefs under indirect rule. We could not, in honour, desert them. But indirect rule, though it was a splendid concept and has proved its usefulness, is either outdated, or breaking down, or proving impracticable of establishment. Its outstanding demonstration was in West Africa, where self-government is now on the threshold and indirect rule has

[1] W. Arthur Lewis, Michael Scott, Martin Wright and Colin Legum, *Attitude to Africa* (Penguin Special, 1951), p. 39.

served its first purpose. Elsewhere, in areas where elected Africans have not yet attained Ministerial responsibility, the great gap between the educated African and his tribal brother, as well as between the more and the less advanced tribes, is an abiding problem. Even where representative members are being added in increasing numbers to the chiefs' councils, the whole idea of indirect rule is often anathema to 'advanced' Africans, and the chiefs' authority is eroded — partly by these Africans and still more by economic changes and stresses. Moreover, the ablest men are not attracted to local government in their territories. They quite naturally seek the wider scope afforded by the development of central government, or in the Civil Service, whose members are precluded from taking on local political functions.

Attempts to build local government institutions on the old foundations are not encouraging. The 1951 African Affairs Report for Northern Rhodesia says that experimental 'parish councils' tend to degenerate into talking shops, and that success too much depends on the personality of a good chief who may and does die.[1] Many individuals retire into intense conservatism in face of new developments. Imagination and ingenuity can soften the impact, but we must not shirk the necessity to be reasonably tough, as we have been at times in our own country. The reconciliation of progress with the maintenance and development of living communities is difficult in the extreme, but the alternative is to stand by and watch communities disintegrate.

If there is substance in the idea that a considerable part of present discontents in the colonies is psychological, we should pay attention to ornament and ceremony. The bread of trusteeship needs some circuses to make it more acceptable. This is not so trivial as it might seem, and is a facet of Liberal opposition to racial discrimination, as well as being something which that intensely practical monarch, Queen Victoria, understood exceedingly well. There is no possible doubt that a feeling of indignity breeds resentment and bitterness. It is not too rash a generalization to say that *the history of the British Commonwealth is the history of a*

[1] *Official Report*, 1953 (S.O. Code, No. 58-1-31-58).

struggle for status, and status has its outward and visible signs which must not be neglected. Both the new leaders in Africa and the new leaders in Asia, although their civilizations, cultural heritages, religious and social backgrounds are so sharply different in terms of duration and stability, need the support of the outward and visible signs of status.

Recently a debate on racial discrimination was initiated by an elected African member in the Northern Rhodesian Legislative Council. His theme was important, but his instances were apparently very small things. He objected that an African holding even a *first*-class railway ticket was forbidden to enter the dining-car; and that Africans might not enter post offices by the same door as Europeans. These apparent trivialities are not so easy to deal with as they sound, and Liberals would not contemplate doing violence to the social conventions of non-Europeans (purdah, for example), though they are prepared to be firm with Europeans. The Liberals are on record on this matter. They require 'the full implementation of the principle that there shall be no racial discrimination in the services and institutions for which Her Majesty's Government or the Colonial Government is responsible' (1955). This at least covers post offices — and a good deal more, for the resolution continues 'just as is here established in courts of law'.[1]

It must not be thought that Liberals are unaware of problems now emerging in territories where advance has been rapid and appears promising. One of the most anxious of these is the reappearance of ancient fissions in the new body politic, whether territorial, or racial, or both. Opposition to the colonial Power produces a temporary unity, but with every advance the dynamic of a common purpose is weakened. This tends to leave a political vacuum, into which the seven devils of old sectionalism can enter. The British problem is the very difficult one of promoting national unity and civic pride while yet leaving latitude for the emergence

[1] The Central African Federal Parliament, on 2 August 1955, rejected a motion by a North Rhodesian African member that federal Civil Service conditions should apply to all Civil Servants according to qualifications and irrespective of race.

of the essential healthy fission of a parliamentary opposition. This difficulty, and the comparative novelty, even in Britain, of the formal entity of an Opposition with a designated Leader, has led many to question whether the British parliamentary system is an exportable product. Here again, however, one cannot put the brake on. For good or ill, the British system is identified in the minds of the colonial peoples with power (reasonably) and material prosperity (less reasonably). Even when they are offered a free choice of any system they care to study and adopt, they usually choose the British way.[1]

Finally the work of promoting cultural pride might helpfully be extended and intensified. It may seem odd anywhere, and especially in a Liberal book, to bracket for praise Josef Stalin, Lord Curzon and Queen Elizabeth I (in respect of her Welsh but not her Irish policy), but all three have made their contribution to thought and practice on the cultural side, whatever reservations one might have about their politics. It is easy, of course, for this kind of thing to be thoroughly 'phoney' (like leaving a volume of Homer on the table when Archbishop Makarios is coming to call), but there is no reason why it need be so. Nor does it have to be 'folksy'. Indian and African films now get awards at international festivals, for instance. The mechanized Muse could lend Clio a hand. We must reject the cynical sophistication of 'intellectuals' and pay greater attention to symbols.

5. SECURITY AND ECONOMIC PROGRESS: THE DILEMMA

This is not the place to expose economic restrictionism or beat the dead donkey of 'Empire Free Trade'. It is enough to say that restrictions, export levies and the like defeat their own ends.[2]

[1] An all-African commission in Ghana was recently given every possible assistance in studying French, Swiss and other systems, with full freedom of choice, but plumped for ours unanimously.

[2] For the sake of strict accuracy, certain war-time restrictions must be excepted, because their purpose was not economic but defensive. But that is no argument for carrying them on after the war. The 'economics of siege' are as unhealthy as the 'psychology of siege'.

K

Attempts to exploit producers degrade their standard of living and curtail the market; attempts to exploit consumers stimulate alternative products and alternative sources of supply. This is not doctrinaire: the facts are there for all who wish to study.[1]

Our problem is to apply the lessons, especially in the uniquely difficult question of land use and land tenure. Here, too, we are inhibited by awful warnings from past history such as the disintegration of native economies precipitated by the honest application of British notions of land ownership to communal land holdings, by abuses of the 'plantation' system, and more recent failures such as the ground-nuts scheme; and we too readily forget the successes of various kinds, such as the activities of the Empire Cotton Growing Corporation in the 1920's, the Gezira Scheme and the Agricultural Society in Jamaica. It has been said often, and weightily, that to give freedom for the sale and purchase of land is the quickest way to destroy native communities and create a landless proletariat.

That can be true, but need it be? And what are the economic facts of the existing situation? Land utilization and land tenures form an enormous and highly technical subject, and the circumstances that confront Commonwealth administrators range over nearly one-quarter of the world in infinite variety. Here we shall only consider some of the broader issues in Africa.

Excluding plantation agriculture, and some special cases like the African-run cocoa economy of Ghana, Africa shows low agricultural efficiency and output, with concomitant low standard of living, low national income and taxable capacity, and a small domestic market. There is heavy pressure on 'good' land, and destruction of potential through soil erosion, generally due to primitive cultivation methods. Native reserves in the Union of

---

[1] E.g. see W. K. Hancock, *Survey of British Commonwealth Affairs,* Vol. II, part I, pp. 113–26, regarding W. African palm kernels, Nigerian and Malayan tin, Malayan rubber, etc.; and, in Britain, the report of the Greene Committee on sugar-beet growing (Cmd. 4871, 1935, and Viscount Astor and B. Seebohm Rowntree, *British Agriculture* (1938), pp. 90–106); and, for E. African cotton, East African Royal Commission 1953–5, *Report* (Cmd. 9475) Chs. 7 and 8.

South Africa have been described by a fair-minded commentator as 'vast agricultural slums',[1] and it would be rash to say that native reserves elsewhere do not sometimes merit the same description — as well as other places that are not reserves and not in Africa. Despite all the research and devoted service that has been given to agricultural problems, the picture remains depressing. Neo-Malthusians may say it is inevitable and talk of birth-control, but there are vast areas where it is not true that the result of British rule has been a huge increase of population. It is not true in Africa.

Meanwhile, a proletariat is creating itself, especially in South Africa. It is a hard and uncomfortable fact that while *apartheid* in all its manifestations is to Liberals the negation of human dignity and freedom, industry in the Union pays the highest native wages in Africa, and this is an economic pull that cannot be gainsaid by noble words. To Africans seeking more than subsistence agriculture can offer, the Rand is El Dorado, and they will continue to flock there from any part of Africa whence it is humanly accessible unless and until there is the offer of something as good or better nearer home. With present prospects of uranium production in the Union, the pull will increase.

Africa is crying out for revenue: for schools and technical services and training; for combating diseases and pests affecting humans, animals and plants; for building communications, hydroelectric projects and harbour extensions.[2] Except where there is mining development, revenue up to now depends mainly on agricultural production and very little on secondary industry. Moreover, the potential of revenue from subsistence agriculture and small local markets is very low indeed, and any increase must come from products entering and able to compete in world markets.[3]

[1] Leo Marquand, *The Peoples and Policies of South Africa* (Oxford, 1952), p. 41.

[2] Lord Milverton once said that 'concrete and steel rails' would be found written on the hearts of African Governors, like 'Calais' on the heart of Queen Mary I.

[3] For a vivid idea of the gulf between the tribal African and the requirements of world markets, see F. Rodsetti, 'The Native — from Magic to industry', *Optima*, June 1955, pp. 46–51.

K2

The producer in Africa is handicapped, too, by natural difficulties such as low or erratic rainfall, leaching, etc., and it is not true that there is much rich land only awaiting development.

In Europe the conclusion to be drawn from such facts would be inescapable: that an agrarian revolution was needed. The same conclusion for East Africa has been drawn by the East African Royal Commission 1953-5 in its *Report*.[1] If much of Africa is not to remain a precarious museum-piece and is to be viable in a modern world, land must pass into the hands of those who will make the maximum economic use of it, withal with the greatest possible safeguards, but also with a clear understanding that neither tribal nor racial rigidities must in the last resort be allowed to restrict the process.[2]

The dilemma of reconciling security and economic progress also appears in the matter of marketing and distribution. In East Africa this is subject to a detailed network of licensing and controls, often directed, like land policy, to the protection of the African as producer and trader, but not always so. The Commission's findings point out all the defects of such systems, which Liberals have attacked for years. In particular they identify the relatively high rate of camouflaged compulsory saving which price stabilization schemes often impose on the producer, and their action as a deterrent to the increased production which favourable world prices should call forth.[3] The Commission do not advocate the immediate and wholesale removal of controls, and make it clear that the aim is expansion of the market, not inflation.

Another vitally important economic question is being thrashed out in the Northern Rhodesian Copper-Belt: that of the right of Africans to advance from unskilled labour to semi-skilled, skilled and technical jobs. Northern Rhodesia's economy (and now, in-

[1] Cmd. 9475.

[2] 'The approach on a tribal basis to questions of land tenure and land use is incompatible with the development of a modern economy, and this applies equally to a purely racial approach to the [White] Highlands question' (p. 397).

[3] Pp. 80-3.

deed, that of the Central African Federation as a whole) may be called 'copper-bottomed' — without the copper-mining revenues, it could not maintain itself afloat. It is elementary justice to enable Africans to share in the benefits of this vast development and elementary idiocy to jeopardize expansion, progress and security by imposing a racial caste system on labour, especially when there is a serious shortage of skilled European labour even at current high rates of pay. The European Mine Workers' Union, with some political support, resisted the sub-division of skilled jobs by which two or three Africans could be trained to take over one European job. It was the old struggle against 'dilution', as in Britain, and the old fetish of the 'White Labour Policy', as in the Union of South Africa. It is totally indefensible, and ultimately suicidal. Both of the big Copper-Belt groups of companies, the Rhodesian Selection Trust and the Anglo-American Group, were willing to employ Africans in a number of categories of work previously reserved to Europeans, but the latter group, having part of its interests in the Union of South Africa, was less able to resist pressure from the European Mine Workers' Union, which also has links with its South African counterpart. In the summer of 1955, the E.M.W.U. abated its opposition sufficiently to offer a transfer of some categories but on the condition that no future enlargement of the listed categories should be made without its consent. The Anglo-American Group accepted this condition, but the Rhodesian Selection Trust (R.S.T.) refused it, although aware that this might lead to a serious situation in its mines. Its courage was rewarded in September 1955, when the E.M.W.U. agreed to the employment of Africans in 24 categories previously reserved to Europeans, and gave up their attempt to veto further African advancement. The Chamber of Mines was able to negotiate a three-year consolidated agreement, and the policy cleavage between the two groups of companies was closed. The fact that some inter-Union trouble has subsequently arisen, when the African Mine Workers' Union began to lose up-graded members to the African Staff Association, is a transitional teething trouble and does not in any way vitiate the principle for which the R.S.T. stood out.

Liberal policy is wholly in sympathy with the R.S.T. Group's attitude, not only in its own area of the Copper-Belt, but wherever similar situations may arise.

Complicated pressures may also arise where there is a constitutional link between more and less developed territories. Central African federation is now a *fait accompli*; but it was not based on the consent of the African majority of the inhabitants. In the cautious words of the *Official Report* for 1953, 'the practical outcome of Federation is being watched intently by Africans, and not without some feelings of uncertainty and misgiving on their part'.[1] We must watch it no less intently and, if need arise, press for the implementation of the various provisions for safeguarding African interests which the Federation's constitution contains.[2] The economic field needs especially jealous watching, for encroachments on the initial basis of federation through economic action can be very subtle. Professor K. C. Wheare has said that power in a federation will ultimately reside where financial power resides. At the start of the Central African federal experiment, great financial power resided in Northern Rhodesia because of its copper revenues, in spite of the greater economic maturity of Southern Rhodesia. Nyasaland was and is, of course, the poor relation in the triumvirate, and the Africans there, and also in Northern Rhodesia, attach great importance to their protected status as a counterweight to aspects of Federal, and Southern Rhodesian, policy which they dislike and fear. Is it or is it not significant that the controversy over the respective merits of the Kariba and Kafue hydro-electric projects has issued in a decision to pigeon-hole Kafue and go ahead with Kariba? The Copper-Belt would have been the immediate beneficiary of Kafue, whereas Southern Rhodesia gains greater advantage from Kariba, especially on a long-term view. It is true that, although the Kafue scheme would have been cheaper, and more quickly completed, the Kafue flats (a seasonal swamp area) had defects as a storage area and the Kafue

[1] P. 1. (S.O. Code No. 58-1-31-53).

[2] The Federation of Rhodesia and Nyasaland (Constitution) Order-in-Council 1953 (S.1. 1953, No. 1199).

scheme therefore had less potentialities for later extension. It is also true that the Shire river scheme in Nyasaland is to be proceeded with. There may thus be nothing sinister in the decision to carry out the Kariba scheme, despite allegations made by Northern Rhodesians that Lord Malvern did not keep faith with them nor even keep their Government fully informed; but the fact remains that Southern Rhodesia's long-term industrial potential has been strengthened at the expense of the Copper-Belt's immediate advantage, and that additional financial weight will in due course accrue to her. To those who are frankly distrustful of the Southern Rhodesian political climate — among whom Liberals must necessarily be included — the shifting of financial weight away from the two Protectorate members of the Federation is something to be keenly and carefully watched. The general question of the location of financial advantage is also relevant to any proposals that may in future be made for setting up other federations.

Developments at the time of the Commonwealth Prime Ministers' meeting in July 1956 were not calculated to allay the Protectorates' anxieties. The Federation's Prime Minister, Lord Malvern, asked Her Majesty's Government to grant to the Federal Government and Parliament complete independence within its own sphere. His proposal included the maintenance, by a formal agreement with the United Kingdom embodying existing constitutional safeguards, of the status of the component territories of the Federation — a political monstrosity at which the mind boggles, and which could hardly survive for long. His request was refused, but the Conference conceded to the Federal Prime Minister the right to attend future meetings — not, as previously, as the personal privilege of Lord Malvern, but as a right conferred on the holder of the office. This concession breaches the sole remaining constitutional convention — equality of status — governing admission to full membership of the British Commonwealth of Nations. While this innovation may serve to ease the entry of non-European Prime Ministers into the Conference circle, and although the Asian Prime Ministers present accepted the change, it must yet be regarded with reserve.

6. THE COLONIES AND THE COMMONWEALTH

It is part of what we have called 'tri-partisan' policy that the progress of colonial territories towards full responsible self-government should culminate with their admission, if they so desire, to the voluntary association of sovereign States called 'the British Commonwealth of Nations'.[1] In the past the policy has been faithfully observed: India, Pakistan and Ceylon opted for the association upon attaining independence; Burma withdrew. But there are breakers ahead through which it may be difficult to steer the policy and maintain its principle intact. It must be said clearly and at once that Liberals stand by the policy without reservations, whatever pressures may arise. The Liberal view is that the Commonwealth is the only effective, voluntary, multi-racial association of States in existence. That is its justification. The citizens of the States composing this association are now also citizens of a virtually world-wide plural society, and they will betray the vital principles of that society if they surrender to sectional pressure from any of its component parts.

Certain consequences flow from this position. The first concerns the three High Commission territories of Bechuanaland, Basutoland and Swaziland. It was contemplated in 1909 that these territories would presently, and without any serious controversy, be absorbed into the Union of South Africa; and legal procedures for this absorption were provided in the South Africa Act of 1909. But Union policy towards its African nationals is today, and for some time past has been, very much more controversial than was ever contemplated in 1909. Most of the electorate of the United Kingdom would now be reluctant to hand over the territories to the control of the Union, but they should keep the issues involved clearly in their minds.

[1] If this name should offend anyone, we must apologize but cannot withdraw because, in the existing confusion of nomenclature, no other title covers the eight States concerned. 'Dominions' is more inaccurate; 'Commonwealth' is held by the Law Officers of the Crown to cover all the erstwhile 'British Empire'.

Basutoland and Swaziland are small areas (11,716 and 6,704 square miles respectively). Bechuanaland is much larger (275,000 square miles), mainly devoted to cattle-raising, but its area includes much virtual desert. Its north-eastern border marches with the Rhodesias, and it has a good and increasing market for beef there and in the Belgian Congo. Swaziland's revenues have doubled in the last four years, and prospects for irrigated farming, afforestation, improved dairying and livestock and further mineral exploitation are promising. Basutoland is simply a poor agricultural country, with no striking prospect of becoming anything else. It is entirely surrounded by the territory of the Union of South Africa. A combined hydro-electric and irrigation project there, using the headwaters of the Orange River, would be practicable, but only by grace of the Union Government, since the main market for power and much of the land to be irrigated would be in Union territory. Swaziland has a short frontier with Portuguese East Africa, but no rail link, and any road and rail development for which finance could be at present foreseen must link up with the Union's systems. Basutoland's external communications can only be *via* the Union. Since 1945 some £15 m. of development funds have been spent or earmarked for the three High Commission territories. By this expenditure, the United Kingdom has shown that it realizes the Africans of these territories must not be forced into a choice between rural stagnation and *apartheid* — otherwise the principle that they are only to be transferred to the Union with their free consent would be a hollow mockery. But if the Union Government were in the future to press to the extreme limit its physical powers of duress over the Basutos and Swazis, we might be faced with a crisis that could rock the Commonwealth.

To mention the application of development funds is to raise a pressing practical problem: how, in politically fluid and sometimes divided and discontented communities, are we to maintain administrative standards and achieve technical advancement? This problem goes to the heart of the British moral dilemma between self-government and abandoning 'the village level' to its fate. Trusteeship is not *tutelle*, its inadequate translation in U.N. offi-

cialese. It is essentially a dual mandate, and if conditions militate
against discharging our duty with our resources as a metropolitan
Power we must enlist additional resources from the rest of the
world.

We include in this notion the enlistment of the economic aid of
the World Bank, the Point Four Plan and the Colombo Plan. But
this is only half the story. The institutional or governmental provision of capital has its political and economic dangers and the
immigration of private capital is often preferable. Private capital,
however, will not readily face the addition of serious political and
administrative uncertainty to economic risks. If we are right in believing in the importance of the psychological element in the 'uncomfortable processes of decolonization', we must apply our ideas
to administrative problems. On the one hand, agrarian, technical
and political revolution can degenerate into exploitation, degrada-
tion and violence without a strong, confident and trusted administration. On the other hand, if we have lost that confidence in ourselves which is an essential part of creative work, we are corre-
spondingly the less fitted to cope with fear, suspicion and insurgent
nationalism.

The fundamental Liberal idea that the Government and the
Civil Service serve the people elicits little response among colonial
populations. To them, Government and its servants represent
power incarnate — British power. It is profoundly suspect in
many colonial eyes, and the fact that there is gross injustice in the
suspicion is in practice irrelevant.

This suspicion hampers us as trustees, and we should seek rein-
forcement to enable us to fulfil our trust dynamically and not
merely conventionally. For this reason Liberals look with favour
on the idea of creating a Commonwealth administrative and technical service on the lines adumbrated in articles in the *Times* of 7
and 8 September 1953. Although the practical difficulties of such a
scheme are real, difficulty is inherent in all change and must not be
overestimated. Some changes in this direction have been unob-
trusively made, when in 1954 the Colonial Service was partially
reorganized and rechristened 'Her Majesty's Oversea Service',

and when the name of Crown Agents for the Colonies was changed. In this context the answer to the question, 'What's in a name?' is 'a very great deal'.[1] There are times when the British affection for preserving the old façade while installing revolutionary new machinery behind it can be overdone, and this is one of them. It should not be beyond our wit to preserve the virtues of the old Colonial Service and add to them the advantages of a Commonwealth Service, open to all qualified members of all races, and launched with such honourable publicity and prestige as to dispel, once and for all, the idea that any Government which draws upon it for service would be tacitly admitting any kind of subordination or inferiority.

By the same token the maximum use should be made of United Nations machinery. It is unfortunate that the Trusteeship Council (largely an Australian concept in its embryo stage) has become a tendentious and even ridiculous organ, forcing the British, more often than they would wish, to take up a position based on the Charter clause excluding the domestic affairs of member States from United Nations jurisdiction. If we are convinced of the need for a line of policy but cannot implement it in a territory because of anti-British and anti-colonial obsessions, we should seek to have it carried out under the aegis of the United Nations. We are well aware that the practical difficulties of this procedure, especially in terms of personnel, would be great, but they would not be insuperable in relation to technical development.

There is one field of technical advance in which Britain has special capacity to help underdeveloped territories. This is in the peaceful uses of atomic energy. The smaller and more industrially 'backward' countries are avid for energy, and it was largely due to their pressure that the Geneva Conference on the Peaceful Use of Atomic Energy was held in July 1955. It would be easy to be beguiled by pipe-dreams of the industrial miracles which might be achieved if atomic power were harnessed to the labour force of

[1] U Nu has said that Burma could have remained in the Commonwealth if the adjective 'United' had been substituted for 'British'.

K3

(say) China. The whole industrial balance of the world *could* be revolutionized, but first there are the revolutionary demands of nuclear engineering on the chemical and metallurgical industries to be met and the personnel to be trained.

But although only the most advanced countries can command the skills needed to develop atomic industrial potential, the results are exportable. Great Britain is already the world's largest exporter of radioactive isotopes. This is a small trade as yet, perhaps half a million pounds value yearly. But we are pushing ahead with the building of atomic power stations. The world's most accessible large uranium deposits are in the 'tailings' of the South African gold mines, and Britain has concluded contracts to buy the first ten years' production. Britain has also offered to develop the Rum Jungle potential for Australia.[1] She has concluded an agreement with India to co-operate in peaceful atomic energy development there (Travancore has extensive thorium sand deposits); and Canada is well ahead with developing its uranium resources at Great Bear Lake, Blind River and Beaver Lodge. The Commonwealth does not lack sources of supply.

Such figures as are available to the lay public indicate that the cost, including overseas installation, of a 'packaged' atomic power station exported from Britain would compare competitively, and even favourably, with the cost of a hydro-electric plant producing a comparable volume of energy. An American authority has said that fusion processes, once tamed for peaceful use, would be still less costly than fission. There is food for thought here for a trustee Power — especially one where the claims of domestic fixed investment have absorbed the bulk of recent saving and left little for overseas investment. Competition for our atomic power stations for export and for home use may well be intense, and the claims of colonial territories crowded out. Moreover, in conditions of limited availability, not many colonial areas would qualify on economic grounds. The North Rhodesian Copper-Belt, with its well-developed mining industry and range of mineral products, is in a favourable position, as would be other areas rich in metals.

[1] Russia is doing a similar service for China in Sinkiang.

Again, a territory where industrialization is under way might be more favourable even than a country where vast capital is already sunk in industry dependent on the traditional sources of power; but a mainly or exclusively agricultural country would be a poor starter in the atomic race. Uranium is not a philosopher's stone with which to turn all colonies to gold. Even with these caveats, however, there remains an inspiration and a challenge to trustee-ship: the possibility of a British initiative which would make the Commonwealth the leader in the practical application of atomic energy for peaceful uses.

It seems in the past to have been the fate of some classes, some peoples and some countries to have been 'objects' of policy, and this attitude on the part of more politically emancipated societies tends to persist towards colonial peoples. It may take new forms, but the essence remains. Conservative paternalism — more often than not a kindly and honourable paternalism — being out-dated, it tends to be succeeded by Socialist regulation and regimentation, more often than not well-meaning and honest, but no less galling to awakening communities. We reject both these policies, to-gether with their basic attitude of treating colonial peoples merely as objects of policy. It is an attitude which encourages the inter-pretation of the clash between progress and security in solely racial terms, until it 'runs like a pathological obsession throughout the daily life and work of the community'.[1]

To say this is not to advocate abdication or defeatism in regard to the natural objects of well-meant paternalism and well-meant Socialism, the people at 'the village level'. The onus of trusteeship remains until the objects of the trust are fulfilled. But Liberals pro-pose firstly to invite the co-operation of the wards of the trust in planning the pace and methods of its fulfilment. We advocate 'the institution of a Consultative Colonial Assembly, meeting periodi-cally',[2] whereat the political and economic development of col-onial territories could be freely discussed by those who have the

[1] *Report* of the East Africa Royal Commission, 1953–5 (H.M.S.O., Cmd. 9475), Ch. 18, para. 5, p. 191.
[2] Assembly Resolution, 1955.

most vital interest in them, the representatives of the colonial peoples themselves, who would be encouraged to 'work out practical means for the fulfilment of their aspirations'.

Secondly — and this applies more to the 'wards' within sight of their 'majority' — Liberals would like to see local colonial representatives take far more part than they now do in the workings of the vast standing machinery of consultation and co-operation of which the Commonwealth disposes. There are many of these bodies on which colonial representation would be wholly appropriate — not representation, as it now often is, by the Colonial Secretary or his designated official, but representation through the presence of an elected Minister or Member of the Legislative Assembly. There are vast possibilities here for training in co-operation and responsibility, for the widening of parochial outlooks, and for an honourable and distinguished share in the working of the Commonwealth. This is not a revolutionary proposal; precedent exists, and only needs to be imaginatively applied. The range of these consultative and co-operative bodies' work is wide and practical, and offers great scope. Recent appointments of High Commissioners (whose offices are of major importance in the Commonwealth's consultative network) for West African territories show that the process has been well begun.

There is precedent, too, for the Colonial Conference proposal in the shape of those held in 1887 and 1897 to mark Queen Victoria's jubilees. Cynics of those days called the Conferences 'amiable jamborees', and we are well aware that our proposal gives plenty of scope to the cynics of today. But the awakened and awakening inhabitants of colonial territories can no longer — and, indeed, should no longer — be satisfied with *ex-cathedra* pronouncements from Westminster and ukases from Whitehall. Where consultation has been used, it has proved its value, and we desire to see the machinery for consultation given a permanent and honourable standing and not confined to visits from Colonial Secretaries or *ad hoc* missions, however successful these may be in their immediate context.

7. PATHS TO A LIBERAL COMMONWEALTH

All men of goodwill can see the goal; the question is how to get there. The situation is almost too fluid, the questions too protean, to grasp. Our old confident sense of mission has waned, but our inexorable responsibility to 'the village level' remains. Willing enough to hand over our power, we seek to ensure that a conscious acceptance of responsibility is transferred with it.

But power and responsibility are political inseparables, and power includes economic power. We must seek every means by which the native's economic advancement can march *pari passu* with his political and economic responsibility. The situations to be met are infinite in their variety, and so must be the methods to meet them.

There is the sub-division of skilled jobs to enable non-Europeans to move up from the unskilled level, as in the instance quoted in the North Rhodesian Copper-Belt. There is the recent South Rhodesian measure to create individual African free-holdings in place of communal tenures, combined with the allocation of funds to enable them to improve their cultivation methods, and the South Rhodesian town-planning policy of freehold house ownership for Africans (admittedly in a 'native purchase area', but progress none the less). There is the chance to get gradually away from hampering communal ownership when there are settlement schemes for reclaimed land, or other reasons for resettlement (e.g. the tenant-farming schemes in Tanganyika). These might also provide opportunities for developing functional responsibilities for chiefs or village councils in connection with the land tenure changes. The relative failure of co-operatives in the Colonies has always been disappointing and puzzling,[1] but recent successes (e.g. in Jamaica) must be studied and adopted. 'Pilot schemes' demonstrating improved agricultural methods have generally proved

[1] 8,626 registered co-operatives, over 1,000,000 members, (total Colonial pop., 82,000,000) over £12 million capital, in twenty-seven territories; but compare 1,885 societies, 250,000 members, £1·25 m. capital in nine territories ten years ago.

their worth, as have hire services for agricultural machinery, and (necessarily long-term) livestock improvement schemes through selection and controlled breeding. Recent agricultural holding consolidation with instruction in more intensive cropping has aroused African enthusiasm in Kenya, as well as African boycotting. We are not limited to our own immediate experience. We can learn much about urban zoning from Canada and Detroit, and about soil conservation from the Transkei and the Tennessee Valley.

Even a superficial look at the successes shows up one common feature: they have come where the local population has realized that these things are done *with* them and not just *for* them. The biggest successes have been where the more educated colonial has responded to this realization, underlining again the need for more education. But the peasant is not a fool, and his leaders learn that they cannot play the fool with his livelihood (e.g. the Ghana Government have quietly resumed the compulsory cutting-out of diseased cocoa-trees against which they fulminated when 'the British' did it). Development and improvement will proceed more quickly if schemes capture the imagination. Why not Five-Year-Plans for agricultural and industrial development launched with *panache* and the inclusion, from the start, of a majority of local colonials in the directing body? Variants of the British 'Public Board' technique might well be suitable, and would afford opportunities to reduce the gap between local and central government bodies. The cardinal fact, to which all our policy and planning should be geared, is that, sooner or later, the mass of the population in any colony will be in control, and the more quickly we give them responsibility in practical planning the better.

Undoubtedly this road is uphill all the way, and undoubtedly those who point to the vast demands which will be made on administrative resources are right. We have already referred to the need to maintain a confident and trusted administration if economic revolution is not to degenerate into exploitation. The vital question is how to maintain the administrative *cadre* in a fluid and uncertain situation. We advocate the Commonwealth Civil Service idea — genuinely Commonwealth, in that its personnel could be used by sovereign as well as dependent territories — to give a sense of security to officers and a sense of equality to users. Pensions could be based on a consolidated Commonwealth Fund. We commend, and desire to see the extension of, the use of U.N. Specialized Agencies and other international bodies (which, for prestige, might be associated formally with the United Nations or its agencies). Where nationalism or suspicion or both might prevent the British doing a needed job, the moral force of the United Nations could be thus enlisted.[1] There are far more of these international organizations than most people are aware of, whose concerns range from pest control and air transport to prison reform, and local colonials should always be associated with their work as well as our old friend 'a British Colonial Office observer'.

It goes without saying that the training of local colonials in administrative and technical service should be pressed on, but this is necessarily a slow process and every possible means of speeding it up must be used. Here the educative value of the association of colonials with international agencies can help, and help, too, to break down parochialism. Few colonials do or can know what world affairs are like. They have been defended, protected and guided by the British, their too sudden *début* into international society can be heady, if nothing worse, and they will be in contact with plenty of bad examples of irresponsibility. If they are to take the worthy place we hope for them on becoming fully independent, a gradual introduction is desirable.

Similarly, the vast range of consultative and co-operative machinery of the British Commonwealth should be used for the same purposes.[2] Since the struggle for status lies at the heart of the British Commonwealth story, constitutional niceties should not

[1] Ruthless moral force if need be, to remedy situations such as the Arab League's liquidation of the vital locust control organization at Jeddah, which has no sin except that it is British (*Times*, 29 April 1956).

[2] Most of the Commonwealth organs do not work by majority decision or vote, but by friendly agreement and compromise — hence their peculiar advantage over other international bodies. *Vide* Heather Harvey, *Consultation and Co-operation in the Commonwealth* (Oxford, 1952).

be allowed to stand in the way, and we insist that colonial association should be as of right to the maximum limit, and not by
patronizing admissions through a back door labelled 'observers'
or some such notion. The same ideas lie behind our advocacy of a
Colonial Consultative Assembly. It is vital that colonials should
learn of affairs outside their own borders.

Power, responsibility and consent: our proposals aim at link-
ing the three in practice as well as in theory. What we cannot
create — although we can foster it — is genuine national consciousness that will overcome traditional fissions and the centri-
fugal forces in plural societies. 'The superior virtue of the British is
almost entirely the accidental one of impartiality'[1] — a rock to
which the weaker sections of colonial populations cling — but
impartiality does not create, it endeavours only to provide favourable conditions for the birth of a nation. We have mentioned
above some instruments for this midwifery. If, as some say, our
parliamentary system (or its federal variants) is not an exportable
product, we believe that is academic. It is too late to change — to
what? — and too late, as Lord Hailey has said, to find the para-
gons to make the change.[2] As he says, we know how it works; we
have put our own faith in it. But we need not hang millstones
round infant nations' necks by permitting the inclusion of discriminatory or privileged positions in new constitutions. Systems
of communal representation are good examples of the possible
conflict between the short-term aim of safeguards for minorities
and the long-term aim of a united body politic.[3] The ultimate aim
must be common citizenship, a common electoral roll and common civil liberties for all.

Finally, there is the proclaimed goal of the right to sovereign
membership of the Commonwealth, the leading group in the great
procession of peoples from Empire to independence; and the right
to refuse it, since the Commonwealth is a voluntary association

[1] Miss Margery Perham, letter to the *Times*, 22 July 1952.
[2] *Listener*, 5 April 1956.
[3] The Reports of the Donoughmore and Soulbury Commissions on
Ceylon illuminate this question.

and none can be compelled to adhere. But we must emphasize two things.

First, how much is illusion in the cry for 'liberation'? Sovereignty does not automatically liberate a people from the real slaveries: from sickness and pests, which recognize no frontiers; from hunger and unemployment, which are subject to no monarch; from ignorance and superstition, which can rule the minds of men technically free. Freedom from these things is something that every colonial people, with our willing help if they will accept it, has to find for itself; it cannot be bestowed by Order-in-Council.

Secondly, membership of the Commonwealth is a magnificent privilege, and not something to be offered and refused like an old shoe. 'Within the city of independent States there are indeed many mansions; there are the slums as well as the fashionable quarters.'[1] Without Commonwealth membership, a newly independent and untested nation would carry little weight in the world. It could too easily be an 'object' of policy in a new context, a mere pawn in the political game of other powers. As a member, it is automatically heir to the fruits of the sacrifices, endeavour and achievement of its fellow-members, and to the respect that they have earned in the councils of the world. This is a heritage without price, for which no price is asked. It is 'independence', and it is something more.

H. H.

[1] C. R. M. F. Cruttwell, *A History of Peaceful Change in the Modern World* (Oxford, 1937), p. 182.

CHAPTER XIV

THE CHALLENGE OF
LIBERALISM

IT is a mark of the malaise of our time that this is called 'the Atomic Age'. True, modern research into nuclear physics, electronics, drugs and biochemistry have made possible a kind of life hitherto unimaginable on this planet; and it is true, too, that man's moral development has not kept pace with his scientific discoveries and is pitifully inadequate to the powers he now possesses. But atomic power, radar, penicillin and vitamins are but means to some end which remains to be defined. More fundamentally significant, and more worthy to give its name to this epoch in man's history, is the world-wide ferment of the human spirit.

Partly as a result of the spread of democratic ideas by means of education, and partly through a recognition of the new possibilities for man made available by scientific discoveries, there has dawned upon mankind at large the notion, dimly but passionately apprehended, that every man and every people has an equal right to consideration. In many lands there is an uprising against privilege of class and inheritance, against racial discrimination and all assumption of racial superiority, against colonialism and the exploitation of the weak. This pervasive movement of the human spirit takes various forms, many perverse and more chaotic. It underlies the upsurge of 'the working classes' in Europe and America, the twin birth of Communism and Fascism, the current turmoil of thought and feeling in Asia and Africa. The very nationalism of that vast region, turgid and selfish as it often is and at open variance with the trend of events towards a common world order, is but a perversion of the claim that all peoples and all persons should be free to realize their potentialities and be valued in and for themselves.

Liberals have always been the challengers of privilege; they have always fought for the enlargement of liberty on the ground of the essential dignity of human nature. This may not yet be called 'the Liberal Age', but it is pre-eminently an age of human aspiration and strife which the Liberals themselves have provoked; and it is they alone that can provide the answer.

Men cry out for freedom, but they also fear it. Moreover, they are often willing to barter it for immediate economic advantage. It is true that liberty implies democracy, but democracy in its turn presupposes a mature and responsible electorate. Without such an electorate a system of universal suffrage will rapidly decay into the tyranny of a party, a demagogue or a bureaucracy. It follows that to be a Liberal one need not in all circumstances be a democrat, though this limitation now applies only to a small and diminishing area in a world of rapid educational advance.

Liberty may decay: it may also be refused as too great a challenge to the resourcefulness and moral responsibility of the individual. And here, to all appearances, Liberals commit the fault of Communists, Socialists and Conservatives in demanding that men should be encouraged to want what they may not want already. Like all political reformers, we claim to be an *élite*. But this claim is an essential element in political philosophy. All such philosophies are based on *a priori* assertions, and inevitably so. '*Ought* cannot be deduced from *is*,' as Hume put it, and we should proclaim our own basic assertion — the belief in the dignity of man as man — without shame or ambiguity.

It follows that the mere fact that liberty is in certain historical situations unpopular cannot and ought not to deflect us from our purpose. And in practice it does not deflect the Liberal purpose. We appeal to the examples of the Liberal elements in the German and Italian undergrounds during the Fascist period who worked violently to destroy régimes they knew to be popular; to the work of the British Colonial Office, surely since 1945 the most effective liberalizing force on earth and almost the only creator in that period of *new* free societies, in its maintenance of remarkably free societies in East Africa, Malaya and British Guiana against popular authoritarian pressures; and to the Aramburu Government in Argentina, which has tried to persuade and coerce a Peronist population to accept a return to parliamentary government. Such 'liberal dictatorships' are cited merely to clinch an abstract case; they are of course exceptional. In most circumstances freedom *is* popular, especially because, in the long run, equality, security and peace (its great rivals in popular affection) are usually aspects of it. In the end the most popular dictatorships decay. We have seen human nature re-assert itself in the Soviet Union since Stalin's death, his most trusted and bloodthirsty lieutenants delighting in foreign travel and easy intercourse with their subjects. Events in Poland and Hungary have shown that minds are not so easily captured and that a mere decade of oppression and propaganda-monopoly have not changed the craving of the common man to be free. And there is the slow thaw in Spain. Clearly, if freedom is less than universally popular in Britain today we must look for special reasons why this should be so.

Liberty is jeopardized through moral inertia; it is jeopardized no less by the development of the machine. Human beings under modern industrial conditions are herded together in enormous cities, their task being to serve and tend machines. Hence the proletariat or largely depersonalized mass-man, the *Verdinglichung* of man. The mass-man is the preordained victim of the tyrant and the boss. The ever-increasing mechanization of industry which may mean, and ought to mean, a great enlargement of human liberty has tended in fact to the depersonalizing of man and the reduction of his human status.

We have, then, on the one side a world-wide demand for freedom and for the recognition of the right of every man and people to equal consideration, and on the other side an unwillingness to rise to the moral responsibilities of freedom, a preference for the easier way of letting 'them' order our lives for us, reinforced by the constant depersonalizing pressure of the industrial order. Hence we find crude nationalisms abroad in many parts of the world and at home political stagnation and a widespread questioning whether 'politics' is worth while. This confused scene is the broad background of the foregoing essays; it is to this world that Liberalism brings its challenge. Only a Liberal policy can meet the needs of awakening Asia and Africa; only a Liberal revival can draw our nation from the political futility in which it is now bogged down.

Liberalism is a political philosophy, not a theory of economics. Its watchword is liberty, and it rests upon the faith that all men are equally worthy of consideration. This faith we derive ultimately from classical humanism as this was made fruitful, dynamic and universal by the religion of the Bible. The political expression of liberty is democracy, and today democracy is the faith of men of various religions and of none. Democracy rests upon the three principles of liberty, order and virtue or, to use the modern term, responsibility. Liberty is the supreme political good, for a man must be free that he may realize the potentialities of his nature. He cannot be free if his whole strength must be given to the provision of the bare necessities of existence, if his livelihood depend upon the whim of his employer, if he have no opportunity to take his place as a citizen, if he have no access to the cultural life of his age and country. The purpose of legislation is the enlargement of liberty and the establishment of regulations within which the citizen can act freely; without order there can be no liberty. The attempt to secure liberty for all men, especially the weak or unfortunate, is an ethical idea. Politics in the Liberal view is a branch of ethics rather than of economics.

The establishment of liberty is not, and cannot be, the first and last end of the other two great parties. Conservatism is not a principle of emancipation. The desire to preserve that which is great and worthy in a national inheritance is no ignoble sentiment, but in practice a Conservative party is resistant to all change and can only tinker, and that belatedly, with the ills or 'crises' of the body politic in a tumultuous world. Men vote Conservative 'to keep the Socialists out' rather than for any cause worthy of their enthusiasm and devotion. The Labour Party is committed to 'Socialism', which is in principle a system of controls and not of liberty. It is concerned with the lot of the under-privileged in our society, but tends to an egalitarianism which, again, is incompatible with liberty, for men are unequal in respect alike of their powers and of their needs, and any attempt to make them equal, except in respect of their right to equal consideration, is a form of tyranny. The Socialist denounces private property, which is the bulwark of political liberty, and would virtually proletarianize society. Liberals, on the other hand, aim at the abolition of the proletariat and the emancipation of workers by making property-owners of them all — no Utopian ideal, for in America it is already within sight of fulfilment.

Political life in this country has reached stale-mate. Conservatism offers little more than a policy of appeasement *vis-à-vis* the great trade unions; the Labour party has no policy to offer beyond worn-out slogans. Both are responsible for constant and serious encroachments on our freedom. Disillusionment and apathy mark our politics. Liberalism comes as a challenge both political and moral. In the previous pages we have offered tentative sketches of what in some of its aspects an unservile State may be. The pursuit of liberty is a cause worthy of us, and the goal is not beyond our reach if we have the moral enthusiasm to work for it.

National policy must rightly and inevitably be self-regarding. A man must do the best he can for himself and his family — but not without any regard for the rights and needs of other people. If we take seriously the Liberal principle that all men and peoples have an equal right to consideration, it follows of necessity that the maintenance and improvement of the present standard of living in these islands cannot be the exclusive and all-dominating concern of British statesmanship. Sir Anthony Eden declared in 1956 that quite apart from our obligations under NATO we should maintain our hold upon Cyprus because of British needs of oil from the Middle East. To all other nations that must have sounded like the language of unashamed power-politics. We can hardly be surprised that Britain, which ought to be leading and helping the awakening peoples of Asia and Africa to freedom and independence, is generally regarded askance as being much more concerned with the maintenance of its own amenities than with the hopes and longings and fierce determinations of the poorer and weaker peoples of the world.

Access to raw materials is declared the right of all peoples by the Charter of the United Nations. As well tell the shivering vagabond under Waterloo Bridge that he has the perfect right to dine off steak and sleep on a feather bed. If we should try to get the Americans to pool their oil resources in the Middle East with ours and to share the available supplies on some equitable scale with the 'free' peoples of the world, then 'the free world' would begin to have some meaning in Asia and Africa, and we should be giving a lead worthy of our calling.

The policy of the two larger parties towards Russia is one of containment and 'peaceful co-existence'. But this is not a Liberal policy. The Communist Party in Russia, like the present government in the Union of South Africa, suffers inevitably from a siege-mentality; it knows itself surrounded by millions crying out for freedom. It must be the policy of a Liberal Britain to hasten the deliverance of the victims of tyranny by any means within our power. They certainly cannot be freed by provoking war. That way is ruled out. But we can believe in freedom; we can proclaim freedom; we can set our own house in order; we can give an example and a lead to the making of a world that is really free. We can, for instance, make illegal all expressions of the colour-bar in this country and wherever our writ runs; we can, and should, do far more for the development of lands dependent on us and for the suppression of all exploitation of non-Europeans in the interests of our insular economy; we can make the racial policy of the Union of South Africa unworkable by offering examples of multi-racial societies that are liberal and free. The revival of Liberalism in Britain would quicken the cause of Liberalism throughout the world.

We are often assured by the cynical and disillusioned that we live in an age of power-politics, and that all idealisms are an agreeable form of self-deception. It may be replied that we do indeed live in a period marked by enormous concentrations of power, political, economic, industrial, financial and military. The moralizing of power is therefore from one aspect the supreme political issue of the time. Liberalism aims at the moralizing of power through the enlargement of liberty.

We are Liberals because we believe the fundamental principle of Liberalism to be right and in accord with the ultimate nature of things. We should be Liberals, therefore, even if all the world seemed to be turning its back on Liberalism. But, on the contrary, there is much to encourage us. It is, first, the principles of Liberalism and of Liberal democracy that have caused the ferment in the world today; and if some of the crude nationalisms and collective experiments in the East and South are far from being Liberal, it is for a Liberal order that the peoples blindly grope, and it is a Liberal order that alone can satisfy their aspirations. Conservatism can have no constructive policy in an era of world-change. Socialism though hydra-headed is in all its forms incompatible with that liberty which man desires and is losing its appeal even in the lands of its origin. Communism as the tyranny of a Party holds its wide empire by force and force alone. Meanwhile the achievements of Liberalism in recent years, grossly under-advertised as they have been, are large and striking. Liberal institutions are taking root in what once seemed the unpromising soil of the Indian subcontinent, in Burma, Malaya and West Africa; there has been a sweeping revival of Liberalism in Western Europe, especially in France, where the Radicals have risen from a point of near-extinction in 1944 to lead more coalitions than any other Party; in 1947 the Liberal International was founded in Oxford, an association of Liberal Parties and groups which has since extended from Europe into Asia and North America; Liberalism has advanced in strength in the United States in the policies of Mr Truman and President Eisenhower, in the waning of Isolationism and the eclipse of Senator McCarthy. This is a more Liberal world than it was in 1945, a vastly more Liberal world than it was in the twenties and the thirties.

Whatever the peculiar difficulties of Liberalism in Britain, the recession of collectivist ideas continues, the day of nationalism is passing, the vacuum grows. It is in the conviction that this vacuum must soon be filled that we have sought to define, chiefly for our own country, the Liberal alternative.

N. M.

INDEX

Abdication crisis (1936), 84
Acton, Lord, 15 n.
Acton Society, 135
advertising, 219–20
afforestation, 244
Africa Bureau, 43
aged, Liberal report on, 14
Agricultural Credit Bank, 251
Agricultural Holdings Act (1948), 75
agriculture, 231–52; its diversity, 50; and co-ownership, 103–4; marketing boards, 245–8
Agriculture Act (1947), 55, 252
Agriculture, Ministry of, 141, 238
air-lines, 205
airports, 42
apartheid, 282, 283, 296, 297 n.
apprenticeships, 297
Arabs, 32
arbitration, compulsory, 203–4
Argentina, 310
Arnold, Thomas, 88
arts, liberty of, 76–8; patronage of, 94
arts graduates, 158
Associated British Cinemas, 77
Astor, Viscount, 290 n.
Atomic Age, the, 308
atomic bomb, 263
atomic energy, 299–301
atomic war, 162, 271–2
Auditor-General, 43
Australia, 278, 299, 300
automation, 191, 202
Avon (Hampshire), 244

Bacon, Francis, 92
Bank of England, 42, 106
Bartlett, Vernon, 48
Basutoland, 296–7
Beaver Report, 130
Bechuanaland, 280, 296–7
Belgian Congo, 297
Beveridge, Lord, 19 n., 116 n., 200
birth-control, 291
birthrate, the British, 170
Bismarck, 20
Blatchford, Robert, 132 n.
Board of Trade, 81, 228, 229
Boyd, Francis, 36
Brandeis, L. D., 74 n.
Bridgewater plain, 244
Brighton, 146

Britain's Industrial Future (1928), 7, 14
British Broadcasting Corporation (B.B.C.), 48–9, 78, 137; and the 'Establishment', 83–4
British Guiana, 280, 310
British Honduras, 271
British Medical Association (B.M.A.), 136 n., 198
British Railways, 86, 106, 107, 139
Budget, 163, 164, 181; its reduction, 183–5
bureaucracy, *see* Civil Service
Burke, Edmund, 30 and n.
Burma, 296, 314
Bustamante, 282
Butler, D. E., 255 n.
Butler, R. A., 36
Byzantium, 276

Cable and Wireless, 42, 106
Cadiz, 13
Cambridge, 234 n.
Canada, 235,278, 300, 304
capital, 163–86, 214–15, 231, 232, 240–1, 285
capital gains tax, 185
Carnegie, Andrew, 92
cartelization, State, 210
cartels, 227
Casement, Sir Roger, 71
censorship, 71
Central African Federation, 280, 285 n., 288 n., 293, 295
Ceylon, 278, 280, 296, 306 n.
Charter of Rights, Trade Union, 79
Chatham House, 43
China, 261, 270, 279 n., 280, 300 and n.
Christianity, 15
Church of England, 83–4
Churchill, Sir Winston, 71
cinemas, 77, 137, 289
civil liberties, 52–87; in trade unions, 196–7; in colonies, 276, 306
Civil Service, 17, 89, 141; its burdens, 37–8; its expansion, 55; its decline in status, 80–1; entrance into, 85; and security, 86–7; and Welfare State, 100; and education, 150; and devolution, 52, 143–4; corruption in, 81–2; and the 'Establishment', 83–4; exchange-system for, 86; Commonwealth Service, 304–5
Clark, Colin, 235 n.
classes, school, 154–5

For Product Safety Concerns and Information please contact our EU
representative GPSR@taylorandfrancis.com
Taylor & Francis Verlag GmbH, Kaufingerstraße 24, 80331 München, Germany